C0001602B8

WILLIAM HALE WHITE (MARK RUTHERFORD)

William Hale White (Mark Rutherford)

A CRITICAL STUDY

BY

IRVIN STOCK

FOREWORD BY
LIONEL TRILLING
COLUMBIA UNIVERSITY

NEW YORK: MORNINGSIDE HEIGHTS
COLUMBIA UNIVERSITY PRESS
1956

Published in Great Britain
by George Allen & Unwin Ltd
1956

Printed in Great Britain

FOREWORD

WHEN William Hale White died in 1913 at the age of eighty-two, he had not achieved anything like fame but he had established himself in the literary life of England as a mind of a peculiar interest, as an intellectual personality to whom a special and delicate respect was gladly paid. His reputation, however, declined rapidly from even this small prosperity. His name, or the name under which he wrote and portrayed himself, Mark Rutherford, was known to me in my college days, but not in a very interesting way, not in a way to draw me to him. He was represented less as a mind than as an instance—he was made to serve as an example of the suffering that might be inflicted on a sensitive soul by a cultural phenomenon of a vanished age, that 'loss of faith' which was characteristic of the nineteenth century. This view of Hale White has recently been canonized in a compendious history of English literature, an American work of some authority. In the single brief paragraph which it devotes to Hale White, it tells us that if his novels are kept in remembrance, 'it will be rather as documents in the history of certain phases of Victorian thought than as works of imaginative literature.'

The opinion is erroneous. It is the expression of the chief bad tendency of literary history, which is to deal with those works of a past age that are less than very great as if they were quite dead and done with, as if they claimed no other attention than to be recognized as cultural facts and correctly ticketed and put in their proper places for easy reference. But there is another and contrary tendency of literary history, the one that justifies this discipline in the face of all the easy conventional contempt for literary scholarship. This is the tendency of literary history to search out what life there may be in the works of the past and to cherish it. Dr. Stock's book exemplifies this right, conserving tendency. It makes plain to us that Hale White is not a mere deciduous fact of the past to be filed in the catalogue of necessary useless knowledge. In this demonstration it is of some consequence that Dr. Stock can tell us of what Hale White meant to Joseph Conrad and to Stephen Crane, to D. H. Lawrence and to André Gide, men who were not likely to respond to what is merely historical or documentary in literature. But it is of still greater consequence in his disproof of Hale White's oblivion, that Dr. Stock himself can respond to what Hale White was and said not only with enthusiasm but with his own grace, vivacity, justness, and wisdom—with, that is, the qualities of mind which are characteristic of the man who is his subject.

Dr. Stock reaches across the barriers of time, of fashion, and of inertia, to greet a mind which speaks intimately to him. And yet, in point of fact he has not had to reach so very far after all—or so it seems to us after we have read his book. Even if we continue to think of Hale White as having chiefly an historical interest, we must see that the opinion I have quoted, that Hale White's books are to be remembered only as documents of certain phases of Victorian thought, is quite inaccurate. The historical significance which Hale White may be said to have is different from this—it lies in his exemplifying for us the natural passage from the Victorian period to the modern period. Hale White's loss of an orthodox religious faith was the central fact of his life, and, like many a Victorian, he devoted his emotional and intellectual energies to recouping the loss, using every device of secular homiletics to overcome the sudden oppressive emptiness of the universe; and, like every Victorian, he set morality and duty at the very heart of the possibility of life. But he differs from his fellow Victorians—he differs from them in some essential and almost indescribable way. One perceives the difference in the quality of his prose. He dispensed with the elaborate stylistic armour of the great Victorians; even in his most solemn passages, his rhetoric has a degree of simplicity and actuality, of relaxation and irony, which we feel to be more characteristic of the literature of the early years of this century than of the literature of the Victorian age. The difference is also to be seen in the things he takes account of. To read, say, the opening chapters of *The Revolution in Tanner's Lane*, to enter the consciousness of the Dissenting printer, Zachariah Coleman, to share with him the acquaintance of Major Maitland, to suffer his disappointment in the smallness of his wife's spirit, and to follow the brilliant exposition of why it was that Lord Byron's poetry meant so much to those who had been brought up in the tradition of Dissent, and then to go on to the delicate account of Mrs. Coleman's bewildered attraction to the Major, of Zachariah's discovery of the beauty of sexual passion in Pauline Caillaud's dancing—this is to experience a shock to our usual conception of the Victorian past, to feel too that the past is far closer to us than we had supposed.

It must be remembered, of course, that Hale White's life falls into two parts, that in which he suffered the Victorian experience and that in which he wrote about it. His dramatic loss of faith occurred in 1852, one of its causes being the young divinity student's reading of *The Lyrical Ballads*. But Hale White did not begin to publish until he was fifty, in the 'eighties, so that it cannot seem strange that there should be found in his work of the following years certain prophetic affinities with, say, the work of Bernard Shaw, that Hale White should, for example, deal with Puritanism in the sophisticated, sympathetic, interpretative way which Shaw was later to use, or that in *Clara Hopgood* (1896) one of his heroines should refuse to marry the lover by whom she is to have a child, finding him to be a person of inferior quality.

The peculiar charm of Hale White's work as a novelist is suggested by something which D. H. Lawrence wrote in 1916. Dr. Stock speaks of Lawrence's admiration for Mark Rutherford as expressed in a letter to Aldous Huxley; and in Harry T. Moore's recent biography Lawrence is quoted as saying that he finds himself 'fearfully fond of Rutherford' because he is 'so just and plucky and sound.' But what I have in mind is a passage in a letter to Catherine Carswell, which Dr. Moore gives at length, in which Lawrence does not mention Rutherford at all but tries in an odd, extravagant, impossible way to define a quality of English literature to which he was especially responsive. 'No, I don't like Turgenev very much; he seems so very critical, like Katherine Mansfield and also like a stale old maid. It amazes me that we have bowed down and worshipped these foreigners as we have. Their art is so clumsy, really, and clayey, compared with our own. I read "Deerslayer" just before the Turgenev. And I can tell you what a come-down it was, from the pure and exquisite art of Fennimore [sic] Cooper—whom we count nobody—to the journalistic bludgeonings of Turgenev. They are all—Turgenev, Tolstoi, Dostoievski, Maupassant, Flaubert—so very *obvious* and coarse, beside the lovely, mature and sensitive art of Fennimore Cooper or Hardy. It seems to me that our English art, at its best, is by far the subtlest and loveliest and most perfect in the world. But it is characteristic of a highly-developed nation to bow down to that which is more gross and raw and affected. . . . No, enough of this silly worship of foreigners. The most exquisite literature in the world is written in the English language.' The categories and examples and judgments of this statement—let alone the absoluteness of its literary chauvinism—may well dumbfound us, but I think we do not fail to know what Lawrence intended. He was trying to suggest, and to erect into a principle, the intensity of his response to a certain openness and lack of rigor, to what amounts to the surrender of the full rights and powers of the literary process, to an immediacy, and homeliness, an indifference to the fully organized literary effect. It is a quality, I think, that goes with a particular response to the natural world of growing things, and of inanimate and commonplace things, with the recognition of the possibility of experience which is not only social and moral. It is the quality that everywhere marks the work of Hale White, who, for all his involvement in the problems of faith, theology, and morality, for all his submission to the hideous abstractness of depressive melancholy, never lost his awareness of the primacy of *things*, of flowers, of insects, of stars; of houses, jobs, cash, manners. 'Think of the Earth!' says Keats's Moneta to the Poet. Hale White thought of the earth.

The objections which are made to Hale White as a novelist are in part those which sometimes used to be made to E. M. Forster as a novelist—very dull objections, it seems to me, based on stuffy pieties about 'the aesthetic' of 'the novel.' Hale White has Mr. Forster's impatience with the prescribed exigencies of the genre of the novel. He is quite as willing as Mr. Forster to suppose that a novel, like an apple, is not much the worse for being cut in half, just as he has Mr. Forster's predilection for sudden death. And there is more that the two men have in common than this happy pragmatic attitude toward the novel—no one, I now know, should write at length of Mr. Forster without taking note of his general affinity with Hale White. So far as I can recall, Mr. Forster has made but a single reference to Mark Rutherford, a rather slighting one. Still it is plain that his Helen and Margaret Schlegal are descended from Rutherford's Clara and Madge Hopgood, that his 'Only connect!' serves as well to denominate Rutherford's prevailing theme as his own; they have in common their undeceived sympathy with the intellectual person and an awareness of his petty isolate pride, and their natural piety or sense of the mystery of the commonplace, and their impulse to affirmation in the face of fully recognized evil and despair.

To Dr. Stock, who has a larger admiration for André Gide than I have yet been able to achieve, it is the analogies that may be drawn between Gide and Hale White that make the surest indication of Hale White's essential modernity. Perhaps they do, but if they do, they also remind us how unabashedly Gide had his roots in the nineteenth century, and that, in speaking of Hale White's modernity, we must recognize that his affinity is with an aspect of the modern that already begins to seem old fashioned. I have in mind that impulse to canvass the possibilities of *salvation* that marks the men of the earlier century. To the writers who make the context in which we may talk of Hale White's modernity, Shaw, Lawrence, Forster, and Gide, the question of salvation is of the essence of their enterprise. How to live—in relation to one's self, to one's neighbour, to the universe; how to be good (or, as we say nowadays, how to be mature); how to be truthful, how to be brave, how to be really alive: the open and explicit (as against the covert and abashed) asking of these questions has come to seem less and less possible. We have lost much of the sense of personal fate, and of the possibility of personal salvation, which animated the great literature of a quarter of a century ago. It has been lost, perhaps, in the questions we now ask about personal or national or racial survival. But another way of accounting for its loss is to observe the diminution of the religious or quasi-religious impulse from which the modern sense of salvation sprang. We have all learned to look askance at the attempts, which began in the nineteenth century and continued into the twentieth, to hold on to the sentiments and impulses of religion even though the dogmas of religion could not be retained; we have learned to regard with satirical skepticism all Open Secrets or Powers-Not-Ourselves or Life Forces, or any of the more or less naturalistic substitutes for an orthodox deity. Very likely we are right to do so, yet we must see how the old religious impulse, continued in elaborate modifications of it, made it possible for the great writers of the first quarter of the century to maintain their belief in the personal fate, in the necessity and possiblity of salvation. They were curious and serious about faith, they were curious and serious about what kept people alive, and willing to live, and out of this curiosity and seriousness they wrote as they did.

'You are the only person who does not mind my being so serious,' Hale White said in his old age to his second wife. *Serious*—it was a word that Matthew Arnold seemed almost sensuously to have loved, and how archaic it now sounds, how elegaic, how impossible! But as Hale White utters it in this touching and desperate sentence, all the dull meanings that have attached themselves to the word disappear and it seems to stand for a quality of mind that is nothing but desirable—we understand that the serious mind is the unembarrassed mind, accepting without abashment its importance and the gravity of its fate, and therefore able to work according to its capacity with wit and force and variousness. Such a mind was Hale White, and we are in debt to the scholars, to Dr. Catherine Maclean in her recent biography and to Dr. Stock in his present critical study, who make it the easier for us to recognize him and to take pleasure in him.

LIONEL TRILLING

ACKNOWLEDGMENTS

IN writing this book I have incurred obligations to a number of people to whom I would like here to express my gratitude. The richest collections of unpublished material by and about Hale White are those of Dr. Reginald Hale-White[1] of London, whose father was Sir William Hale-White, the novelist's eldest son, and Mrs. Dorothy V. White of Sherborne, Dorset, widow of the novelist. Not only were these collections most generously made available to me but from Dr. Hale-White I heard much that was interesting about his grandfather, and by Mrs. White's talk, as well as by her distinguished writings, I was led to a deeper understanding of her husband's temperament and of the 'religious world' in which he was most at home. A number of valuable letters were shown me by Mrs. Irene White of St. Albans, Hertfordshire, widow of Hale White's youngest son, and Mrs. Gladys A. Easedale of London, both of whom also had many fine memories of the novelist to share, and by Viscountess Robert Cecil of Sussex. I must acknowledge too the illumination derived from talks with the novelist's daughter Miss Mary T. Hale-White, his granddaughter Miss Cecily Hale-White, and Dr. Catherine M. Maclean, whose forthcoming biography of Mark Rutherford is eagerly awaited by those who know her other writings.[2] To the generosity and friendliness of all of these I am indebted not only as a scholar but as a visitor to England whose stay they helped to make one of the pleasantest periods of his life.

To M. Pierre Chevrillon of Paris and Bournand, Viènne, I am also grateful both for help and hospitality, for I read his intelligent and instructive study of Hale White (as yet unpublished) in his beautiful thirteenth-century Commanderie at Bournand.

There remain to be mentioned the obligations I have incurred at home—that is, in America. I would like to thank Professor William York Tindall for valuable suggestions, Professor Lionel

---

[1] Some time after the death of Hale White, his two eldest sons and his daughter added their father's middle name, with a hyphen, to their last name.

[2] This book has appeared since the above was written. See the bibliography.

Trilling for general enlightenment along the lines of my study and for encouragement, and Professor Susanne Howe Nobbe, a constant support to me in matters both large and small, in matters of morale as well as of scholarship. Then there are my friends Mr. and Mrs. Jack Davis, Dr. and Mrs. Isadore Traschen and Mr. Martin Lobenthal, and my sister Mrs. Evelyn Prieto, to whom thanks are due for helpful criticism of various chapters of the book, and Mrs. Jean Soichet and my sister for typing.

Finally, I want to thank my wife—for typing, for criticism, and for much more.

CONTENTS

CHAPTER I

Introduction to the Work

I

'THE man who digs up unnecessary authors, histories, biographies is a public nuisance,' William Hale White remarked in his 'Black Notebook.' 'He adds to our burdens, already too heavy to be borne.' [1] In now attempting to bring Hale White himself again into view, the present writer is sensible that he risks appearing to be such a nuisance. When a man is so little read, the suspicion is not unlikely that he deserves no better, that he is, in fact, unnecessary. It may be prudent, therefore, before launching into a detailed consideration of his individual works, to give the reader some preliminary grounds for hope that the job is worth undertaking. This will be done first by a brief appeal to several authorities whose opinions should carry weight, and then by an introductory glimpse of the nature and quality of Hale White's work as a whole. It is my own opinion that the nature of that work—that is, the human problems dealt with and the ideas and attitudes brought to their investigation—is far more congenial to modern readers than its rural, Puritan, 'Victorian' surface might suggest; and that its quality, as writing, is remarkable.

Let us begin, however, with the simplest identification. Hale White was born in Bedford, England, in 1831, and was, like his parents, a devout Dissenter for his first twenty years. After two years of study for the ministry he was expelled for heretical views on Biblical inspiration and from then on gradually ceased to attend any religious institution or to accept literally any religious dogma. He spent most of his adult life as a civil servant, supplementing his income for a time by writing newspaper columns, and he died in 1913.

[1] W. H. White, 'Black Notebook,' an unpublished journal in the possession of Mrs. D. V. White.

He did not begin to write seriously until the age of fifty, and he has left us, not counting works of technical scholarship, eleven small volumes. The first two, *The Autobiography of Mark Rutherford* (1881) and *Mark Rutherford's Deliverance* (1885), are largely an account of his own most important experiences in the guise of fiction. They pretend to be the posthumous autobiography of a poor London clerk and former minister edited by a friend called Reuben Shapcott. The 'friend' speaks of having reason to suppose that other manuscripts are lying about among the belongings of the late Rutherford, and sure enough, there followed four novels: *The Revolution in Tanner's Lane* (1887), *Miriam's Schooling* (1890), *Catherine Furze* (1893) and *Clara Hopgood* (1896), and three volumes called *Pages: More Pages* and *Last Pages from a Journal* (1900, 1910 and 1915). These *Pages*, the third coming after Hale White's death, contain short stories, essays and aphoristic 'notes' (as he calls them) extracted from two unpublished notebooks, the 'Black' and 'White' notebooks. The double pseudonym was a disguise sincerely intended and Hale White's identity did not for a long time become generally known. Among his last books appeared a short defence of Wordsworth against the charge of apostasy from the supposed political and intellectual radicalism of his youth (1898) and a critical work on John Bunyan (1904). He was also the author of translations of Spinoza's *Ethic* (1883) and his *Emendations of the Intellect* (1895),[1] and it is interesting to find in the preface to the Modern Library edition of Spinoza that 'it was desirable to use White's translation because it is the most accurate and elegant extant,'[2] a remark unaccompanied by any hint that he had other claims to distinction as well. Finally, there appeared in 1924 two more books which are of great interest to admirers of Hale White: these are a volume of correspondence called *Letters to Three Friends* and *The Groombridge Diary*, in which his second wife gives a detailed record, full of his talk and his letters to her, of his last seven years.

In spite of Hale White's obscurity, others, as I say, have shared my

---

[1] Hale White preferred to write *Ethic* without the *s*. The second Spinoza work is also known as *Correction of the Understanding*.

[2] Joseph Ratner, editor, *The Philosophy of Spinoza*, New York, Modern Library edition, Random House, 1922, p. vii.

view of his merit. The fact is, since 1880 when his books began to appear, his admirers, though they have not been many, have been choice. What is more, there has often crept into their comments on him a note almost of indignation at a neglect they have found it hard to understand. Of the first two books William Dean Howells declared that they 'may yet mark a new era in fiction . . . they carry so deep a sense of truthfulness to the reader, they are so far in temper from any sort of mere artistry, they are so simply and nobly serious. . . . We could not give too strong an impression of this incomparable sincerity.'[1] Matthew Arnold[2] and Swinburne[3] and later Joseph Conrad[4] and Stephen Crane[5] admired his work. Edmund Gosse called him a 'genius' and complained, 'It appears to us that no author of anything like his rank has in our time been so continuously neglected by responsible criticism.'[6] H. W. Massingham considered him the 'one imaginative genius of the highest order'[7] produced by English Puritanism since Bunyan. Arnold Bennett called *The Revolution* 'the finest example of modern English prose,'[8] and D. H. Lawrence remarked of our author, 'I *do* think he is jolly good—so

[1] William Dean Howells, 'The Editor's Study,' *Harper's New Monthly Magazine*, LXXII (February 1886), p. 485.

[2] In a letter of June 24, 1913, now in the possession of Mrs. D. V. White, John W. Gulland, Member of Parliament, wrote to Mrs. White: 'My colleague here, William Jones, the Welsh Whip, used to be a teacher in Wales and Matthew Arnold was his Inspector. They had talks on literature and Arnold always "enthused" over Mark Rutherford and told Jones on no account ever to miss anything that Mark Rutherford ever wrote.'

[3] On September 22, 1909, W. T. Watts-Dunton wrote to Hale White of 'your "Mark Rutherford" books which both Swinburne and I read with profound admiration.' (W. H. White, *Letters to Three Friends*, edited by Dorothy V. White, London, Oxford University Press, 1924, p. 362 n.)

[4] In a letter of September 3, 1904, quoted in G. Jean-Aubry, editor, *Joseph Conrad: Life and Letters*, London, 1927, I, p. 335.

[5] See John Berryman, *Stephen Crane*, New York, William Sloan Associates, 1950, p. 248.

[6] Gosse was reviewing *Pages and More Pages from a Journal* in the *Morning Post*, London, November 14, 1910.

[7] H. W. Massingham in his 'Memorial Introduction' to *The Autobiography of Mark Rutherford*, 3rd edition, London, 1923, p. vii.

[8] A. Bennett, in the *New Statesman*, XXII (October 13, 1923), Supplement, p. viii.

thorough, so sound and so beautiful.'[1] J. M. Murry has noted that his style, 'very near perfection,' took its character from 'a mistrust of words, a sense of responsibility to personal truth,' and the 'heavy obligation [placed by Hale White] on the written word of sincerity to deep personal feeling.'[2] This critic's grasp of his subject's literary character merits further quotation. That the following is not mere praise but an exact description of a certain kind of writer will, I hope, become clear. Murry speaks of 'the manifest oneness of Mark Rutherford. His letters, his novels, his journals are radiations from a simple living centre, function—to use a mathematical term—of one unchanging soul. . . .' His work is 'secure against decay because it was moulded by a true man in his own image. He digged down to bedrock in his soul and his work rests unshakeable on that firm foundation.'[3]

There are others, but I will close the list with the comment of André Gide, who has created a vogue for Hale White in France which, slight as it is, is yet the most marked anywhere at the present time. This too must be quoted at length for it will be the text for much of what follows. Coming, moreover, from a mind peculiarly 'modern'—in its freedom and complexity—it will help to confirm the suggestion made above of the relevance of Hale White's work to our own culture and its problems. The comments are all from his *Journal*.

October 8, 1915: Wonderful integrity of the book [*The Auto-biography*]. I do not know any work that is more specifically Protestant. . . . The exquisite qualities of Hale White's style . . . are the very ones I would like to have.[4]

January 24, 1916: I read in Rutherford . . . a passage about the devil and hell that just happens to back up my thoughts wonderfully. 'The shallowest of mortals is able now to laugh at the notion of a

---

[1] *The Letters of D. H. Lawrence*, edited by Aldous Huxley, New York, Viking Press, 1932, p. 83.

[2] J. M. Murry, in *Daily News and Leader* (London), October 8, 1915.

[3] J. M. Murry, *To the Unknown God: Essays Toward a Religion*, London, Jonathan Cape, Ltd., 1924, pp. 260-2.

[4] *The Journals of André Gide*, translated by Justin O'Brien, 4 vols., New York, Alfred A. Knopf, 1947-51, II, p. 101.

personal devil. No doubt there is no such thing existent; but the horror at evil which could find no other expression than in the creation of a devil is no subject for laughter, and if it do not in some shape or other survive, the race itself will not survive.'[1]

May not this entry be a clue to the devil which dominates *The Counterfeiters*, already at this date being considered?

And, finally, of *Catherine Furze*:

March 8, 1936: I do not think this book can find many readers in France; less and less: palates spoiled by too many spices can no longer taste what is pure. . . . I find in *Catherine Furze* the so specifically Protestant qualities and virtues which awakened such profound echoes in me, when, for the first time, I read his two little volumes: *Autobiography* and *Deliverance*. Here honesty and integrity become poetic virtues, beside which everything seems camouflaged, inauthentic, and overloaded. The human soul may be compared to palimpsests: here is read the original writing, so difficult to make out through the accumulation of retouchings and additions. The very style of William Hale White (Mark Rutherford) is exquisitely transparent, scintillatingly pure. He develops to perfection qualities that I wish were mine. His art is made of the renunciation of all false riches. He is apolitical, because there is no politics without fraud.[2]

So admired, then, Hale White may well be thought to deserve more attention than he has received. He deserves it for various reasons: because of his value as the historian of a segment of English culture not elsewhere, except to some degree by George Eliot, so understandingly or so vividly preserved; because of a dramatization of the problems of moral freedom as subtle—and almost, for his time, as daring—as that to be found in the work of André Gide, with whom he has, in fact, a startling affinity; and because of the beauty of his art, in its style and its dramatic clarity and power. A word or two must be said about such matters by way of proper introduction. And yet it is not in these that his most striking quality, the ground of a unique and peculiarly poignant appeal, is to be discovered. They

[1] *Ibid.*, III, pp. 337-8.   [2] *Ibid.*, III, pp. 337-8.

are, as it were, the literary by-products of something that is not in its originating impulse or final effect literary at all. Just so might we find various literary and intellectual merits in a sermon—I mean the passionate sharing of his insight by a spiritual leader who has suffered much and understood much and wishes rather to help others than to demonstrate his abilities; just so might we find them in the talk of one who has met his dearest friend after a long absence and at last, in private and free from the need to show cleverness or to hide weakness, utters what has lain close to his heart; and yet in neither case would it seem better than frivolous to regard them as most important. We will therefore postpone our consideration of the above characteristics, the kind he shares with many good novelists, until after we have tried to understand what he shares with almost no one at all.

II

The comments I quoted recurred often to the word 'sincerity' or to some equivalent. There is, of course, a sense in which any serious writer is sincere—honesty is a basic condition of his profession and some kind of truth its necessary raw material—but we are rarely impelled, except perhaps in mitigation of the charge of failure, to place that word in the centre of a critical portrait. With Hale White, however, it must in fact go in the centre: it is the chief distinction of his work and the source of his finest effects. What it helps us express in his case is the feeling he gives of an especially intimate relationship between the man and his writing. In order to understand the unique qualities of the writing, we must for this reason start with the man himself.

And the first thing we must note about him is that by the age of fifty, when he began to write, he had experienced so much unhappiness that life had come to mean for him chiefly the endurance of suffering. 'As we get older,' he wrote to a son, 'we find that endurance is the exact synonym for life.'[1] This is sometimes uttered as a commonplace: for him it was the most immediate of realities. He had been poor and for nearly twenty years had had to work from

[1] Unpublished letter to Jack Hale-White, dated August 8, 1889, copy in the possession of Dr. R. Hale-White.

the time of rising to the time of sleeping to support his wife and four children. No one has described better than he the anguish—an ignoble anguish—of having to give up one's life to a boring and degrading job while all higher gifts rust unused or become mere sources of pain. Worse than this was the fact that while she was still in her twenties, his wife became ill with disseminated sclerosis, a progressive paralysis that did not kill her for thirty years but that gradually crippled and blinded her. Most of those thirty years she spent in wheel-chairs or in bed. And though amid her sufferings she preserved a courage that could shame her husband, he was never able to forget for an instant the terrible visitation. That he should have been oppressed by it is natural enough, perhaps, but there was a special reason for his vulnerability to misfortune. He had a trial that multiplied the difficulties of every other, and that, indeed, required little support from circumstances to steep his life in gloom. From his early manhood he was afflicted with a tendency to what he called 'hypochondria,' that is, depression, which was not the occasional 'bad mood' we all know but an attack of horror and panic that lasted for long periods at a time and that, when not actually upon him, was being, as it were, consciously held at bay. It is interesting that the state recurs so often in his fiction, sometimes named, sometimes not —and even in his criticism, where it is seen to be involved in the work of favourite writers—that we are reminded of the sexual abnormality in Proust which ends by turning up everywhere. Of course, it was a sickness. He spent much money on doctors (though in vain), and he does not fail to point out the questionable validity of the ideas about life, produced by it, suggesting that they ought not to be regarded as 'mere logical inferences'[1] but rather as symptoms which must disappear with returning health. Nevertheless, it was impossible not to regard this 'hypochondria' most often as the opening of a window on a terrible and undeniable reality, on a vision not less true because the usual pleasures and preoccupations of health (that 'divine narcotic'[2]) mercifully conceal it. The terror of it affected nearly everything he said and did, and those who get to

[1] W. H. White, *The Revolution in Tanner's Lane*, New York, Dodd, Mead and Company, 1899, chap. xiv.
[2] *Ibid.*

know him well can see its influence in the most unlikely places in his work. It made more precious the simplest pleasures of life, and his serious reflections not only derived from it a kind of desperate urgency but were, by it, forever challenged for their true helpfulness to the soul which struggled and suffered.

It is this which accounts for the chief demand he made on the works of the mind—in art, philosophy, even religion: Do they help men to live? Exclusive preoccupation with the separate disciplines themselves tended to make him impatient all his life. 'Poetry, if it is to be good for anything, must help us to live,' he remarks in his *Pages from a Journal*. 'It is to this we come at last in our criticism, and if it does not help us to live it may as well disappear, no matter what its fine qualities may be.' [1] As a rule, we are right to reject such a demand that art, or any other intellectual pursuit, be primarily useful, because it is so often made by those with too narrow a notion of what men need or of the manifold ways in which they can be served. But not only was the demand made in his case by one well aware of the peculiar sanctions and seductions of the intellectual life; it was also made by one who sought help for problems of the utmost complexity, for problems, indeed, which are often insoluble. What he sought above all was help to endure uncrushed life's unavoidable pain, and for this it is not things or society that must be changed— the usual notion of those who demand art as 'a weapon'—but only, if possible, oneself, one's ideas. It is the help ideally offered by religion. And in fact his abnormal need intensified all the influences in his education which had made religious thinking natural to him. For it is an important characteristic of religion that, while it deals in ideas which link the individual to mankind and to the universe, these ideas are related directly to the emotional life. They are attempts (whatever else they also are) to help him understand and endure his inevitable sorrows. This is the reason Hale White never lost his reverence for true faith, his nostalgia for a time when his own could have been perfect, and his sense of the special value of those many religious insights that do not depend on the acceptance of systems of dogma but are clearly the insights of men grappling directly with the eternal problems. And this is why the Bible became

[1] W. H. White, *Pages from a Journal*, 2nd edition, London, 1910, p. 108.

for him the most precious of all books, forever read and reread, though he did not get to know it rightly, he tells us, until after he was expelled from his seminary for questioning its unique inspiration.

If religion had been ideally the source of this help, the nineteenth century had, for men like him, destroyed its perfect sufficiency, and such men now sought its consolations also in philosophy and literature. It is significant that the philosopher who meant most to Hale White was Spinoza. Spinoza attempted to reconcile the great helpful ideas of religion—its identification of virtue with inner peace; its lesson of self-forgetfulness, or rather self-discovery, in the higher, the greater, the whole; its lesson of the necessary and healing acceptance of reality (or God's will)—with the demands of the rational intelligence and the facts of nature, and thereby to provide the grounds for 'a joy continuous and supreme to all eternity.'[1] This was exactly the problem of Hale White, who liked to emphasize that admitted human motive for Spinoza's philosophic quest. And though Spinoza aimed at joy, it was not a joy available to the weak; he led us toward a love of God which does not demand, as the celebrated proposition has it, that God love us in return. One can understand how a man whose life had taught him that inner peace was not in fact going to be made easy by a God of prompt rewards might be struck by such an idea.

In other intellectual fields, too, he sought—religion, one is tempted to say, but, at any rate, this same help to live. In his essays, which range among the works of scientists and at least one polar explorer, as well as of poets and novelists, he is quick to notice the sense of trouble—sometimes, as with Bradley, the eighteenth-century explorer, it takes the form of physical danger—and the medicine used against it: so often, and not only with Bradley, courage. This gives even to his literary criticism, even, indeed, to his most rigorous philosophic reflection, an amazing note of repressed personal feeling. Not that literature as pleasure, using the word in its widest sense, was beneath his notice. On the contrary, like all pleasure it was thrice precious to one whose life so desperately needed sweetening. There

[1] *Ethic of Benedict Spinoza*, translated by W. H. White and Amelia H. Stirling, 4th edition, London, 1910, Preface, p. v.

is clear personal gratitude in his remarks on Scott, for instance, whose wonderful tales he had read aloud to his wife and children. (So insistent a 'practical' emphasis may after all engender a doubt as to whether he was aware of what the art of literature is in itself. Let me not move on without at least a hint that he was. To a friend who told him she did not 'understand' poetry because she was interested in 'what is said,' not in 'the way it is said,' he wrote that the distinction was a fallacy.

The noblest office of genius is *realization*, the making *ex*-plicit the world in which we live, and form, therefore, is emphatically reality. . . . There is a passage in Milton—indeed, there are many in the poems of this miraculous master, in which accent alone is tremendous fact.

> 'Grasping ten thousand thunders, which he sent
> Before him, such as in their souls infix'd
> Plagues.'

He deserts the ordinary rhythm of heroic blank verse in the last eight syllables: they are all slow and their slowness is a great definite creative act.[1]

This statement is one of many which show how his ultimate choices were never made simple by inability to see and feel what 'opposed' them.)

One thing more must be understood about the man if we are to understand the reason for his special qualities as a writer. It is the abnormal intensity of his longing for a friend with whom he could share what in youth he called his 'heartfelt thinkings.' [2] 'It is not those who have the least, but those who have the most to give who most want sympathy,' [3] he said, and he speaks in *The Autobiography*, after explaining that the reserve often charged against him was due

---

[1] Unpublished letter to Miss Sophie Partridge, September 3, 1904, copy in the possession of Mrs. D. V. White.

[2] Unpublished letter to his father, May 3, 1853, copy in the possession of Dr. R. Hale-White, quoted below, p. 43.

[3] W. H. White, *Clara Hopgood*, New York, George H. Doran Company, undated, chap. xix.

to a longing for self-revelation which had generally been rebuffed, of 'a dream which I had . . . of a perfect friendship.'

I always felt [he goes on] that talk with whom I would, I left something unsaid which was precisely what I most wished to say. I wanted a friend who would sacrifice himself to me utterly, and to whom I might offer a similar sacrifice. I found companions for whom I cared, and who professed to care for me; but I was thirsting for deeper draughts of love than any which they had to offer; and I said to myself that if I were to die, not one of them would remember me for more than a week. This was not selfishness, for I longed to prove my devotion as well as to receive that of another. How this ideal haunted me! It made me restless and anxious at the sight of every new face, wondering whether at last I had found that for which I searched as if for the kingdom of heaven. It is superfluous to say that a friend of the kind I wanted never appeared.[1]

As it happens, such a friend did finally appear. And though he was old and she was young, mutual recognition was instantaneous and she became his second wife. Her diary of the seven years they had together at Groombridge, Kent, before he died, tells the story of a union of minds as perfect as any in the history of literature—this in spite of painful troubles due to the difference in age and circumstances or to his unfortunate temperament. And to this woman when she came he said a strange thing: 'If I had been given you when I was thirty I would never have let the public hear a syllable from me.'[2] The inference is clear that when at the age of fifty he sat down, not at first to the comparative frivolity of story-telling, but to share in secret the history of his own inner struggles and the modest 'deliverance' he was able to find, he had chosen the anonymous reader for his perfect friend. It is a fact that the voice—the style—we hear in this work is that of a man alone with such a friend and uttering at last what he had never been able to tell a living soul. And when he offers a reason for making public a tale so 'commonplace'

[1] *The Autobiography*, chap. ii.
[2] Quoted by Mrs. D. V. White in *The Groombridge Diary*, London, Oxford University Press, 1924, p. 176.

and so sad, it is something as distinct from the usual motives for a literary career as this:

I have observed that the mere knowing that other people have been tried as we have been tried is a consolation to us, and that we are relieved by the assurance that our sufferings are not special and peculiar, but common to us with many others. Death has always been a terror to me, and at times, nay generally, religion and philosophy have been altogether unavailing to mitigate the terror in any way. But it has always been a comfort to me to reflect that whatever death may be, it is the inheritance of the whole human race; that I am not singled out, but shall merely have to pass through what the weakest have had to pass through before me. In the worst of maladies, worst at least to me, those which are hypochondriacal, the healing effect which is produced by the visit of a friend who can simply say, 'I have endured all that,' is most marked. So it is not impossible that some few whose experience has been like mine may, by my example, be freed from that sense of solitude which they find so depressing.[1]

We are now in a position to understand that 'sincerity' which so many readers have found peculiarly characteristic of his work. It comes from this: that he writes at the impulse of such strong personal feeling, out of so pressing a sense of the gravity of man's condition and the urgency of his need, that all considerations of mere craft seem to become subordinate, or else to disappear. And it is because he was able to divest himself of pride as few men have ever been, and to confess (though in disguise) the existence within him of one who suffered and struggled, and who did so not as a 'hero' but as an ordinary man, that he makes so powerful an appeal to that same unheroic self hidden in all of us, exciting responses more intimate and more moved than are common in literature.

This—so to speak—non-literary character of his work accounts for its chief literary qualities. It accounts for the remarkable style, which is a simple communication, undistorted by the slightest striving for

---

[1] *The Autobiography*, chap. i.

effect and absolutely faithful to what has been intensely felt and clearly seen. 'If the truth is of serious importance to us we dare not obstruct it by phrasemaking,' he wrote. 'We are compelled to be as direct as our inherited feebleness will permit. The cannon ball's path is near to a straight line in proportion to its velocity. "My boy," my father once said to me, "if you write anything you consider particularly fine, strike it out."' [1] The beauty that results is impossible to imitate because one of its main characteristics is an unparalleled purity and naturalness of English: there is no self-assertive twisting of the idiom to take hold of. It comes to seem merely a beauty of personality. But though the naturalness, purity and simplicity of his writing are most often noticed, these alone would be nothing without the emotion which is equally pervasive. One finds in his work many explicit demands for the right to express intensity, lest moderateness of expression tell its own kind of lie. 'There is more insincerity,' he remarks in *The Revolution*, 'in purposely lowering the expression beneath the thought, and denying the thought thereby than in a little exaggeration.' [2] The restraint of his style, like his self-discipline in general, is a visible conquest, and sometimes his short definite sentences resemble nothing so much as the speech of a man who must speak coldly between clenched teeth lest he be over-mastered by emotion. This could, of course, become oppressive, but in his case it has not, because the conquest has been achieved; the man who speaks so is also a man of mind, aware of more than one perspective on his own experience, and capable of irony directed at himself and of humour. When *his* voice vibrates, we are at a point safely beyond sentimentality or a self-pity that is not justified. In fact, while his expressions are always simple and modest, they are clearly meant by an extremely conscious mind in their widest possible signification. This sets up a tension which is one of his chief effects and which can thrill, like understatement.

The art of his novels, too, takes much of its character from this unusual seriousness and intensity. He has described this art himself, unintentionally, in the following remarks to a son:

[1] W. H. White, *The Early Life of Mark Rutherford by Himself*, London, Oxford University Press, 1913, pp. 30-1.
[2] *The Revolution*, chap. xi.

Art is art in proportion to its distinctness. Noble art is distinguished from base art by the perfect clearness of the conception which it aims to embody. I do not assert that there are not other contrasts, but this is perhaps the most striking. The vehicle may be obscure, but in the writer or painter the intention is definite and vivid. Otherwise what burden lies on him to speak or paint? Only because he sees or thinks with intensity and consequently with a definition superior to that of ordinary mortals does he become great. . . . The sum and substance, to put it in other words, is *realization*. Whatever we have to speak, let it be bounded by a precise limiting line, so that the thing spoken is marked off from the vague, from chaos, from all other things with absolute precision. . . . Perhaps I could have concluded all I had to say in one word. Our actual *experience*, not what we can invent or dream: and no step a hair's breadth beyond what is real and solid for us, proved and again proved. This should be the character of all our speech.[1]

Exactly such clarity of definition—proceeding from just such warmth of response—appears in his characterization, though this can be of the utmost subtlety, in his development out of it of dramatic clash and climax, and in the underlying conception of the meaning of it all which determines the form of a work. Though he writes in the discursive tradition of George Eliot, which permits him to interrupt and comment at will, his novels have the speed and economy of those of Turgeniev, whom, indeed, he admired. His comments, for that matter, tend rather to increase than to dilute intensity, for he hardly ever interrupts unless he must: he seems driven by emotion to utter his larger thought. The reader may have noticed how sometimes, even before one knows what is to be said, the mere fact that a writer is being thus driven to generalize can in itself be moving.

The intimate relation between his writing and his character accounts, finally, for the peculiar unity of his work noticed by Murry. Never the professional fulfilling merely some literary purpose, he brought to every utterance nothing less than his whole self.

[1] Unpublished letter to Jack Hale-White, dated August 29, 1893, copy in the possession of Dr. R. Hale-White.

This is why, as has been suggested, his highest flights of philosophic reflection are charged throughout with the emotion which was their human origin and are often, oddly, as poignant as his accounts of love or pain. And this is why he can pass directly from such heights to the most humbly practical concerns—the pathos of the workman's fleeting Sunday, or how to break the habit of drink—without the slightest air of incongruity. Such concerns, being for him the true basis of all the rest, are seen naturally in a larger perspective that exposes their furthest meaning and unites them with what is highest. As he wrote of a character, 'his passion was informed with intellect, and his intellect glowed with passion. There was nothing in him merely animal or merely rational.' [1] For those to whom the novels fully reveal themselves, therefore, it is likely that the writer will at last be overshadowed by the man. They will be moved again and again to a response that is more than aesthetic, more than intellectual, and, drawn first perhaps by the quiet triumphs of his art, they may find that the slightest essays or notes, the letters, and not least the lovely *Groombridge Diary* of his second wife, so full of his wise and passionate conversation, grow as precious to them as the ripened works themselves.

All that I have so far tried to make clear can be summed up by a passage from one of his late stories. The passage concerns a certain friend of the narrator called Robert, who has chosen to give up the woman he loves in order to be true to a spiritual vocation which must bar her from his life forever. Though we are shown his particular trouble, however, the significant thing for us now is its intensity and its result.

---

[1] *Pages*, p. 191. In a perceptive criticism of *The Autobiography* in *The Groombridge Diary* (p. 66) Mrs. D. V. White says: 'I noticed in this chapter (V) a good illustration of his favourite sudden transition from the "particular" to the "general," the small to the great. These transitions produce a marked effect upon his style, which is very orderly, and yet full of strange surprises, every sort of climax, cadence and attack. Here, sandwiched in between an apparently trivial story about Mr. and Mrs. Hexton, and an apparently bald description of Mr. Hexton's way of life, is this sentence: "I do not believe there was a single point in Mr. Hexton's character in which he touched the universal." . . . *Immediately before:* ". . . a plate fell down and was broken; everything was in confusion; I was ashamed and degraded." *Immediately after:* "If he had kept bees. . . ."'

What made the separation especially terrible, both to Veronica and Robert, it is hard to say. Here are a couple of lines from one of Robert's letters to me which may partly explain: 'There is something in this trouble which I cannot put into words. It is the complete un-folding, the making real to myself, all that is hidden in that word *Never*.' Is it possible to express by speech a white handkerchief waved from the window of the railway train, or the deserted platform where ten minutes before a certain woman stood, where her image still lingers? There is something in this which is not mere sorrow. It is rather the disclosure of that dread Abyss which underlies the life of man. One consequence of this experience was the purest sincerity. All insincerity, everything unsound, everything which could not stand the severest test, was by this trial crushed out of him. His words uniformly stood for facts. Perhaps it was his sincerity which gave him a power over me such as no other man ever possessed.[1]

This is the power of Hale White.

III

But it is not, this power, by any means the whole story. The reader may even be relieved to know that Hale White did not look exclusively into his own heart, but that, like most novelists of impor-tance, he also recreated a solid world inhabited by people other than himself. He did this with such vivid and subtle accuracy, indeed, that his work has marked value as history.

His world is chiefly that of the Dissenting lower middle class in the East Midlands of England. He grew up in this region—in Bunyan's own town of Bedford and in the Calvinist sect of Independents—and his stories rarely stray far from this centre of his most lively memories. He writes, therefore, of a people whose relation to a religious tradition is one of the most important facts about them. He was among them, moreover, at a time of greater and more disturbing changes in belief than had been seen for generations. The Higher Criticism—that study of Biblical texts which suggested that they

[1] W. H. White, *Last Pages from a Journal*, edited by Dorothy V. White, London, Oxford University Press, 1915, pp. 43-4.

were the work of fallible men rather than the infallible word of God
—the advance of geology, which cast doubt on the Biblical history
of the earth, and the new conditions of life introduced by the
Industrial Revolution, were terrible blows to religious funda-
mentalism. It is the results of these blows on character and social
relationships in the world of Dissent which furnished Hale White
with the materials for his stories.

He shows us that there were roughly three ways to respond.
There were those who closed their minds entirely to new ideas, as in
self-protection, and this produced the rigid mechanical dogmatism,
sometimes sincere, sometimes hypocritical, which has been the
target of so much criticism. (Remember Dickens's Mr. Chadband,
or Gosse's *Father and Son*, or the attack of Matthew Arnold in his
St. Paul and Protestantism.) There were others who rejected their
religious heritage just as absolutely for a 'free thinking' that could,
of course, be extremely intelligent and adequate to many of life's
problems but that could also be thinking of the shallowest, easiest
and, what is worse, most blindly complacent kind. And there were
still others who could not reject what seemed true knowledge and
true ideas, but who found it painful and at last unnecessary to give
up their religion altogether. These, to adapt the words of Hale
White, committed the heresy of seeking the meaning of dogma,
that is, of regarding their religion as a language of symbols, a mode
of expressing wisdom eternally applicable to human life, that
required only to be properly translated. And if this seemed to put
their religion on a par with any of the historic accumulations of
wisdom, whether in religion, philosophy or literature, a very
plausible case could be built to show that the Judeo-Christian insights went deepest, covered more and were more helpful than all
others. It was to this category, as we shall see, that Hale White himself belonged, so that in spite of his expulsion from the Dissenting
college, his work can constitute for a secular generation an introduction to the profound meaningfulness of religious formulations and
ways of thought. There was also a fourth kind of relationship to
religion, and this was the perfect faith of those wholly untouched by
the new ideas because ignorant of them or uninterested. In other
words, it had been possible, and was still so here and there though

sceptics might deny it, to find in one's religion all the room needed for a rich and intelligent life, to find that it gave life a meaning which included all that was important. There were many such believers whom Hale White honoured, some by whom he was, indeed, deeply influenced. It is a special interest of his fiction that he shows with the most delicate inwardness what beauty, wisdom and peace such faith can sometimes make possible.

Religion, moreover, has never been an isolated matter, but involved, often inextricably, with social status and attitudes and political convictions. The period to which Hale White's fiction is chiefly devoted begins in his father's time, around 1815. The Industrial Revolution and the just-ended war with Napoleon had brought about a severe economic depression: violent uprisings were not uncommon. And yet it was also a time of such intense political reaction that the radical was treated as practically a traitor or an agent of defeated France. Workers' political clubs had to go underground, and they were hounded by Government spies and *agents provocateurs*. Most prominent among the radicals, or the mere wild protestors, were the Dissenters. The Manchester weavers who gathered to petition George IV for political and economic relief and were shot down by the militia at 'Peterloo' were Dissenters, and intensely devout. Even the pulpits of their ministers were then not too lofty a sphere, as they later became, for the expression of political opinion. The drama of this state of affairs is preserved in all its excitement in the pages of Hale White, who goes on to show us how for many the coming of better times meant also a blunting of political consciousness, a growing snobbery, for they could now hope to rise in status, and the gradual transformation of their religion into a social form which made the Higher — the Anglican — Church increasingly seductive.

The Dissenting community in the period he describes was therefore a much richer mine of human material than the familiar caricature of it would lead one to expect: rich in external conflicts, as those with different relations to the common traditions came together, and rich too in the more interesting and painful internal ones, as men for whom vital matters were at stake in their development changed and grew. It is Hale White's value for us as a social historian that he suffered these conflicts himself or watched the suffering of those he loved, and being gifted with great psychological penetration, could present them to us from the inside in all their variety and intensity. Because of him that vanished society need not be peopled for us exclusively by bigots and hypocrites, but also by recognizable and complex human beings.

The reader will by now have recognized his similarity to George Eliot. The resemblance between their work is often striking. But if the greater quantity of life which Eliot so masterfully recreates and organizes entitles her to superior rank as a novelist pure and simple, she is not the greater writer. Partly because of the peculiar non-professional relationship to writing already described, Hale White's scope was deliberately narrowed to those things alone which in fact or in imagination he had intensely experienced. And the result has been not only limitation but a psychological subtlety, a wisdom, a force and precision of language, and a dramatic power she never matched.[1]

IV

Even more than by the society he recreates, however, the reader of today is likely to be interested by Hale White's thought. And here it will help us to be aware of another affinity, one which has already been mentioned in these pages and which will suggest at once a peculiarly modern complexity. I mean his affinity with André Gide. Though the *milieux* in which the two writers discover and embody

[1] I will later quote Mr. E. A. Baker to disagree with him. But his voluminous *History of the English Novel* is full of insight and intelligent enthusiasm, and I am glad to be able to welcome here his partial confirmation. 'All of Mark Rutherford's fiction put together would hardly exceed in bulk George Eliot's *Middlemarch*,' he writes. 'He worked not so much on a smaller scale, as with a finer pen, and with a suggestive word, left to the imagination what she would have dwelt upon for page after page. Perhaps he left too much to the imagination. *Catherine Furze* could have been expanded to much advantage. Comparison is inevitable; their themes, their characters, and both their problems and their solutions are so similar, and they all but coincide in their times and places. It would be absurd to deny that in weight and creative fertility she was his superior. But the converse, equally unqualified, would be just as absurd.' (*The History of the English Novel*, London, H. F. and G. Witherby, Ltd., 1938, IX, p. 114.)

C

their meanings could hardly be more different, these meanings themselves are surprisingly alike, finding expression often in almost
identical formulations. Here are several passages from the work of
Hale White which will at once demonstrate the resemblance, and
provide the basis for a definition of Hale White's central ideas. For
readers of Gide they will hardly require comment.

Each person's belief or proposed course of action is part of himself,
and if he be diverted from it and takes up with that which is not
himself, the unity of his nature is impaired, and he loses himself.[1]

The symbolism of an act varies much, and what may be mere
sport in one is sin in another.[2]

The universe is so complex that nothing is true save a word fitted
to a particular occasion.[3]

There is no human truth which is altogether true.[4]

The curse of every truth is that a counterfeit of it always waits on
it and is its greatest enemy.[5]

We are compounded of sincerity and insincerity in every thought;
the laughter of the brightest, the prayer of the most devout, is tainted
with insincerity, not because we have not the will, but because we
have not the strength to be otherwise.[6]

Remember the aged La Perouse in *The Counterfeiters*, who suggests
that no matter how hard we try to hear the voice of God, it is only
the devil we can succeed in hearing, that is, only our selfishness,

[1] *Clara Hopgood*, chap. xviii.
[2] *The Revolution*, chap. iii.
[3] W. H. White, editor, *Selections from Dr. Johnson's 'Rambler,'* London, Oxford
University Press, 1907, p. xviii.
[4] *Clara Hopgood*, chap. xxviii.
[5] W. H. White, 'Principles,' *Mark Rutherford's Deliverance*, 11th edition, London,
undated.
[6] W. H. White, Introduction to T. Carlyle, *The Life of Sterling*, World's Classics
edition, London, Oxford University Press, 1907, p. xx.

whatever the noble profession in which it comes disguised. But if Hale White mistrusts the self, he also defends it:

It is impossible totally to exclude the 'I' in our most unselfish acts. We ought not to torment ourselves because we cannot exclude it. We must not set pleasure so sharply over against unselfishness.[1]

The practice of self-denial is good; it may be learnt. More difficult than self-denial is enjoyment, rejoicing in that which ought to delight us. This perhaps may be partly learnt, but not without the severest self-discipline.[2]

Was it not in just this 'puritanical' manner, on reasoned and moral grounds, that Gide forced himself toward the delight an older morality had taught him to shun? 'It has long seemed to me,' we read in *Fruits of the Earth*, 'that joy is rarer, more difficult and lovelier than sadness . . . [and] not only a natural need . . . but also, indeed, a moral obligation.' [3]

Perhaps life is too large for any code we can as yet frame, and the dissolution of all codes, the fluid, unstable condition of which we complain, may be a necessary antecedent of new and more lasting combinations. One thing is certain, that there is not a single code now in existence which is not false; that the graduation of the vices and virtues is wrong, and that in the future it will be altered. We must not hand ourselves over to a despotism with no Divine right, even if there be a risk of anarchy.[4]

There is one statement, finally, in which the resemblance between the two writers is most vividly shown, and in which Hale White's thought—the conflict which drives it forward, and the way this conflict is resolved—is most clearly expressed. It comes from an essay called 'Principles.'

[1] *Last Pages*, p. 297.
[2] *Ibid.*, p. 311.
[3] André Gide, *Fruits of the Earth*: translated by Dorothy Bussy, New York, Alfred A. Knopf, 1949, p. 222.
[4] *Pages*, p. 76.

What we have once *heard*, really heard in our best moments, by that let us abide. There are multitudes of moments in which intelligent conviction in the truth of principles disappears, and we are able to do nothing more than fall back on mere determinate resolution to go on; not to give up what we have once found to be true. This power of determinate resolution which acts independently of enthusiasm is a precious possession. . . . One would like to have a record of all that passed through the soul of Ulysses when he was rowed past the Sirens. In what intellectually subtle forms did not the desire to stay clothe itself to that intellectually subtle soul? But he had bound himself beforehand, and he reached Ithaca and Penelope at last. . . . After six months [at a long and difficult task] I began to flag, and my greatest hindrance was, not the confessed desire for rest, but all kinds of the most fascinating principles or pseudo principles, which flattered what was best and not what was worst in me. I was narrowing my intellect, preventing the proper enjoyment of life, neglecting the sunshine, &c., &c. But I thought to myself 'Now the serpent was more subtile than any beast of the field,' and his temptation specially was that 'your eyes shall be opened, and ye shall be as gods.' I was enabled to persevere, oftentimes through no other motive than that aforesaid divine doggedness, and presently I was rewarded.[1]

The reader may remember Vincent in *The Counterfeiters*, for whom the devil had to provide an ethic to 'legitimize' his behaviour, because Vincent 'continues to be a moral being and the devil will only get the better of him by furnishing him with reasons for self-approval.'[2] But the passage bears an even more marked resemblance to the labyrinth chapter of Gide's *Theseus*, which, like the above essay, is one of its author's most complete and significant utterances. Gide's labyrinth is that of self-indulgence, in which each of us can lose himself if he risks it without a thread that will link him, as Theseus is linked to Ariadne, to the past, to duty, to his own best resolves—to something, in short, held above his immediate desires.

[1] 'Principles,' *Deliverance*.

[2] André Gide, *The Counterfeiters*, translated by Dorothy Bussy, New York, Alfred A. Knopf, 1927, p. 130.

For the place is difficult to escape from because it is filled with vapours which 'not only act on the will and put it to sleep; they induce a delicious intoxication rich in flattering delusions. . . . Each [victim] is led on by the complexities implicit in his own mind to lose himself . . . in a labyrinth of his own devising.' [1] Thus even our highest powers can be put in the service of the Sirens, proliferating marvellous reasons for a self-indulgence that will destroy us. It is interesting that Hale White ends here too with the devil—the serpent —so dear to both writers as a symbol of the self, with its subtlety and its temptation of pride. But if each requires the self to be thus held in check, it is not by a chain fashioned by others, not by a principle heard from without. It is by a principle inwardly heard, and by a thread of which the *spool* remains in the hero's own hands.

The source of the affinity between Hale White and Gide has perhaps already been made plain. It is the Protestantism in which, as it happens, both were strictly nurtured. Though each cast off early the orthodoxy in which he began, each retained what was capable of a life outside the orthodox forms. In brief, they retained the two great ideas which Protestantism, though it often distorted or even contradicted them, has made important in our culture. (These ideas are also human, needless to say, and others have found them elsewhere.)

The first idea is that of the primary importance of the moral problem. How should I live, is the question signalizing Bernard's emergence into manhood, which is thus shown to mean also into an awareness of moral responsibility. He wants at last not simply to be free and to enjoy himself, but to live right and to use his freedom for an upward progress. Bernard's question is at the bottom of most of what our two authors have written, and it is the tendency of each— for the moralist tends to become a generalizer—to formulate his answers into guiding principles. At the same time, however, beside this need to seek the right and be in it, each has kept with him from his Protestant heritage another element equally crucial. This is the idea of 'the priesthood of all believers,' the idea that no *other* priest, but only himself, only an 'inner voice,' can be the proper judge of the individual's moral rectitude. Of course, as our writers show us, these

[1] André Gide, *Two Legends: Œdipus and Theseus*, translated by John Russell, New York, Alfred A. Knopf, 1950, pp. 85-6.

two ideas must often stand opposed. For the general principles which each is forever deducing from experience must forever be tested against fresh experience, lest some vital difference has arisen in self or situation, or lest what led one man upward lead the next man down. The conflict between these two movements of the mind, the perpetual criticism passing back and forth between principles and changing particular contexts, has been for both Gide and Hale White the motor, as it were, for an ever deeper and more audacious exploration of the moral life. It has made that life eminently adventurous for them, made it one for which, if freedom of conscience is necessary, that same freedom creates endless dangers and difficulties. But it has also enabled them to avoid the two typical extremes, so prevalent today. For, on the one hand, it sets them apart from those who live by principles they have placed once for all beyond question, and who would suffer reality to be distorted or simplified rather than that a principle be doubted. And on the other, it sets them apart from those who cynically reject principles altogether and give themselves up instead to the immediate cues of every new context or of personal appetite.

Now there are certain traditional modes of attack on both these attitudes. The preoccupation with moral questions, for instance, is supposed to be narrowing, and, in literature, anti-aesthetic. Thus, E. M. Forster speaks in his *Aspects of the Novel* of 'that tiresome little receptacle, a conscience, which is so often a nuisance in serious writers and so contracts their effects—the conscience of Hawthorne or of Mark Rutherford.' [1] But this is rather like complaining that the requirements of literary form are a nuisance and contract a writer's effects. In fact, the moral conscience, like form, like many rules and regulations, is what makes effects possible, because it gives definition to the mere chaos of experience. If nothing were right or wrong, good or evil, if there were no *ought*, then all would be one and nothing would make any difference. It is the lack of a conscience that is the real literary handicap, because it means the lack of a mode of discrimination—and even of a motive for discrimination, that is, of interest in life. (Forster himself, I need hardly say, rejoices in a con-

---

[1] E. M. Forster, *Aspects of the Novel*, New York, Harcourt, Brace and Company, Inc., 1927, p. 206.

science of particular firmness and delicacy.) Of course, any complaint about too narrow or simple-minded a morality, which means too narrow or simple-minded a view of human experience, would be entirely legitimate. But it should be remembered—Gide is the great example, but Hale White is another—that for the subtle mind a conscience is precisely a goad toward further subtlety.

Far more serious has been the attack on the other idea, that of the 'priesthood' of each man for himself; we have witnessed indeed a steady decline in the prestige of the free conscience, and not only in the comparatively unintelligent realm of politics. In a famous and influential essay, T. S. Eliot, for instance, seemed to see the Protestant 'inner voice' as *necessarily* in conflict with principles—which were presumed to be *necessarily* derived from some outer authority— never itself, in its 'best moments,' the author of them. It is the voice, he told us, which 'breathes the eternal message of vanity, fear, and lust.' [1] Yet the self-exaltation of Protestantism was never at its best either pride of self or lust for self-gratification. The self was exalted, not as an object of worship, but as an instrument for use, the only reliable instrument in matters as complex and changing as those of the soul. The purpose for which it was used remained precisely a search for the altar on which it might not vainly be given up, the soil in which the grain of corn might 'die' and bear fruit. It has always, in fact, been a development peculiarly characteristic of the Protestant tradition that to a God personally descried and freely chosen the self should be utterly abandoned.

The price for this assumption of personal responsibility has not been small. It accounts for the introspective gloom which marks so much of Protestant culture and the sounds of anguish it frequently emits. (The progress of Bunyan's Pilgrim would have been less agonizing, as well as less thrilling, if it had led at the outset to a centre of authority where the burden of decision could be shifted to others.) It accounts too for the frequent eccentricities which rise to make a mock of human freedom. But the reward is at least commensurate with the price, for it is nothing less than the liberty to maintain a personal relationship with the Highest, with reality,

[1] T. S. Eliot, 'The Function of Criticism,' *Selected Essays*, 2nd edition, London, 1946, p. 27.

justice and truth. Thus Hale White, in his freedom, sometimes pined for the certainty and security it denied him, and Gide has perhaps been led by his into eccentricity. But, in return, each has been enabled to stay honest, to explore deeply the new paths his new experience has opened for him, and, most important for us today, to learn and show that freedom is not incompatible with morality, or with a *self*-discipline which can keep it moving 'upward.'

In spite of their profound affinity, however, a word must be said of their differences, which, as will appear, are also great and interesting. They flow, chiefly, from this: that Hale White explores the moral life with his eye on human suffering, from which it is his main concern to seek deliverance; Gide, acquainted though he is with suffering, tends to regard it as failure: it is his pride to concentrate rather on his goal of happiness, and to seek it happily. The result is that Gide seems to write for human strength, inspiring courage and leading to joy; Hale White for inevitable human weakness, mitigating terror and assuaging pain. Though their insight into the nature of moral problems is remarkably alike, Gide uses his to open the way before us, and Hale White seeks instead to show us where we can legitimately rest, what amid the dangers of the way can support us when we fall. What he finds, like the discoveries of Gide and for the same reasons, can never be offered as absolutely sure. There are extremities, moreover, in which no tool or weapon of the mind has ever availed, and since he will not lie, he can only counsel us in these to remember that others have passed through them and to endure. But testimony exists to the admittedly peculiar fact that his books have done more than delight and liberate; they have consoled. Earlier in time and different in temperament, Hale White does not carry us so far nor in so many directions as Gide, who is the greater of the two, as he is surely one of the greatest forces for intellectual and moral liberation among the writers of our period. But if the French writer is the more dazzling and instructs us more widely, it is the English writer whom we can love.

CHAPTER II

Life–Part 1

BECAUSE of the intimate relationship I have mentioned between our author's personal experience and his writings, a preliminary sketch of his life will be useful.

He was born in Bedford on December 31, 1831. He thus began his life in a Puritan culture and ended it in a culture which was substantially our own—scientific, liberal and secular. This is of first importance, for his work is, among other things, a translation into modern idiom of the doctrines of Puritanism. 'Even if Calvinism had been carved on tables of stone and handed down from heaven by the Almighty Hand,' he was to write, 'it would not have lived if it had not been found to agree more or less with the facts, and it was because it was a deduction from what nobody can help seeing that it was so vital, the Epistle to the Romans serving as the inspired confirmation of an experience.' [1] He was able to convey the 'experience' beneath the Puritan formulae because his own life gave him both the closeness to the subject and the distance from it which accurate translation requires. To this point, however, another must immediately be added. He rarely speaks of the actual Puritanism of his own youth without irony or anger, and this often looks like mere self-contradiction. The same doctrine, for instance, which he suggests in *The Revolution* is a picture of terrible reality—that of the predestined damnation of the many—becomes, when he tells of his seminary studies, a 'terrible invention,' [2] parroted without dismay only because no one took it to heart. In fact, there is no contradiction. It was precisely because they were not connected by his teachers with experience, as, freed from the tyranny of literalness, he was later to connect them, that the Puritan forms and formulae of his youth seemed gratuitously cruel.

[1] *The Revolution*, chap. i.   [2] *Early Life*, p. 60.

His middle name came from his mother's mother and was supposed by some to indicate a connection with the Carolean Chief Justice Sir Matthew Hale. But his kind of pride, when it showed itself at all, tended to look elsewhere. On that connection he made a point of throwing doubt, while concerning his paternal ancestors he once wrote his second wife as follows:

I have been told they lie buried in Wilshamstead Churchyard. Wilshamstead is [a] small remote agricultural village in Bedfordshire. They were Bedfordshire folk, and Bedfordshire was the headquarters of Puritan and Cromwellian Independency. This survived. My grandfather had his windows smashed by an angry Tory mob during the Napoleonic Wars because he refused to illuminate for British victories, and my father also had his windows destroyed because he was a member of Lord John Russell's committee at the borough election during the time of the Reform Bill. I seem to have come of an honest set, but socially nothing much above farmers, who may have been, and indeed very likely were, officers in Oliver's army.[1]

The Puritan culture evoked in such a passage has been charged with being unintellectual or anti-intellectual. On the whole, the charge has been either false or misleading. It was not a culture given especially to the arts or to the tasting and proliferating of ideas for their own sakes. But ideas, conscious and related principles, were its informing spirit, and it was the attempt to bring actual life in line with ideas which chiefly characterized it. During the period of its vitality the allegiances of the Puritans, religious and political, were not mechanical, but thought through and related to each other. There was no divorce between the life of the mind and conduct. Integrity was therefore the Puritan's outstanding quality, and though grace of manner, whether in behaviour or language, was not a conscious end, grace of a peculiarly attractive kind did result from the genuine conformity of acts and words to inner and outer realities.

The Independents—now more commonly known as Congregationalists—were a sect of Dissenters or Nonconformists, so called

---

[1] *The Groombridge Diary*, p. 196.

because they refused to acknowledge the authority or conform to the dogmas and practices of the Established Church of England. To them the hierarchical form of that Church was contrary to Scripture. The state of a man's soul, they felt, was a matter between himself and God, and salvation could be attained, or realized, only through an inner struggle of which no outsider could possibly be a judge. However useful the priest, by reason of what learning he might have, could be in some matters, he was in this merely a struggling pilgrim like all others, and no more likely than the most ignorant of his parishioners to be touched by Divine grace. (The Puritan is supposed to be especially limited in his view of human nature and human life, but this idea involves precisely an awareness of their complexity: of such awareness, indeed, *The Pilgrim's Progress* is sufficient proof.) For this reason the Independents were loosely and democratically organized. Each congregation was an independent unit, selecting its own ministers, criticizing them freely and making its own regulations.

The Independents were Calvinists, and the fundamental doctrines of Calvinist Dissent were those of St. Paul, particularly as these were re-emphasized by Luther and Calvin. Man, it was held, rendered inherently imperfect, or sinful, by the Fall, is incapable of living according to God's law and must, as a matter of strict justice, be damned. In order that God's mercy might save man without conflicting with His justice, Christ has paid the price of man's guilt, and this price redeems every sinner who *believes* that it will do so, who has faith. But faith is not to be won by an exercise of will. It is a free gift of God, a work of grace, and God has known from the beginning who is to receive the gift and who not: it is, as it were, part of each man's original nature. A handful, in fact, are to be saved, and the rest damned, nor have the mere creatures any right to protest, since their Creator owes them nothing.

We shall see, as we go over the novels of Hale White, how much in all this may be read as permanent truth, alien as may be to some of us the form in which it is expressed. A key may here be given, however, to the 'secular' meaningfulness of religious formulations. Explanation must be read as if it were symbolic description. If it is hard to accept the idea of a God who preordains the salvation of only

a few of His creatures and the damnation of all the rest, it may be
less so to accept the 'secular' idea to which this exactly corresponds:
that more of us do, in fact, suffer than find peace and that our fates
result from a combination of temperament and circumstances over
which we have only the most limited control. (Are we entirely
determined, or only partly? The Puritan puzzled over this problem
in his way just as we do in ours.) The Calvinist God is cruel because
reality is so. 'Let us . . . remember that these men [the Puritans] did
not idly believe in such cruelty,' Hale White tells us, again in *The
Revolution*. 'They were forced into their belief by the demands of
their understanding, and their assent was more meritorious than the
weak protests of so-called enlightenment.'[1] Religious formulations
are thus the expression of *insight*, of things really seen in life, in teleo-
logical terms; and it is in the kinds of things seen, in the elements of
experience shown—as with the penetration of genius—to be related
that the unique wisdom of religion is to be found.

The consequences of these ideas for our own culture are well
known. Among other things they led to the modern sense of the
value and rights of the individual, which means to political democracy. 'This theological individualism of the Puritan doctrines,'
wrote Halevy, '. . . constituted no small factor in the republicanism
of the Cromwellians.'[2] And Tawney, going further, calls them 'a
theory of individual rights which, secularized and generalized, was
to be among the most potent explosives that the world has known.'[3]
It is no wonder, then, that the opposition to Dissent was not a purely
religious matter, but took on from the first, and until well into the
nineteenth century, the character of political repression. In a very
real sense the family of Hale White were, during his youth, members
of an oppressed minority. Here is the picture as one historian of
Dissent gives it:

The condition of the Nonconformists at the beginning of the 19th
Century was such as is very difficult to realize today. They were still

[1] *The Revolution*, chap. ix.
[2] Élie Halevy, *A History of the English People: Book III, Religion and Culture*,
London, Penguin Books, 1938, p. 24.
[3] R. H. Tawney, *Religion and the Rise of Capitalism*, West Drayton, Middlesex,
Penguin Books, 1938, p. 229.

under the ban of the law; they were unable to hold any public office; the national universities were closed to them; they could not be married in their own churches nor be buried save with the rites of the Church of England. They were compelled to pay church rates for the support of the Establishment, and, if their worship was tolerated, it was only in specially licensed conventicles.[1]

Such a state of affairs might alone have ranged the Dissenters alongside the political radicals driving for popular rights, if their doctrines had not already predisposed them to sympathy with republican ideas. As Selbie goes on to say, 'The cause of freedom in religion was bound up with the liberties of democracy. Whatever may be thought to be the case today, historically, at any rate, Nonconformity was committed without question to all those causes which are now grouped under the name of liberal.'[2]

And as late as the 1830's, in Bedford, there were still Puritans who lived up to their noblest traditions, both religious and political. One example Hale White had, as we shall see, in his own home. Another was the minister in charge of his family's chapel, Bunyan's Meeting,[3] during his infancy. This was the Reverend Samuel Hilliard, a minister long remembered, John Brown tells us, as a passionate and eloquent preacher. He not only taught a religion that was seriously intended to influence daily life, but he was also, in traditional Nonconformist fashion, an active republican, openly supporting Lord John Russell in 1832.

By the first decades of the nineteenth century, however, the Puritan doctrines had become for the majority a passively accepted legacy of phrases and rituals, a legacy which preserved their community but left the inner life largely untouched. And it was a symptom of decay that Dissenters had changed in their political attitudes as well. 'We can watch,' says Halevy, 'between 1792 and 1815 an

---

[1] W. B. Selbie, *Nonconformity: Its Origin and Progress*, London, Williams and Morgate, 1912, p. 198.

[2] *Ibid.*, p. 200.

[3] Bunyan himself was a Baptist, but the chapel called 'Bunyan's' or the 'Old Meeting,' built on the site of St. John's Church where he preached from 1656 onward, was Independent, or Congregational.

uninterrupted decline in the revolutionary spirit among the sects.'[1]
At Bunyan's Meeting Mr. Hilliard was replaced by the Reverend
John Jukes, who remained the minister during Hale White's boyhood and youth and who began the process that estranged his father
from their religion. Mr. Jukes was diplomatic, unimaginative—a
mediocrity. He avoided all controversial subjects and his theology,
of which his sermons were a smooth, dull recitation, reflected rather
the desire for easy comfort than the felt and inwardly consistent
vision of life's tragic realities that had been the religion of his
predecessors. He taught, Hale White remembered,

what was called a 'moderate Calvinism,' a phrase not easy to understand. If it had any meaning, it was that predestination, election, and
reprobation were unquestionably true, but they were dogmas about
which it was not prudent to say much, for some of the congregation
were a little Arminian, and St. James could not be totally neglected.
[The Arminians held that salvation could be won by the proper
works and beliefs and by repentance, and St. James that, 'faith, if it
hath not works, is dead, being alone.'][2]

'It was not the gifts of the minister,' Hale White tells us, 'certainly
after the days of my early childhood, which kept [the] congregation
steady. The reason why it held together was the simple loyalty
which prevents a soldier or sailor from mutinying, although the
commanding officer may deserve no respect.'[3]

There were thus the two kinds of Puritans before Hale White's
eyes as he grew up, one for whom the sermons of Mr. Jukes were a
sufficient religion and another more closely resembling the Puritans
of the best times. Each kind recurs in his work. And each is pictured
with the vividness of intimate knowledge, because his mother
belonged to the first and his father to the second.

William White, the father, was a remarkable man, acknowledged
by the writer to be a chief influence on his life. It is undoubtedly
from him, as I say, more forcefully than from anyone else, that Hale
White learned how religion in general and Calvinism in particular

[1] Halevy, *op. cit.*, p. 48.   [2] *Early Life*, pp. 16-17.
[3] *Ibid.*, p. 16.

could make sense to an intelligent mind, and perhaps we can partly
account for the warmth of his loyalty to his cultural heritage through
the fact that it is also an aspect of his loyalty to his father. In the
'Black Notebook' he was to write, 'What I have felt the want of
more than anything else in this life is wise counsel for particular
occasions, of somebody who could *advise* me. Principles I could get
by the bushel anywhere. My father was able to help me best.'

White, born in 1807, was a bookseller, the last in Bedford to do
his own binding, and a man of deep, if narrow, culture. He loved
poetry 'of a sublime cast' [1] and to him this meant not only Milton
(his great favourite) but also Byron. We are told that this strict
Calvinist, who became Superintendent of Bunyan Meeting Sunday
School, would recite long passages of Byron aloud as he worked at
the composing desk in his printing office. But he was not only a man
of culture, he was active in public life, a leader both in politics and
in the struggle of Dissenters against discrimination. A prominent
Whig, he was considered one of Bedford's best public speakers.
During the election of 1832 he was on one occasion besieged with
the Whig Committee in an inn by a Tory mob, and on another, as
we have already seen, had the windows of his house broken. As for
the religious struggle, White defeated almost singlehanded in 1843
a movement to require all schoolteachers under the Bedford Charity
to be members of the Church of England, a step that was feared to
be only the first toward the total exclusion of Dissenters from the
schools. His newspaper letters on this affair, written in reply to a
member of the opposite camp, were reprinted in a pamphlet entitled
Bedford Charity Not Sectarian, and it was with regard to this pamphlet
that Hale White made the remarks on style quoted in Chapter I.
Indeed, we may see in the novelist's style one of the chief signs of
the father's influence, for White wrote an English very much like
his son's, simple, pure, direct, yet often eloquent.

White did not remain loyal to Bunyan's Meeting. His dissatisfaction with Jukes, as has been said, was what first took him away from
the Meeting House, but not long afterwards he gave up his belief in
the literal truth of Calvinism altogether. Hale White tells us it was
Carlyle's *Sartor Resartus* and *Heroes and Hero-Worship* that caused his

[1] *Ibid.*, p. 37.

father's final change, doing so not by direct attack on dogma but merely by inciting intellectual growth. A picture of what his mind then was is preserved in a brilliant pamphlet he wrote in 1852 in defence of his son when Hale White and two others were expelled from a Calvinist seminary for heresy. The young men had dared to question the idea that the inspiration of the Bible was different from that of other books, that its authority lay elsewhere than in its 'mere' truth. This pamphlet, called *To Think or Not To Think*, distinguishes between true belief, which is voluntary and really affects one's behaviour, and mechanical assent to authority, asserts with Coleridge that 'whatever finds me bears witness for itself that it has proceeded from the Holy Spirit,' and concludes that by its tyrannical dogmatism the school condemned itself to retain only the fools and the hypocrites.

White's public activity did his business no good. He was forced to close his shop, and when he left it, he was in debt. But shortly afterwards, as a return for his services in the Liberal cause, he was given by Lord Charles Russell the post of Assistant Doorkeeper—he soon became Doorkeeper—of the House of Commons. Adding to his income by writing newspaper letters on House debates, he eventually paid his Bedford debts in full. In both these jobs of his last years he distinguished himself. In the House he won the esteem and friendship of many famous statesmen, becoming too the invaluable mentor of newcomers. At a dinner given in honour of Lord John Russell and attended by Sir David Dundas, the Solicitor General, he was one of the speakers, and Russell's brother, Lord Charles, tells us in an obituary notice, 'His [White's] was the finest speech, and Sir David Dundas remarked to me as Mr. White concluded, "Why there is old Cobbett again, minus the vulgarity!" '[1] As for his journalism, the newspaper letters were afterwards collected into a book entitled *The Inner Life of the House of Commons*, a remarkably lively and intelligent picture of nineteenth-century English statesmen in action.

On his retirement in 1875 he received a gift from the members of the House, testifying to their high appreciation. He died in 1882. In concluding the sketch of him in the Early Life, Hale White writes:

[1] *Early Life*, p. 34.

My father was a perfectly honest man and hated shiftiness even worse than downright lying. The only time he gave me a thrashing was for prevarication. . . . His portrait, erect, straightforward-looking, firmly standing, one foot a little in advance, helps me and decides me when I look at it. Of all types of humanity the one which he represents would be most serviceable to the world at the present day.[1]

Of his mother, Hale White tells us only a little, but it is enough to establish her type clearly. She was 'by no means democratic,' but had 'a slight weakness in favour of rank.' [2] She took great satisfaction in having managed to know some people who lived in a 'park' near Bedford. 'It was called a "park" but in reality it was a big garden with a meadow beyond. However, and this was the great point, none of my mother's town friends were callers at the Park.' [3] It was, in fact, his mother's preference for people who did not stand behind counters that was responsible for what he calls 'the great blunder of my life,' [4] the decision that he study for the ministry. Her persuasion had also another motive: a son of her brother was already being trained for that profession and 'she desired equality with her sister-in-law.' Hale White adds at last, it is true, 'Besides, I can honestly declare that to her an Evangelical ministry was a sacred calling, and the thought that I might be the means of saving souls made her happy.' [5] This, however, hardly alters the picture. We see her as devout, but with a religion that must have been as different even from her husband's orthodoxy as outright scepticism would have been. Much of Hale White's work is clearly personal in origin, much of it deals with marriages made unhappy by the intellectual gulf between husband and wife, and there is a tendency to suppose his own marriage is always the source. In fact, we may see in his father's the origin of his most unhappy fictional marriages, those in which the gulf can never be bridged because one spouse is mentally commonplace and unfeeling. There is another kind, however, one in which the guilt belongs to the self-centred intellectual who eventually restores family happiness by recognizing the supreme

[1] Ibid., pp. 36–8.   [2] Ibid., p. 42.   [3] Ibid.
[4] Ibid., p. 55.   [5] Ibid., p. 56.

D

human virtues he had overlooked. For this, as I will show, he may indeed have had a basis in his own marriage.[1]

Both his parents being then devout Independents, Hale White's memories of his childhood Sunday, with its family prayers, its Sunday School, its interminable services in the packed and airless Bunyan's Meeting, its cold dinner and its prohibition of most of life's amenities, were as dreary as anything in Gosse's *Father and Son*. Sundays, however, though their gloom seemed endless, came only once a week, and religion aside, Hale White's childhood was a happy one. Bedford was still rural, with open country easily accessible. There was also the River Ouse, with its swimming, boating and fishing in summer and its skating in winter. There was never, he told his second wife, thinking ruefully perhaps of what came later, 'by nature a happier child.'[2]

Two of his boyhood memories are worth recording, for they crop up in his work. One is that of a certain aunt in Colchester, a woman whose 'singular originality'[3] irritated her neighbours. She was a person who would often take a mile-and-a-half walk to church at five in the morning, and then sit down on its porch to read George Herbert. This aunt was not of Hale White's family, having married, surprisingly, his uncle, a baker who was 'a good kind of man, but tame.'[4] What the aged Hale White recalled with most vividness was her generosity. 'The survival in my memory of her cakes, ginger-bread and kisses has done me more good, moral good—if you have a fancy for the word—than sermons or punishment.'[5] We will meet again this combination of deep religiousness, eccentricity and generosity in the character of Miss Leroy in *Mark Rutherford's Deliverance*.

In the second memory there is a significance for his whole life. He felt this himself, and it recurs in the *Early Life*, in talk set down in *The Groombridge Diary*, and in the story 'Michael Trevanion,' while its meaning is symbolized frequently elsewhere. Already a good

---

[1] My information on the father comes chiefly from the *Early Life*, *The Groombridge Diary*, and obituaries in the *Birmingham Post*, November 3, 1882, and the *Bedfordshire Times and Independent*, March 11, 1882.

[2] *The Groombridge Diary*, p. 71.   [3] *Early Life*, p. 11.

[4] *Ibid.*   [5] *Ibid.*, p. 12.

swimmer, he had set out to swim to a boat about a hundred yards from shore. He had reached it and was returning when suddenly the 'mad conviction' came to him that he would never get back.

There was no real danger of failure of strength, but my heart began to beat furiously, the shore became dim and I gave myself up for lost. 'This then is dying,' I said to myself, but I also said—I remember how vividly—'There shall be a struggle before I go down —one desperate effort'—and I strove, in a way I cannot describe, to bring my will to bear directly on my terror. In an instant the horrible excitement was at an end, and *there was a great calm*. I stretched my limbs leisurely, rejoicing in the sea and the sunshine. This story is worth telling because it shows that a person with tremulous nerves such as mine, never ought to say that he has done all that he can do. Notice also that it was not nature or passion which carried me through, but a conviction wrought by the reason. The next time I was in extremity victory was tenfold easier.[1]

In *The Groombridge Diary* he calls that 'mad conviction' a 'hypochondriacal fancy.'[2] And though what he refers to as hypochondria, a tendency to fear and depression amounting often to despair, did not set in till a later occasion, this episode perfectly reveals its nature. In a situation where pleasanter possibilities existed and were even probable, he became convinced of the worst. And his salvation lay not in arguing with his fear but in ignoring it and proceeding on the dogged assumption that it was wrong. It lay in *faith*. It is true that he here says it was faith in a conviction wrought by the reason, but his writings will show us how often it was at least the appearance of reason which faith had—doggedly, not reasonably—to oppose, for the fear and gloom of a reasoning man never fail to produce 'reason' and 'evidence' to support them.

When he was about fifteen the question arose of what he was to become. He himself had already decided. He had been studying art at the Bedford Grammar School, and he wanted to be an artist. Indeed, he wanted so desperately to continue studying art that when he was overruled there were even tears—'and he thought,' wrote his

---

[1] *Ibid.*, pp. 53-4.   [2] *The Groombridge Diary*, p. 95.

wife, recording a conversation, 'that tears at that age meant a great deal.' [1] But he had also been teaching Sunday School, and, for reasons we have seen, his mother preferred to find in this the indication of what his profession should be. It was decided that he become a minister.

Before entering on his studies, he had to undergo a ceremony called 'conversion.' That is, he had to prove to Bunyan's Meeting that he had become convinced of his sinfulness, innate and acquired, and of his salvation through Christ, who had Himself paid the price to ransom all believing sinners. Like the young Gosse, he was spared the necessity of testifying to any dramatic awakening because he 'had enjoyed the privilege of godly parents.' [2]

I can see myself now—I was no more than seventeen—stepping out of our pew, standing in the aisle at the pew door and protesting to their content before the minister of the church, father and mother, protesting also to my own complete content, that the witness of God in me to my own salvation was as clear as noonday. Poor little mortal, a twelvemonth out of round jackets, I did not in the least know who God was, or what was salvation.[1]

(This, by the way, is one of those ironies his work will appear to contradict, for *Catherine Furze* is precisely a demonstration of the real human meaningfulness of the theory of 'conversion.')

He began his studies around 1849 or 1850 at the Countess of Huntingdon's College at Cheshunt and a year or so later transferred to New College, St. John's Wood. In neither of these schools did he learn anything of value. The secular teaching was superficial and perfunctory, and the religious a mechanical assertion of doctrine. The chief text for the latter was, of course, the Bible, but this was studied merely as a compendium of dogmas to be accepted and memorized without discussion. On February 3, 1852, the Principal, Dr. John Harris, examined Hale White's class on his recent inaugural lecture. Its subject had been the inspiration of the Bible, and speaking for English Dissent he had declared:

[1] *Early Life*, p. 28 n.   [2] *Ibid.*, p. 58.
[3] *Ibid.*, p. 59.

The mind of the Reformation protested against human dictation only that it might yield itself the more unreservedly to the Divine Authority of Scripture. We profess to represent that mind; and with the same sheet anchor out our vessel can ride in safety. But to tamper with it is suicidally to cut and fray the strands of our cable while a storm is threatening and there are breakers ahead.[1]

During the examination two members of the class, Hale White quickly associating himself with them, rose and 'asked some questions about the formation of the canon and the authenticity of the separate books.' [2] The Principal stopped them at once. 'I must inform you,' he said, 'that this is not an open question within these walls. There is a great body of truth received as orthodoxy by the great majority of Christians, the explanation of which is one thing, but to doubt it is another, and the foundation must not be questioned.' The three rebels were brought before a committee and were asked questions like 'Do you believe a statement because it is in the Bible, or merely because it is true?'[3] Their answers were such that on February 13 they were expelled.

There were many influences abroad at that time that might have started the young Hale White on the path to 'heresy.' Some have been mentioned in Chapter I. But Hale White gives all the credit for his own development to Wordsworth. Opening a volume of Wordsworth for the first time at eighteen, he came on the words, 'Knowing that Nature never did betray The heart that loved her,' and these words, he says, 'were a signal of the approach of something which turned out to be of the greatest importance, and altered my history.'

It was a new capacity. There woke in me an aptness for the love of natural beauty, a possibility of being excited to enthusiasm by it, and of deriving a secret joy from it sufficiently strong, to make me careless of the world and its pleasures. Another effect which Wordsworth had upon me, and has had on other people, was the modifica-

[1] Quoted by H. A. Smith, *The Life and Thought of William Hale White*: doctoral dissertation, University of Birmingham, England, 1939, p. 97.
[2] *Early Life*, p. 64.   [3] *Ibid.*, p. 65.

tion, altogether unintentional on his part, of religious belief. He never dreams of attacking anybody for his creed, and yet it often becomes impossible for those who study him and care for him to be members of an orthodox religious community. At any rate it would have been impossible in the town of Bedford. His poems imply a living God, different from the artificial God of the churches. The revolution wrought by him goes far deeper, and is far more permanent than any which is the work of Biblical critics, and it was Wordsworth and not German research which caused my expulsion from New College. . . . For some time I had no thought of heresy, but the seed was there, and was alive just as much as the seed-corn is alive all the time it lies in the earth apparently dead.[1]

It is likely that Carlyle also had a hand in his change, as he had had in that of his father. An essay in *Pages from a Journal* informs us that his enthusiasm for Carlyle's work in 1850 led him to write to the great man. The answer he received, dated March 9, 1850, tells him, 'Be not surprised that "people" have no sympathy with you,'[2] and we may suppose that Carlyle too had by that time started thoughts in him which he could not share with his orthodox fellows.

The sense of isolation was destined to grow. Expelled from college, he was also cut off from the only intellectual and social community he knew. He was untrained, moreover, in any way that might make easier his adjustment to the world outside Bedford and Puritanism. He went to London to look for work. The first job he got was as a schoolmaster in a private school at Stoke Newington. He stayed only two days, but he never forgot the experience, for here 'there fell upon me what was the beginning of a sorrow that lasted all my life.'[3] Even in his old age he spoke of it (to his wife) with the fascinated precision of detail with which we recall a nightmare. He was received at the school by a servant, given a cold supper in a dimly lit empty classroom, and then shown to his room, a garret reached by a ladder which was to be pulled up after him. It was while he stood at the garret's window, looking out toward the 'dull glare' of London in the distance and listening to its 'deadened

[1] *Early Life*, pp. 61-3.   [2] *Pages*, p. 3.
[3] *Early Life*, p. 80.

roar,' that the 'sorrow' came—an attack, it seems, not merely of loneliness but of pure horror of life. It was not till he had found a substitute and fled from the school to the home of a friend that 'the horrible choking fog' [1] departed from him. But it was to return, and it remained at best, as I have said, his life's constant background.

He went back to London, tramped the streets miserably for some days looking for work, and at last met with success at a well-known address, 142 Strand. This was the office of John Chapman, publisher of heretical books and editor of the *Westminster Review*. Hale White's account of the interview tells us much about both. Chapman tested him for a required degree of heresy as, at his New College trial, he had been tested for orthodoxy. He asked the young man if he believed in miracles.

I said 'Yes and no.' I did not believe that an actual Curtius leaped into the gulf and saved Rome, but I did believe in the spiritual truth set forth in the legend. This reply was allowed to pass, although my scepticism would have been more satisfactory and more useful if it had been a little more thorough.[2]

He did not like his work at Chapman's. In fact, as we shall see, he never liked any of the work he did for pay. This was not because he was lazy and self-indulgent, for he never did less than his best, but because he always responded too intensely to the pricks of life, and because his hunger for free private thought, study and expression was always so imperious. The job with the publisher was especially 'disagreeable,' however. He not only kept Chapman's accounts, he had to go out and sell his books to bookdealers. He liked the job so little that even Chapman's offer of a partnership could not keep him when, in 1854, a friend got him a clerkship at the Registrar General's office in Somerset House. It is significant that he preferred such a retreat from the public life and challenges of the publisher's office, though the clerkship paid little and though he could not have expected it to be other than in fact he found it, excruciatingly dull.

But during the two years at Chapman's there was one memorable consolation. Living in Mrs. Chapman's boarding-house, he had as a

---

[1] *Ibid.*, p. 82.   [2] *Ibid.*, pp. 82-3.

fellow-lodger a young assistant editor of the *Westminster Review* named Marian Evans. She was not yet the famous George Eliot, but he felt and responded to her genius. He responded to more: she had a gift for sympathy that was a particular boon to 'an awkward creature [like him] unaccustomed to society,'[1] to a creature, we might add, who was not merely shy but whom life and reading and thought generally stimulated to abnormal intensities of feeling. (A college friend remembered how his voice used to tremble, as with repressed emotion, when he delivered sermons, and he tells us himself that poetry could make him break into tears.) Miss Evans would reply 'even with eagerness to a trifling remark I happened to make and give it some importance.'[2] She played Beethoven and Gluck to him, and once, 'I was, I am afraid, a little incoherent in my thanks.'[3] Did he fall in love with her, as, in *The Autobiography*, his counterpart, Mark Rutherford, falls in love with her, Theresa? We don't know for certain, but he went so far as to find her 'attractive personally,' which, from what we are usually told, was a great length to go: 'Her hair was particularly beautiful, and in her grey eyes there was a curiously shifting light, generally soft and tender but convertible into the keenest flash.'[4] And to his second wife he said, 'I could worship that woman.' When he left Chapman's, a mixture of shyness and self-torturing perverseness prevented him from keeping up the friendship—the story is told in 'Confessions of a Self-Tormentor'—and for this he never forgave himself.

Hale White had been expelled for heresy in a way that intensified his first rebelliousness against his Puritan past; and at Chapman's he was working in an atmosphere, except for Marian Evans, full of 'emancipated' notions and literary cleverness. But neither rebelliousness nor emancipation nor cleverness was able to simplify his thought or dry up his feelings, as they so often do with bright young men. The proof of this is in a letter he wrote to his father, the earliest one we have. The letter is worth quoting because it reveals so well what he then was and because, its overwrought Carlylean tone aside, it can stand as a strangely apt prologue to the work begun almost thirty years later:

[1] *Early Life*, p. 84.   [2] *Last Pages*, p. 132.
[3] *Ibid.*, p. 134.   [4] *Ibid.*, p. 132.

142 Strand
3 May 1853

Dearest Father

Your note in turn, I need scarcely say, fills me with great joy, and
yet not without pain intermingled, for instantly the thought rises up
that you are a long way off and then vain wishes come that you
were here or I with you. With all that you say I most cordially agree,
most especially with what you say about cold negativism. Mr. Chapman is nothing so much of a negation merely as many of his books
are, but I see, and must see infinitely more of this heartless emptiness
both in books and men than I ever saw before, and this drives me
back again to all my old eternal friends who appear more than ever
perfect, and Jesus above them all. Granted that all that the Strausses,
Foxtons and Newmans have made out is correct—that there is no
miracle, that Palestine's laws of nature were really England's, and so
on, yet I turn round on them and say 'You cannot deceive my eyes.'
Here are words in these Gospels in black and white, and such words
I maintain were never spoken before. No literary world here full of
attempts at book or sentence making, no writing for the sake of
writing, no thought of publishing here, no vain empty cleverness,
attempted merely for the purpose of glorifying the writer in the
reader's eyes, but the simple solemn words, spoken as by one conscious of eternity round him and over him, to beings whose life is
an awful thing 'coming from eternity and going to eternity again'—
Oh, after all the soul rests in calm satisfaction *on* the *soul*—nothing
short of this—and if you feel in a book that the writer's *heart*, his own
real truest thought is not present, there is no rest but a vague dissatisfaction and disquiet. But on the Bible I can repose and feel none
of this disquiet and discontent. The writer's *soul* is there, his own
most real experience and consequently on that I rest. In nine-tenths
of the books I read I feel just as a magnet I should think feels when
there is a card put between it and a piece of steel, as if it would long
to pierce through the covering and get at the real true metal. So in
books you feel as if a film were between you and the author which
you could not pierce, as if you would give anything to get really
at the heartfelt thinkings of the man. In the Bible I feel now at

length do I see the real soul. Here I am heart to heart, hand to hand with a real human being. I embrace no clothed, disguised man but feel the blood beating and the touch of the warm flesh. . . .[1]

We know to whom he owed that longing to pierce beneath the 'clothes' to the soul in contact with 'eternities.' But to that grasp of the indestructible wealth in the Bible he was led by an influence greater than Carlyle's, by a man of whom he flatly declared to his second wife, 'He *made* me.' [2] This was the Reverend Caleb Morris, an Independent minister, a Welshman, a man of 'extraordinary genius.' [3]

Hale White met him first in 1849, when Morris was forty-nine years old, but the period of most fruitful contacts was after 1850 and especially the first London years. In this period the young Hale White attended his services in Eccleston Square Chapel to which Morris drew crowds (though 'a strangely nervous temperament . . . with an obscure bodily trouble, frequently prevented him from keeping his engagements' [4]) and the even more memorable gatherings on the Sunday at Morris's home. There in 'his remarkable way . . . he would take some story from the Bible and oblivious of everything except just what concerned his nearest self, would pour out unrestrainedly to a few friends his unpremeditated thoughts.' [5] Hale White remembered, too, exciting walks down the Strand, Morris again holding forth intensely, now and then pausing to act out an idea, and altogether unconscious of the passers-by. 'Nothing was too common for him, and he has taught me in the crowded streets of London lessons suggested by what he saw in them, which came closer to me than those derived from the laborious study of many big volumes.' [6]

A partial explanation of his influence (which touched many besides Hale White) is this capacity for just and passionate utterance.

---

[1] Unpublished letter, copy in the possession of Dr. R. Hale-White.
[2] *The Groombridge Diary*, p. 27.
[3] *Ibid.*, p. 16.
[4] *Early Life*, pp. 85–6.
[5] *The Groombridge Diary*, p. 27.
[6] *Last Pages*, p. 248.

Having heard continuously all the most noteworthy speakers of my day [Hale White tells us]—Roebuck, Cobden, Bright, Gladstone, Binney—I affirm unhesitatingly that Caleb Morris was more eloquent than any of them. His eloquence was not extravagant, nothing was laid on, it never went beyond his subject, but it was equal to it; it was the voice of the thing itself. I shall never forget a sermon of his on the prodigal son. He dwelt not so much on the son as on the father, and he almost acted, with perfect restraint but with overcoming tenderness, the daily longing for the child's return, the looking out—'Shall I see him today?' He pointed out that this parable, although it taught us the depth of God's love, was a glorification of human love. I can feel even now the force which came from him that night and swept me with it, as if I were a leaf on a river in flood.[1]

This is exactly the sermon of the Reverend Mr. Cardew in *Catherine Furze*, though it is evidence of Hale White's grasp of life's complexity that he views it there ironically, showing us how such beautiful ideas can also lead to danger. And here are two more remarks from sermons of Morris that will be worth remembering when we come to that novel. 'There is no sincerity where there is no emotion; no dull man can be sincere.'[2] And: 'The Christ the Jews expected did not come; the Christ they did not expect did come; the Christ men expect will not come.'[3]

The message thus persuasively presented to the young Hale White came at an opportune moment, though it was surely in some respects like that he had been learning elsewhere. 'Hale was then about one-and-twenty,' Mrs. White says, 'and apparently for the time being at loose ends.' He told her that 'had it not been for Caleb Morris he would have settled down in the church or else broken away from creeds altogether.'[4] Morris indicated, that is, a road *between*, doing so, as we see, not by attacking dogma, but merely by emphasizing the permanent truths beneath the forms. It was the great nineteenth-century lesson of conservative rebellion from formal religion, a rebellion that left intact the connection with its vital meanings. It

---

[1] *Ibid.*, pp. 244-5.
[2] *Ibid.*, p. 247.
[3] *Ibid.*
[4] *The Groombridge Diary*, pp. 28-9.

may be true, as Mrs. White suggests, that 'the pupil follows the master because they are both already on the one road,'[1] but we can date from Hale White's exciting London contacts with Morris his secure possession of a religiousness, if not a religion, invulnerable to attacks from left or right. More than half a century later, showing his wife those notes from Morris's sermons, he told her, 'This was the world in which I have lived, not the world of the clever critics or of literature or art for its own sake, nor yet the world of professedly dogmatic teachers, but a religious world.'[2] It was Morris more than anyone else who, during this moment 'at loose ends,' reconstituted that world for him, and he continued to read the Bible all his life (at one period going through it regularly again and again) as Morris had taught him to do.

A second friend of importance to him in those early London years —important in a similar way—was Mrs. Elizabeth Street, who was also a disciple of Morris. She was an extremely busy housewife and mother, engaged also in business, but he loved to visit her, and the reasons are set forth in a beautiful 'Letter on the death of Mrs. Street' written for his children in 1877 at his first wife's request. They are reasons which tell us much about him, and her type, too, recurs in his work: it is an example of the religious personality untouched by the epoch's religious controversies. 'Amidst all kinds of turmoil and perplexities' she was always ready to talk with him about what lay above or beneath them, about the 'general laws' of life. 'Even in that dingy Searle Street, she literally, as the Bible has it, walked with God.' She was also cheerful and had a striking air of inner unity and peace.

She in early life had been formed by Mr. Morris's influence mainly upon one type of character: a Biblical type. She had not been distressed and distracted by the anarchy of the present time, which, being a time without a religion, has not been dominated as religious times are by the supremacy of one ideal. . . . She was a religious woman. I don't mean that she went to church or chapel. The word includes many things, and it is difficult to say exactly what it means,

[1] Dorothy V. White, 'Occasional Notebooks,' unpublished.
[2] *The Groombridge Diary*, p. 15.

although if the irreligious man and the religious man are placed side by side the difference is so manifest. To one man the world is a collection of material facts. To the other it is incessantly awful and mysterious.[1]

But he was also drawn to Mrs. Street's house by someone else: her young niece, who was charming and musical and whom he was to marry.

[1] W. H. White, 'Letter on the death of Mrs. Street,' unpublished MS. in the possession of Dr. R. Hale-White, London.

CHAPTER III

Life–Part 2

IN that section of *The Autobiography* which deals with the Chapman episode of Hale White's history, Mark Rutherford loves Theresa (who, as I have said, is clearly a portrait of the young George Eliot) at a time when he is in love with and committed to another woman. With so much in that work taken from life, may we suppose that such a conflict was also something Hale White personally experienced? I think we may. For we have seen how warm was his feeling for Marian Evans in 1854, and we know that he too was at that time committed to someone else. The woman he was to marry—we learn this from Sir William—was in 1854 already paying the long visits of a fiancée to his parents. And I think we may safely go even further in our speculations. It seems to me that Hale White must also have experienced Mark Rutherford's indecision when he realized that his fiancée Ellen could not share his intellectual life, and Rutherford's later gratitude for Ellen's supreme human virtues. It is true that Hale White married his fiancée, while his fictional counterpart was separated from Ellen for many years. But that is not necessarily a significant difference, and in fact, Ellen, who begins simple, cheerful, pious, and whose character and faith are deepened by a life of suffering, seems to me a deliberate portrait of the author's wife.

The woman he married on December 26, 1856—he was twenty-five—and took to live first in Heathcote Street and afterwards at 69 Marylebone Road in London, was a Miss Harriet Arthur. Here is a description of her by her second son, Jack.

She was slightly made, with delicate small hands and feet, short-sighted blue grey eyes, a great abundance of bright brown hair braided and coiled behind her head. . . . She had been well taught as a girl: of French her knowledge was good; she gave me my first lessons in that language from Noel's and Chapsal's grammar, and I still possess the tiny volume of the New Testament in French she had at school. Some Italian she knew also, I believe. She loved simple lyrical poetry, but music was, I think, her best medium of expression. When I first remember her, she had no longer the strength for continued effort even in music, but she had been a pupil of Sir Charles Hallé, and my father's sisters, both of them lovers of music and competent musicians, used to tell me that her playing on the piano when she was younger was wonderful.[1]

He tells us too that 'she was naturally cheerful'; this he saw through the affliction of the terrible illness which began some years after the marriage, and we may therefore suppose the trait was a marked one. Moreover, 'Love and Piety filled her soul. Such words of counsel as I remember to have received from her were in keeping with her whole life, simply wise, earnest and unworldly.'

Jack Hale-White is concerned in his memoir to disprove the suggestion that his father's own experience lay behind his tales of unhappy marriages. 'To my father,' he says, 'her relationship was one of devotion, almost of adoration. She was absorbed in him.' Further:

It was during my mother's lifetime . . . in that home where her afflictions were a daily addition to his own, but where her patience, piety, and unsophisticated, unworldly nature were always before him, that his best and most valuable work, the real message he had to deliver to the world, was thought out. I do not say that she influenced his intellectual conclusions or the contents of his books: that was not in her power: but there was nothing in her that ran counter to them: quite the contrary.

Hale White himself tells us the following in a conversation recorded in *The Groombridge Diary*:

She was a pupil of Hallé and played very well, very 'accurately': nothing 'profound' would she attempt. He said that as a young man

---

[1] Jack Hale-White, 'William Hale White, "Mark Rutherford," 1831-1913, Notes by his Second Son,' 1931, unpublished MS. in the possession of Dr. R. Hale-White, hereafter to be referred to as Jack's 'Notes.'

he was enthusiastic about poetry, more so even than in after years: used to wander about London streets at 6 o'clock in the morning, reading Tennyson's *Maud* and so on. His wife did not understand that kind of poetry; she liked Cowper, and he used to read Cowper aloud to her. He said several times that 'it was impossible to help loving such a tender affectionate creature.'[1]

From all this—and we may perhaps judge of her capacities in music rather from Hale White's account than from his sisters'— certain conclusions rise of themselves. Whatever the young man found in his bride, it would seem that he did not find the fullest intellectual companionship. Though so much is unmistakable, however, it is equally so that he came upon human qualities which more than made up for what she lacked, which taught him, indeed, that those of the intellect were not after all of the very first importance. In 1888 he wrote to his son Jack, with direct reference to his wife:

As I get older I more and more learn to set store upon the virtues which are not intellectual but emotional and moral. . . . How continually, after thinking about anything do I come back to the Bible. I recur now to the preference of Jesus for the simple and not for the philosophers; for Peter, Mary, Mary Magdalen, and not for the priests and the Greeks. The simple too have saved the world.[2]

As it happens, the height to which such qualities can rise did not have to be deduced merely from their muffled operation in ordinary life. Their terrible occasion came about five years after the marriage, when the disease which was to test 'the stalk of carle hemp' in both of them, made its first appearance. Disseminated sclerosis is 'an incurable disease of the nervous system,' their eldest son, Sir William, tells us. And he goes on:

Slowly she [his mother] became paralyzed in the legs, so that both indoors and out of doors she had to be taken about in a bath chair; next the paralysis spread to the arms so that she could not write and hardly feed herself. The disease, marching on, made her almost blind

---

[1] *The Groombridge Diary*, p. 93.   [2] Quoted in Jack's 'Notes.'

during her last few years, but it did not kill her till 1891. For thirty weary years she endured but never once complained. To all of us she was more than a saint for she awakened in us not only reverence but great love.[1]

In March 1891, a month before she died, Hale White wrote to his oldest and closest friend, Mrs. Colenut, that his wife had been through one of her worst attacks of 'utter prostration,' but that 'her patience and self-forgetfulness for others, even when she can hardly speak, are extraordinary.'[2] She died on June 1, 1891, and two months later he wrote to Mrs. Colenut as follows:

The [outsider] sees of course nothing but the death of a woman to whom death was a release. *I* think of five and thirty years ago, and think too that *this* history has ended as all things end. Furthermore you can hardly imagine what it is to be at once deprived of an outlet for what you feel most intimately. Much as children are loved, it is impossible to impart to them all one hopes or fears. My poor wife daily heard from me what nobody now can hear, and offered a sympathy which nobody else can give. The world, aware of so small a portion of what was in her shy, unpretending soul, would have been astonished perhaps that she could be of such service to me, but she was for me and not for the world. The lesson of her heroic patience and unselfishness was obvious to everybody, and that daily teaching has also departed.[3]

Nothing that is known of Mrs. White belies this judgment, which does honour to both. Coming from a man so much of whose life could not be shared with her, these remarks to his son and his friend are clearly a fruit of that wisdom which has learned to put aside the irritable and greedy self. To imagine, however, that the *young* Hale White possessed such wisdom at once and without intermission—

[1] Sir William Hale-White, 'Notes about W. Hale White (Mark Rutherford), Personal Reminiscences by his Eldest Son, W. Hale White,' 1932, unpublished MS. in the possession of Dr. R. Hale-White; hereafter to be referred to as Sir William's 'Notes.'

[2] *Letters*, p. 49.

[3] *Ibid.*, p. 50.

E

that he accepted what she lacked of depth or extent of culture, of quickness of response or penetration of mind, without any gestures of disappointment and annoyance, or any moments of silent pain— to imagine this is to imagine a prodigy indeed. I think that he did have such feelings, but that his history was more or less the same as those of Mark Rutherford and Ellen and of Mr. and Mrs. M'Kay in *The Autobiography* and the *Deliverance*, of Miriam and her husband in *Miriam's Schooling*, of Mr. and Mrs. Cardew in *Catherine Furze*, and of the couples in the stories, 'James Forbes,' 'The Sweetness of a Man's Friend,' and 'A Dream of Two Dimensions.' The self-obsession and self-pity which are the intellectual's occupational disease gave way, whether soon or late, to understanding and remorse. The life situation was perhaps never so clear-cut nor so dramatic as the situations of the stories, nor is it likely that Hale White's development was quite so simple. We may suppose that warring attitudes were present in him, as in all of us, from beginning to end, but that the less generous, the more childish, learned to be silent before his maturing will, while the most sincere gratitude for what she was took all the foreground. And it is surely his own wife who is responsible for the passionate celebration of woman's love which we get in the *Deliverance*.

In 1857, the year his first son was born, Hale White was appointed Registrar of births, deaths and marriages for Marylebone, and a year later he was transferred to the Admiralty. There he remained, rising in 1879 to the post of Assistant Director of Naval Contracts. His eldest son, Sir William, naturally concerned with his father's standing as a man amongst men, insists on the difference between him and the pathetic Mark Rutherford, who found office work detestable, hated the obscenity with which his beer-drinking colleagues often fought the terrible monotony, was able to endure it only by separating his real and his office self completely, and never attained any success. There was certainly a difference which deserves emphasis. Hale White was extremely efficient, not only as an employee but also as a chief exercising responsibility. 'He left his mark on the Contract and Purchase Department,' Jack tells us, '. . . in the form of improved organization,'[1] and when he retired in 1892 he received a commen-

---

[1] Jack's 'Notes.'

dation from his chief which led to an increase in his pension. This said, in part:

My Lords desire me to express to you their sense of the able and conscientious manner in which you have performed your duties as Assistant Director of Naval Contracts, and their regret at parting with so valuable an officer. They cannot speak too highly of your services in connection with the Patents Committee, a peculiarly intricate and difficult subject, your thorough knowledge of which was of great advantage to the service. My Lords feel sure that you carry with you into a well-earned retirement the esteem and respect of your colleagues.[1]

In short, unlike Rutherford, and in spite of the handicaps of a devotion to books and the life of the mind, he seemed at last a practical success, and he was not without satisfaction in this. Though he rarely talked to her of his writings, he once showed his second wife the letter of commendation. 'He is actually the least bit PROUD of it,' she wrote. 'To see him proud is a funny sight, as funny as it is rare! He even allowed that it was a most unusual thing for the Lords to step out of their way to praise a subordinate.'[2] And in his will he left the letter, and all other papers relating to his civil service career, to his eldest son, directing him to preserve them. 'I know why he did this,' Sir William tells us, 'because he wished his descendants to see that he had done his life's work in a way in which he believed work should be done, and he was proud of this.'[3]

Such a record must indeed stand against a too simple identification of Hale White and Mark Rutherford. But it does not make it impossible, nor even unlikely, that Rutherford was a picture of a truer self which the efficient civil servant concealed, a self that would have surprised his colleagues. As it happens, that truer self did surprise them. When the books which were surely its most authentic fruits were at last identified as written by William Hale White, one of his former colleagues actually declared he would not have believed Mr. White had it in him. From this we may guess that Hale White too

[1] *The Groombridge Diary*, p. 325 n.   [2] *Ibid.*, p. 352.
[3] Sir William's 'Notes.'

had adopted Rutherford's 'stratagem' of keeping his real personality a secret from the office. There is, in fact, little doubt that for all his success, it is his own feelings and experiences that we get in Rutherford's office history. Jack tells us that it was not until 1879 that his civil service salary alone could support the family—he could hardly have felt much of a success before. And those who know Rutherford will, of course, remember this from *The Groombridge Diary*:

> He told me that when he was a young man at the Office, he had to endure plenty of such talk [obscene joking], but he never joined in it, and never laughed at it, never at least if he could possibly help it. I asked Hale what they thought of him for never joining in. He said, 'Oh, of course I got called names—Pious, I think that was the word.'[1]

We will see below how other, and worse, miseries of Rutherford's working life are duplicated in his author's. But it is perhaps enough to cite this flat declaration: 'He said he had been so many years in the Admiralty: "I never liked it," '[2] an attitude toward clerical work which his temperament alone, as we have come to know it, makes easy to understand.

The chief disadvantage of the civil service, however, was the fact that it paid so little. By 1869 there were already five children to support (two others had died in infancy), to say nothing of the expense of doctors, nurses and housekeepers incident to his wife's illness. For over twenty years Hale White had to use up most of his leisure on extra work. The preaching he did in the early days falls perhaps partly into this category of work done to augment his income. Mark Rutherford, we remember, forced out of the sect of Independents by his altered views, accepts an offer to preach among the Unitarians at D—— where the income is £100 a year. He does so because 'the money in my pocket was coming to an end, and . . . I did not suppose any dishonesty would be imposed on me.'[3] Hale White, too, became a Unitarian minister—in 1853-54 he had preached occasionally at Ipswich—and his second wife has discovered

---

[1] *The Groombridge Diary*, pp. 264-5.   [2] *Ibid.*, p. 2.
[3] *The Autobiography*, chap. viii.

that Rutherford's term at D—— is based on a term the writer spent as a Unitarian minister at Ditchling in 1856-57. Of course, it would have been more than the pay alone which drew Hale White to such work. His books make sufficiently clear that preaching can be a powerful form of self-expression, one to which, moreover, his kind of interests and insights were peculiarly appropriate. But in *The Autobiography* Rutherford discovers at last that the Unitarians of that time and place were as hidebound in their way as the Independents in theirs and that religion as wisdom was not what they wanted. When the term at Ditchling was over, Hale White gave up preaching for good—gave up for good, we may say, all hope of finding his kind of religion in any established institution. From then on it was with the pen that he sought to add to his income or to share his thought.

His first appearance in print was in *Chambers's Journal* for March 6, 1858, with an article about one of his jobs called 'Births, Deaths and Marriages.' In the same period he wrote a number of biographies for the *Imperial Dictionary of Universal Biography*—his contributions fall in the sections for F and G. As may be expected, none of these youthful writings has permanent value, though the student of Hale White will be interested to see even so early his characteristic modesty and purity of style, his irony, his intensity. In the portrait of Benjamin Franklin, quite sympathetic on the whole, this sentence occurs: 'He seems not only to have printed, but to have written, a variety of loose things about this time, and even to have plunged, we cannot say head over ears, for the waters were rather shallow, into metaphysics and controversial theology.' [1] And the essay on Garrick concludes in a way to remind us not only that Hale White honoured emotion, but that he was a Puritan.

His beautiful portrait, his works, the testimony of his friends all show us a soul overflowing with humour and love and a genius for abandonment which explains the echo of his fame which has been prolonged even down to our day. It is to him we chiefly owe the restoration of our great national poet and the purification of the

[1] W. H. White, 'Benjamin Franklin,' *Imperial Dictionary of Universal Biography*, 6 volumes, London, 1857-1863, II, p. 479.

stage from that filthy licentiousness with which it had been disgraced since the time of Charles II.[1]

In 1861 he found a kind of extra work that was permanent and that made other kinds unnecessary. With his father to help him get into the House of Commons for political news, he began to write weekly London columns for provincial newspapers. 'I applied to nearly 100,' he told a friend, 'and at last two replied.'[2] He generally had at least two, and for a time even three columns a week to write. He liked this job, we are told, even less than his clerical work. He found it painful to have to conform to a newspaper editor's idea of the interesting, as well as to dash off 'lively' comments on matters that seemed to him to call for study and reflection. That he felt himself misrepresented by his journalistic writings is indicated by his refusal in his later years to permit any of them to be reprinted. Yet one who glances through them must be sorry that he refused and must hope the job will some day be done. Not only is it our sole source of information about his mind of those years; that mind is already mature, and already interesting. The style is the one we know, though less perfectly economical, and there are many reflections worth preserving about literature, morals and manners.

Chiefly, however, he wrote about politics. And this was due not only to the nature of his job, but to his own lively political consciousness. Gide calls him 'apolitical,' but though this is appropriate to what he became, he was quite the reverse for a good part of his mature life, and his books often have politics and political passions at least among their subject matter. A word is in order, therefore, about his political development.

'I think,' said W. D. Taylor, 'that Mark Rutherford must have written all his novels with some sentences from the notorious speech

---

[1] 'David Garrick,' *ibid.*, III, p. 563. According to H. A. Smith, he also wrote for the same work lives of William Franklin, the Emperor Galba, Aelius Gallus (Praefect of Egypt, 258 B.C.), Gallus (Roman Praetor, 67 B.C.), Caius Sulpicius Gallus (Praetor, 169 B.C.), Theodore Gaza: Saint Genevieve, Genseric (King of the Vandals), George of Trebizond, M. A. Gordianus (Emperor, A.D. 237), Pius F. Gordianus and Gorgias, the rhetorician.

[2] Letter to Mabel Marsh, dated September 27, 1903, copy in the possession of Mrs. D. V. White.

of Mr. Robert Lowe against the 1866 Reform Bill in his head. "Let any gentleman consider the constituencies he has had the honour to be connected with. If you want venality, if you want drunkenness and facility to be intimidated, or if, on the other hand you want impulsive, unreflecting and violent people, where do you look for them in the constituencies? Do you go to the top or to the bottom?" ' [1] Gide's view of the novels as 'apolitical' is, of course, more just, for there is clearly somewhat more in their author's head than such a speech. But Mr. Taylor's remark could certainly be true of Hale White's first separately printed work, a pamphlet published in 1866 entitled *An Argument for an Extension of the Franchise: A Letter Addressed to George Jacob Holyoake, Esquire*. This essay, part of the movement for universal manhood suffrage which ended in the Reform Bill of 1867, shows a commitment to the fight for democracy as warm as his father's had been on the occasion of the Reform Bill of 1832. Hale White attacks the arguments of men like Lowe with logic, angry wit and great polemical eloquence. He declares that for all their education, the upper classes have invariably chosen wrong in politics, having to be forced to accept any necessary progressive measure; that it is they, not the poor, who are the more easily tempted to political dishonesty; and that the poor have a knowledge far more important to a nation's welfare than Greek or Latin: the knowledge of their own conditions. 'The nation as a whole,' he says, 'is wiser than any arbitrarily selected portion of it,' [2] and the lower classes should be entreated, not forbidden, to share in the responsibility of government.

For a long time Hale White continued aggressively liberal.[3] On December 2, 1876, he was writing in the *Birmingham Post*, apropos of 'secret societies':

[1] W. D. Taylor, 'Mark Rutherford,' *Queen's Quarterly*, XXV (October, November, December, 1917), p. 159.

[2] W. H. White, *An Argument for an Extension of the Franchise: A Letter Addressed to George Jacob Holyoake, Esquire*, London, 1866, p. 11.

[3] This word is used in the American sense—to denote the attitude that society unfairly favours the rich and powerful, that it can be made more rational and more just through political action and that such action should be the responsibility of all its members.

The secret society particularly to be dreaded is that which is made up of all the persons who have something to gain by war. All over Europe there are loan contractors, shipowners, colliery-proprietors, and an immense number of military people whose one ambition is money or glory and who know that a war would bring both. Who shall say how much of the war fever and war-like writing is not due to these people, directly or indirectly? A gigantic capitalist, if war comes, can, by writing a sheet of notepaper, put hundreds of thousands of pounds perhaps in his pockets, the sufferers being the needy taxpayers for whom he negotiates the loan. He commands voices in newspapers and in Cabinets, and he and his fellows are more to be feared infinitely than all the Carbonari, Illuminati, Communists or Socialists.

Even as late as the Boer War he is still showing political excitement: his opposition to the war would have done credit to an old-time radical Dissenter or to a liberal of the 1930's.[1] He distributed anti-war leaflets, and to a friend he wrote:

If Mr. Chamberlain wants a grievance and has any superfluous courage, let him attack the brewers at home. There is not a vested interest here which is not impugnable. . . . Pray stir up everybody who has a conscience to protestation. All art, literature, seems to me to be a mockery now, mere trifling.[2]

In spite of the foregoing, he ended, however, in complete political disillusion. And this disillusion was not really a contradiction of his basic early attitudes. For more important in these than his liberalism had been his demand for allegiance to ideas and principles held above the claims of the moment, his demand for political integrity. On December 13, 1879, he wrote in the *Birmingham Post*:

The faith in an idea has now departed from amongst us, and there is no more certain method of scoring a success in the House than by deriding 'mere theory' and 'coming down to practical politics.' . . . The consequences of this scepticism—for scepticism it is of the most

---

[1] See footnote 3, p. 57.   [2] *Letters*, p. 192.

fatal kind—is the present confusion in [our] own legislation, the multitude of silly ineffectual permissive compromises, and the ever increasing crowd of half measures which do not work.

Such an allegiance to principles, though it began by putting him beside the liberals, led him finally to a loss of faith in the 'people' and even in politics—'this weltering chaos called politics which is nothing more than the eddying conflict of individual greed.'[1] This does not mean that he sank into simple reaction. An essay called 'Apology' in *Pages from a Journal* states beautifully his final position. And the following excerpts are far truer to the complex mind of the novelist than was the downright Argument, so sure of its political solutions.

The disease is often obvious, but the remedies are doubtful. The accumulation of wealth in a few hands, generally by swindling, is shocking, but if it were distributed tomorrow we should gain nothing. The working man objects to the millionaire, but would gladly become a millionaire himself, even if his million could be piled up in no other way than by sweating thousands of his fellows. The usurpation of government by the ignorant will bring disaster, but how in these days could a wise man reign any longer than ignorance permitted him? The everlasting veerings of the majority, without any reason meanwhile for the change, show that except on rare occasions of excitement, the opinion of the voters is of no significance. But when we are asked what substitute for elections can be produced, none can be found. So with the relationship between man and woman, the marriage laws and divorce. The calculus has not been invented which can deal with such complexities.

The voices now are so many and so contradictory that it is impossible to hear any one of them distinctly, no matter what its claim on our attention may be. The newspaper, the circulating library, the free library, and the magazine are doing their best to prevent unity of direction and the din and confusion of tongues begets a doubt whether literature and the printing press have actually been such a blessing to the race as enlightenment universally proclaims them to be.

[1] W. H. White, *Spinoza*, 4th edition, Preface, pp. xxviii-xxix.

The great currents of human destiny seem more than ever to move by forces which tend to no particular point. There is a drift, tremendous and overpowering, due to nobody in particular, but to hundreds of millions of small impulses.[1]

This is a 'defeatist' position, perhaps, on which it would be dangerous for us to come to rest, but it is at least the 'defeatism' of wisdom, and it is worth something to have cleared away so much political cant. His final conclusion, from a letter to *The Speaker* of February 10, 1906, is that 'organization and parties will not save society. There is but one salvation, and that is the slow process of saving individual human souls.'

With the journalism become a regular thing, Hale White's life settled into a routine that changed little in twenty years. It was a life of hard work, anxiety and gloom, which he endured as with gritted teeth because, as he wrote to a friend, 'there is such a thing as duty, which exists and is imperative apart from all other motives. [2] He told his second wife that

he used to go to the House after work. His dread, terror, was lest he should not finish his office duties in time, for, if he failed in that he knew he should never get promotion. This was a perpetual nightmare, and the strain on the nerves was very bad. After the House he came home to supper, then must write out his reports; home to an invalid wife. He said that he told me all this (so egotistical he thought it!) because it explained so much in him.[3]

And Jack's 'Notes' complete the description of his routine:

I see him now coming home between six and seven in the evening, and running upstairs to prepare for the evening meal, after which he would often work upon his articles. He retired generally quite early, slept badly, and rose early; often by 4 o'clock. The fire place in his study had a row of gas jets around the base to enable him to light the fire easily; after his bath he made himself a cup of cocoa in an aetna, and then, in those early morning hours, he read and wrote as his own

[1] *Pages*, pp. 79-81.   [2] *Letters*, pp. 23-4.   [3] *The Groombridge Diary*, p. 72.

spirit moved him, not as the journalist from whom a weekly task was expected. Nevertheless, when he had an article to finish, even these hours were invaded, and he would rouse me up at six o'clock to meet the newspaper train on its arrival at the station and bring him the morning's papers. Sometimes the article was finished in the waiting room at Victoria Station on his way to the Admiralty.

Jack speaks of the cloud that hung over their home, and Miss Mary Hale-White, a daughter, has emphasized in a conversation with the present writer the joylessness of her childhood. Even without the father's difficult and worried working life there was reason enough for this. There was the mother's terrible illness, worsening day by day. There was the succession of housekeepers this made necessary and the resulting loss of privacy—a particular sorrow for husband and wife. There was Hale White's own constant bad health. This was partly physical—a chronic dyspepsia—and partly nervous, the nervousness aggravated by his insomnia. (It was the insomnia that enforced his early bedtime which, during the week, left him hardly a moment with his wife and children.) Sir William tells us that like other bad sleepers he believed that certain foods were a help to him: for a while he felt the need of a daily drink of gin and water, a detail that recalls the growing reliance on wine which terrifies Mark Rutherford. Above all there was his tendency to sink into long periods of nearly crippling depression, a tendency to which dyspepsia and insomnia no doubt contributed, if they were not the whole cause. What he wrote to a friend in 1887 can stand as typical of these periods whenever they occurred. He speaks of

my wretched self over which the same shadow rests, darkening every day and darkening the house too. It is very sad when the master of the household to whom everybody in it—at least it has always been so here—looks for guidance and stimulus, falls into silence and despair. It would be different if I had a wife energetic and active, able to take my place, but her disease, rendering her unfit for all exertion, makes the position very dismal.[1]

[1] Unpublished letter to Mrs. Colenut dated December 24, 1887, copy in the possession of Mrs. D. V. White.

The atmosphere of the White home was enlivened very little by social intercourse. The wife's illness was one reason—it was a source of embarrassment, or it made visits difficult to repay. The husband's peculiar schedule was another. But the most important reason was surely the temperament of the master of the house. 'When life is ruled by standards such as his,' Jack remarks, 'congenial friendships become rare.' [1] This is true, but the observation of Sir William that he was 'shy' to a degree that was 'difficult to overcome' [2] is perhaps less misleading. For he did not despise the simpler pleasures of sociability any more than he did all others that were harmless. On the contrary, he placed an almost excessive value on non-intellectual pleasures, because he needed them like a medicine. Ordinary visitors fell away or neglected to appear because he did not know how to attract them, though he often longed to do so. He was too serious, too intense. ('You are the only person who does not mind my being so serious,' he told his second wife after a passionate discussion of the Temptation in the Wilderness. 'I can't *help* being serious.') [3] This does not mean he was solemn, for, as Jack says, 'he was quickly alive to the humorous and could laugh with heart and soul.' But he could not take things casually. His pains and pleasures tended to be agonies and exaltations. He leaped to the heart of matters too quickly for those who had been content to stay on surfaces. He meant all he said too deeply for those who hardly ever meant anything much.

There is often this compensation for such an unsociable temperament: if it makes ordinary pleasant acquaintances impossible, it is peculiarly suited to friendship. 'My dear friend,' he writes to Mrs. Colenut on March 26, 1878, 'life is getting short and every day I feel impelled closer and closer to friends, and to make more of them.' [4] Friendship as a kind of passion is a recurring subject in his books and we can see his own capacity for this in his *Letters to Three Friends*. These friends are in different ways his kind of people; Mrs. Colenut and Miss Partridge, not intellectual but quick and deep in human understanding, and interested in life, which they saw, like him, through the medium of a religious background; and Philip

---

[1] Jack's 'Notes.'   [2] Sir William's 'Notes.'
[3] *The Groombridge Diary*, p. 125.
[4] Unpublished letter, copy in the possession of Mrs. D. V. White.

Webb, more a representative of the world of culture, being an architect and an artist and a reader of literature, yet at the same time more warm-hearted than 'clever.' We can see in these letters that he 'can't *help* being serious,' but we see this means, too, that he turns to his friends not in idle chat or out of obligation but with a kind of hunger for human contact and out of the impulse to share what means most to him. This is why the letters are so similar in quality to his books: they have the same combination of pressing emotion and clear restraining thought, the same utter simplicity, and, apparently resulting from this, the same simple but intense style.

As a parent he was, we surmise, rather formidable, and this for two reasons. The first is that his standards for behaviour were puritanically high and strict. Explaining to his eldest son in 1874— the boy was seventeen—that he does not go to church because 'I do not know anybody who can teach me anything there which I want to know,' he added:

But on the other hand there are many things in which I am far more strict than church-going people. I cannot tolerate deceit, sensuality, filthy conduct, harshness or brutality. I insist on perfect truthfulness, perfect tenderness, perfect purity, perfect kindness and perfect reverence for the great God who made us. This is the religion of Christ and of all really religious people in all times, whether Jew, Greek, Roman or English.[1]

He was merely stating an ideal, no doubt, but a father who could state such an ideal so gravely must have had his difficult side. He was as strict a Nonconformist in his own way, indeed, as his ancestors had been in theirs. None of his children was baptized at birth, and Jack tells us he was not permitted to attend classes in Scripture history at school. He was set to learn Virgil's Eclogues by heart instead, a task for which his father, who loved Virgil, might well have been responsible. It is interesting that Hale White's strictness partly spoiled his children's Sundays as his father's different kind had spoiled his own. His daughter has told the present writer how specially deprived

[1] Unpublished letter dated March 2, 1874, in the possession of Dr. R. Hale-White.

and lonely she used to feel as she watched the other children through the window go off to Sunday School, church or chapel.

The second reason for his occasional oppressiveness as a father is that, whatever the demands he may have made on his children, his feeling for them had all the intensity characteristic of his emotional life in general. This was not always a fault, of course. In his letters to his youngest son Ernest, perhaps because Ernest had inherited, as he said, his own 'fatal temperament,' [1] and needed reassurance, or perhaps only because these letters alone have not been pruned for publication, we find an anxious tenderness almost feminine in its warmth. 'Goodbye,' he ends one letter when Ernest is eighteen, 'my dearest, dearest boy, my best best best love and kisses to you.' [2] And again, two years later: 'Comfort yourself by thinking of my love for you, and if it is any consolation to you, know that your departure upset me almost as much as it has you, for I love you profoundly and you have been a great blessing to me and a companion as well as a son.' [3] But this warmth, though generally more restrained in its utterance, if not concealed altogether, could grow uncomfortable. He had a dangerous tendency to hold what he loved too close, as though each step toward a separate life threatened his own abandonment. His eye was quick to detect the signs of another's restlessness in his presence, even when these did not exist, and the feeling of being left behind, of being left out, while those dear to him had fun elsewhere and with others, was for him a common one: it results in some of his most beautifully poignant pages.[4] Thus, when his eldest

[1] Omitted portion of letter to Mrs. Colenut dated January 23, 1889, in *Letters*, copy in the possession of Mrs. D. V. White.

[2] Unpublished letter to Ernest White dated March 22, 1887, in the possession of Mrs. Irene White.

[3] Unpublished letter to Ernest dated January 9, 1889, in the possession of Mrs. Irene White.

[4] The following pencil note in one of his little black pocket-books was probably jotted down, Mrs. White tells us, when she had left him alone for an evening in order to give a party to her club of teenage boys: 'The most excusable weakness is the despair, even an active despair, which overwhelms me, old, suffering, hopeless, solitary, during dark December days while [I] know that others are rejoicing. At this moment, as I lie here wakeful in the silent night, the dancing is beginning, the brilliantly lighted room is alive with excitement and fluttering expectation.' (*The Groombridge Diary*, pp. 397-8 n.)

son became engaged, though the girl was a person he was able to take quickly enough to his heart, it was his pain rather than his pleasure that received most emphasis in his letters. 'As for my own feelings, apart from my sympathy with him, I have been the victim of the strangest emotions,' he wrote to a friend. The event, he said, had been a self-revealing shock. 'The steel plate is wrought with care and to all appearance is solid throughout and free from flaw, but lo! the hammer is swung, the test applied and it is mere sheet-glass. I am struck dumb with my own ignorance of myself.' [1] He could not even forbear to risk dampening his son's happiness. He wrote to him:

I believe you love your mother—let nothing be said about me to whom you owe so little compared to what you owe to her. . . . But you must think of us. It is not all bliss to us—simply because your joy reminds us of a whole life's joy missed through her illness. What she has denied herself God only knows. Your mother and I think you are the most blessed of men to have obtained such a girl. [2]

The final sentence is significant—it means he could struggle against such feelings. But they were a dangerous element in his relations with those near him, and we shall see how they added much pain to the last great love of his life.

[1] *Letters*, p. 26. The words 'apart from my sympathy with him,' omitted from the published letter, are restored from the copy in the possession of Mrs. D. V. White.

[2] Unpublished letter to Sir William, dated July 28, 1884, copy in the possession of Dr. R. Hale-White.

CHAPTER IV

Life–Part 3

NATURALLY, his life was not only one of gloom or moral earnestness or passion. On Sundays and holidays, when he was free, the atmosphere of the White home often changed wonderfully. He would read to the family, which had seen him so little all week, read from books like Kingsley's *The Heroes*, Carlyle's *Reminiscences*, above all the novels of Scott. He loved music, as we know: when young, he had played the flute. There was a period when he played the organ to them all on Sunday mornings—the instrument belonged to a cousin who had left it with them for a time—and he went frequently to the Saturday popular concerts at St. Jame's Hall. 'When he came home he would turn over the programme again and whistle the arias with exquisite precision and feeling.'[1] He loved the English countryside and often took long walks with his sons. Jack writes:

[1] Jack's 'Notes.' About Hale White's feeling for music Dr. Stone, whose recent books I read after finishing my own, makes a point that should not go uncorrected. 'In spite of his professions to the contrary,' Dr. Stone writes, 'Hale White's love of music was not very deep. Both Mrs. D. V. White and Dr. R. Hale-White [a grandson] attest to this.' (*Religion and Art of William Hale White* ('*Mark Rutherford*'), Stanford, California, Stanford University Press, 1954, p. 185, n. 7.) But when I asked Mrs. White if she had in fact confirmed Dr. Stone's view of her husband's affectation and hypocrisy in this matter, her reply, dated January 27, 1955, was as follows: 'I am quite sure my husband was fond of music. It would never enter my head to doubt it. He would never have pretended to like it! Nor pretended about anything at all! The only possibility is that I might have laughingly alluded [in speaking to Dr. Stone] to the fact that after we were married he was very keen that I should practise on the piano every morning after breakfast, and that *this* was not from love of the music, which of course he would not hear, being in another room, but from the instinct of holding the reins, that instinct of which I was dimly aware but naturally (I mean by *nature*) disregarded.' The interested reader is advised to look up the references to Bach, Mozart, Scarlatti or simply 'music' in the *Letters to Three Friends* or *The Groombridge Diary*. These will leave no doubt that Hale White's love of music was sincere and intense.

66

Among the happiest times I have ever spent were those when I was his companion on summer holidays, or wandering with him in the lanes round about his abodes at Ashstead, Crowborough, Hastings and Groombridge, or over the country near Cockermouth and Bassenthwaite when I lived in Cumberland. When I was a boy he would take me with him into the country and read aloud as we walked. Among the books so read was Morris's translation of the *Aeneid*, then recently published. One entrancing holiday of later years was spent alone with him in the Scilly Isles, where we used to accompany Captain White, the hale and hearty superintendent of the Coastguard Station—no relative of ours—on his rounds in his yawl. I remember the lodgings at St. Mary's with sunshine falling through the passage from the front entrance to the door at the back where the pretty daughter of the house leant at ease, cleaning the shoes, and my father quoting:

> 'Scrubbing requires for true grace but frank
>   and artistical handling
> And the removal of slops to be ornamentally
>   treated.'

At such times all his deep enjoyment of Nature, and of what was simple and great in mankind, of Literature, Art and Science, came out: his talk became animated, discursive and inspiring as I have known no other man's to be.[1]

It was, however, in those early morning hours when he could 'read and write as his own spirit moved him' that he found the chief consolation for his life's difficulties. It was then he acquired that culture, surprisingly rich for so busy a man, which makes itself felt throughout his work. English literature he came to know thoroughly; he read Goethe in German, and also the Bible, preferring the Kautsch translation to all others because of its accuracy; Montaigne, Rabelais, Voltaire and Rousseau he read in French, Virgil in Latin, and one finds among his writings quotations from the Greek, though this was not a language in which he was ever at home.

He was also deeply interested in science. This is worth bearing in

[1] *Ibid.*

P

mind: though he inhabited a 'religious world' it was a world in which science was not only no threat but had an honoured place. When in 1864 his cousin and friend the Reverend W. T. Chignell (a Unitarian minister) was attacked in the papers for too liberal a sermon, Hale White replied in a letter:

In what attitude shall the human mind face a new discovery of science? Shall it ask whether it is true, or shall it ask whether it accords with what we have previously believed. . . . The world . . . is every day pronouncing pretty strongly as to which side it will take, and marches on in its own grand way, discovering new truth after new truth, and leaving the so-called defenders of the faith to follow in the rear and find out as they have done in the disputes about the seven days of the Mosaic creation, about the sun and moon standing still, about the authenticity of the Pentateuch, and in earlier times, about the discoveries of Galileo and Columbus, that if they can't get the new light to accommodate itself to their eyes, they must even accommodate their eyes to the new light.[1]

His attitude to science was not, however, only the respect of a thinker; he found it personally congenial. 'I have heard him say,' Jack tells us, 'that the objective life of scientific investigation would have suited him better than any other, and that if he had been given the necessary training in his youth, he would have given up everything for science.'[2] What attracted him most of all, as he suggests repeatedly in letters and books, was the necessity science imposes for turning away from the inner abyss of feeling and dream, for sticking to facts and earning thereby a knowledge which is useful and indisputable.[3] For one too apt to suffer from the sort of questions left behind by a discarded religion and generally insoluble outside it—

[1] Letter to the Editor, *Exeter and Plymouth Gazette*, London, January 6, 1864.
[2] Jack's 'Notes.'
[3] In an unpublished letter to Jack dated July 9, 1888, copy in the possession of Dr. R. Hale-White, he writes: 'Stonehenge, after you get acquainted with it, is wonderful, but I find that it disposes me to indefinite, vague misty sentiment, and this I try as much as possible to avoid. It is bad for anybody, trebly bad for me, and I would rather acquire some distinct piece of information about Stonehenge than be the victim of the shapeless emotion which almost overpowers me as I look at it.'

questions about ultimate meanings and purposes—science was a medicine and a relief, and his bent for it a development that was self-protective. This is exactly the point made in *The Autobiography* about the 'butterfly-catcher' whom tragedy had plunged into those un-answerable questions and whom the methodical study of butterflies had restored to sanity and content. (It is such a relation to urgent emotional needs, as I have pointed out, that gives all his intellectual pursuits their peculiar and attractive warmth.) Hale White's own 'butterfly-catching' when at last he had time for it, was to be astronomy, in which he became, Jack says, a 'competent amateur.' To look ahead, he went so far as to put up in his garden an astro-nomical telescope—this was in 1892—and in 1895 he read a paper before the British Astronomical Association on 'The Wilsonian Theory of Sun-spots.' The present writer has seen notebooks of astronomical observations containing coloured charts, notations of time and elaborate mathematical figuring which Hale White kept over long periods, and he can testify to their scrupulous care for detail and their beautiful neatness if not to their accuracy.

The principles and methods which science demands are not, of course, limited to science. Hale White was equally 'scientific' in his attitude to literary scholarship. Not the least admirable element of Ruskin's genius for him was his 'patient industry and his love of fact,'[1] and of another scholar he wrote: 'His accuracy and his methodical habits made him very attractive to me although he was High Church and conservative. . . . It is really a great virtue, when-ever we think of anything or when anything is presented to us, to be able to say to ourselves, "Is it so?" Indeed, it is the virtue of all virtues.'[2]

Of his own possession of this virtue, at once intellectual and moral, he has left a record in two volumes of pure scholarship. To anticipate again, he began in 1894 or 1895 a six-year study of Wordsworth and his epoch, which was stimulated by his friendship with Thomas Hutchinson and J. Dykes Campbell, Wordsworth and Coleridge scholars respectively, and which produced his study of Words-worth's 'apostasy' (to be discussed later) as well as the two scholarly

[1] Unpublished letter to Jack dated October, 1894 (day omitted), copy in the possession of Dr. R. Hale-White. [2] *Ibid.*

works. The latter are *A Description of the Wordsworth and Coleridge MSS. in the possession of Mr. T. Norton Longman*, published in 1897, and *Coleridge's Poems, Facsimile Reproductions of the Proofs and MSS. of some of the Poems*, edited by J. Dykes Campbell, with Preface and Notes by W. H. White, published in London in 1899. The *Description* is a comparison of various texts with manuscripts and letters showing the changes made in the *Lyrical Ballads*, and the *Poems in Two Volumes*. In the preface he remarks: 'Some of the details may appear insignificant, but the value of a detail is not to be measured by its external importance. The intermixture of handwritings, for example, is remarkable evidence of the intimacy of the relationship between Coleridge, Wordsworth and Dorothy, and shows how much the *Lyrical Ballads* owed to their love and friendship.'[1]

Many of those early morning hours were also devoted to the study of philosophy. References to Aristotle, Bacon, Bruno, Maimonides, Hegel, Kant, Mill and others occur often in his letters, his journals and his books, and it is clear that he devoted to them much absorbed study. There is one philosopher, however, whose importance to him outweighed that of all the rest. This was Spinoza, to whose work he turned for the first great intellectual task undertaken after his marriage, and to whom he went back again and again until the end of his life.

The first edition of Hale White's translation of the *Ethic* appeared in 1883, but in his preface he tells us that it had been made twenty years before, when the time was not yet ripe for its publication. He was therefore a young man of thirty or thirty-one, with two children, and working days in the civil service and evenings on his journalism, when he sat down in the time he had left to that long translation from the Latin. The job could hardly have been lightened by any strong hopes of profit or prestige, for the name of Spinoza was not yet of much importance to the general public. It could only have been a labour of love, a labour of gratitude, and this can easily be believed even without the testimony of his subsequent writings, for the work of Spinoza was precisely calculated to answer his deepest

[1] W. H. White, *A Description of the Wordsworth and Coleridge MSS. in the Possession of Mr. T. Norton Longman*, London, Longmans, Green and Company, 1897, p. v.

needs, as it answered those of many of his contemporaries who were in a similar intellectual position. Since Hale White's work is saturated in Spinoza's philosophy, a word about this, as he saw it, will be useful.

The great attraction of Spinoza for the nineteenth century in general and for Hale White in particular lay in the fact that he had created a majestic and on the whole reasonable scheme designed to remove the contradiction that then seemed to exist between religion and science. To remove this contradiction as Spinoza does it, however, is to answer needs that are not limited to any particular epoch but are human and permanent. Though his language may 'date' and his system be found shaky, men will always be eager to translate the former and overlook the latter, for 'there is something in Spinoza,' as Hale White points out, 'which can be superseded as little as *The Imitation of Christ* or *The Pilgrim's Progress*, and it is this which continues to draw men to him.'[1]

It may be said that Spinoza explores and systematizes those insights by which men attain to maturity. His great accomplishment was to make the universe and its impersonal necessities—which are for him God and His will—the centre of our thinking, instead of the self and its shortsighted desires. The God he reveals is not a superhuman Person, brooding over each individual soul with human emotions of love or anger, but rather Nature, in its laws as well as in the matter they organize. To use Spinoza's terminology, he is Being absolutely infinite, that is, infinite Substance, consisting of infinite attributes, of which 'thought' and 'extension' are the two revealed to man. Hale White found this insight particularly liberating. It removed the gulf between spirit and matter, between the soul or mind and the body, since accompanying that formulation is the statement that 'the mind and the body are one and the same individual, which at one time is considered under the attribute of thought and at another under that of the body.'[2] As man's body is part of infinite Substance extended—that is, part of God in his aspect as the material universe—so his mind is part of infinite Substance thinking, God's mind, the vast orderliness of the Universe. From this it follows that the more we know about nature and ourselves,

[1] *Pages*, p. 32.   [2] Quoted in *Last Pages*, p. 89.

the more we know about God, at least in so far as He makes Himself visible to the finite intelligence. To the question, Why bother with the idea of God at all? Hale White answers for Spinoza that to begin with that Idea, as we address ourselves to the study of nature, is the same as beginning with the assumption of order so necessary to scientific investigation.

All such speculation, however, is subordinate in the *Ethic* to 'that which, let us never forget, was the object for which it was written. What Spinoza was most anxious to do was to teach the true doctrine and treatment of human vice and human virtue; to show that hatred, anger and envy "have certain causes through which they can be understood, and certain properties which are just as worthy of being known as the properties of any other thing in the contemplation alone of which we delight." '[1] And 'in such knowledge lay salvation. He felt that the things on which men usually set their hearts give no permanent satisfaction, and he cast about for some means by which to secure a "joy continuous and supreme to all eternity." '[2]

He begins by denying that the ordinary notion of freedom of the will makes sense. As Hale White paraphrases him, 'the will is determined by the intellect.'[3] A man who knows what a triangle is is not free to believe that it has four sides. His freedom is the freedom to acquiesce in the necessity revealed by his intelligence. 'I call that thing free which exists and acts solely from the necessity of its own nature,' Spinoza wrote in a letter to Schuller. 'I call that thing coerced which is determined to exist and to act in a certain and determinate manner by another.'[4] And Hale White comments: 'What Spinoza means is that the free man is bound by the necessity of his own nature to assert the truth of what follows from the definition of a triangle and the stronger he feels the necessity the more free he is. Hence it follows that the wider the range of the intellect and the more imperative the necessity which binds it, the larger is its freedom.'

In genuine freedom [he goes on] Spinoza rejoices. 'The doctrine is of service in so far as it teaches us that we do everything by the will

---

[1] Preface, *Ethic*, 4th edition, p. lxviii.   [2] *Pages*, p. 33.
[3] *Ibid.*, p. 40.   [4] *Ibid.*, p. 41.

of God alone, and that we are partakers of the divine nature in proportion as our actions become more and more perfect [i.e. more in accord with the nature of reality] and we more and more understand God. This doctrine, therefore, besides giving repose to the soul, has also this advantage, that it teaches us in what our highest happiness or blessedness consists, namely, in the knowledge of God alone, by which we are drawn to do those things only which love and piety persuade.' In other words, being part of the whole, the grandeur and office of the whole are ours. We are anxious about what we call 'personality,' but in truth there is nothing in it of any worth, and the less we care for it, the more 'blessed' we are.[1]

For Spinoza evil-doing and suffering result from coerced actions, actions to which we have been hurried by passions not understood, whereas right doing and joy come from actions which are voluntary, because we have understood that they are necessary, that is, are the will of God. Those who do evil literally 'know not what they do.'[2] The good action is not a mere avoidance of the bad, but, more positive than that, it is the fulfilment of a desire which springs from the understanding. 'No one delights in blessedness,' Hale White quotes Spinoza, 'because he has restrained his affects (passions), but, on the contrary, the power of restraining his lusts springs from blessedness itself.' And on this Hale White comments: 'This is exactly what the Gospel says to the Law.'[3] The propositions which concern this point he declares in the essay 'Revolution' to be among the most crucial ideas in his own intellectual life. They are: 'The actions of the mind arise from adequate ideas alone, but the passions depend upon those alone which are inadequate. From this it follows by direct deduction that the more perfection a thing possesses, the more it acts and the less it suffers, and conversely the more it acts the more perfect it is.'[4]

Finally, the man who understands that everything happens according to the Divine necessity will not sorrow or hate or even spend himself in pity, but will try to do well and rejoice. He will repay hatred with love and generosity. 'He who wishes to avenge

[1] Ibid., p. 44. [2] Ibid.
[4] Ibid., pp. 42-3. [4] Last Pages, p. 60.

injuries by hating in return does indeed live miserably. But he who
on the contrary strives to drive out hatred by love, fights joyfully
and confidently, with equal ease resisting one man or a number of
men and needing scarcely any assistance from fortune. Those whom
he conquers yield gladly, not from defect of strength but from an
increase of it.'[1] These words are Spinoza's and they will perhaps
suggest to those repelled by his coldly systematic manner that this
conceals something warmer and more interesting.

One can understand, at least, with what special interest such ideas
must have been encountered by the thirty-year-old Hale White, a
man incurably moral and deeply in need of a reasonable basis for that
'repose' of the soul which religion had once made possible. Here is
how he concludes the preface to the fourth edition of his Spinoza:

It is impossible after familiar acquaintance with him, to live for a
single day as we should have lived without him. He was the first to
protest against the ordinary treatment of wrongdoing—the theological treatment, we may say [i.e. he related it to ignorance rather
than guilt]—although it is current beyond the limits of theology, and
will survive it. It was he who relieved men, or who did his best to
relieve them from the trouble and despair consequent upon what is
really a dual government of the world [matter *vs.* spirit], and it was
he who gave a vitality and a practical meaning to the great doctrine
of the Unity of God. Lastly, he may be said to have contributed
something towards a truly human religion.[2]

The translation of the *Ethic* finished, Hale White put it away for
twenty years, and during most of this period there were nothing but
trifles to show for all his reading and all his thought. He was a civil
servant and, in his own eyes, a hack journalist, and that was all,
though his thirties passed and then his forties. The fact is worth
mentioning, because there can be little doubt that he had dreamed
otherwise and that the mediocrity of his existence was a source of
pain. An obsession like his with the life of mind and of books is
rarely unaccompanied by the hope, if not of fame, at least of personal

---

[1] *Pages*, p. 45.
[2] Preface, *Ethic*, 4th edition, pp. xciii–xciv.

accomplishment. Indeed, it is surprising, considering how common it must be, that we do not have more pictures of the anguish of those gifted individuals who see all their promise drown in the encompassing ocean of life's duties, a subject quite different from the familiar one of the misunderstood artist. We may be sure such anguish was Hale White's because we know the discrepancy between the life he led and the promise he had, because he did keep turning to writing of one kind or another when he had time, and finally, because that feeling is an important part of the story of Mark Rutherford. I believe that the following paragraph from the essay on Job, which is included in the volume containing the *Deliverance*, may be taken as pure personal revelation:

Happy is the man, no matter what his lot may be otherwise, who sees some tolerable realization of the design he has set before him in his youth or in his earlier manhood. Many there are who, through no fault of theirs, know nothing but mischance and defeat. Either sudden calamity overturns in tumbling ruins all that they had painfully toiled to build, and success for ever afterwards is irrecoverable; or, what is most frequent, each day brings its own special hindrance, in the shape of ill-health, failure of power, or poverty, and a fatal net is woven over the limbs preventing all activity. The youth with his dreams wakes up some morning, and finds himself fifty years old with not one solitary achievement, with nothing properly learned, with nothing properly done, with an existence consumed in mean, miserable, squalid cares, and his goal henceforth is the grave in which to hide himself ashamed.[1]

Such reflections, however, if they do indeed refer to himself, belong to that blackest darkness which precedes the dawn, for they were set down at a moment when the process was already under way which would, in his own life, belie them. In 1880, a year after he had risen to the comparative security of his last civil service position, his mornings turned suddenly fruitful. First came four essays all published in the *Secular Review*: 'The Genius of Walt Whitman' (March 20), 'Marcus Antoninus' (July 3), 'Ixion' (November 11), and

---

[1] 'Notes on the Book of Job,' *Deliverance*.

'Heathen Ethics' (November 27). And then, in 1881, appeared *The Autobiography of Mark Rutherford*, a work written, he told his second wife, 'at extra-ordinary high pressure.'[1]

Each of these essays expresses ideas which are among the themes of the story of Mark Rutherford and, since they are not easily available, it will be useful to spend a moment on several of them here. Whitman, we are told in the first, comes as an antidote to the 'miserable modern sentimentality which discerns nothing in our own time worth seeing . . . a sentimentality morally pernicious, because, under its influence, life passes away like a dream, all the messages of the Present lying entirely disregarded.'[2] Instead of uttering the prevalent 'weak despair,' the complaints about the 'advancing ugliness of cities,' the insistence on life's 'insoluble riddles,' he teaches a glad acceptance of ordinary daily life, he teaches courage and faith. 'He believes that thought will be its own cure; that if we are afflicted by doubt, we must not hesitate—least of all must we stop short and hide ourself in a fiction: but that we must go forward.' And Whitman's faith goes so far—in the 'Prayer of Columbus'—as to affirm the value of our upward striving even in the face of death and defeat. But to grasp that value, Hale White reminds us, we must forget the self and consider the progress of the whole.

Of course, as the writer was well aware, it is the tendencies of men like Hale White himself that Whitman opposes. In the 'Marcus Antoninus' he describes that type of man: exactly such a one was the emperor-stoic. And the description is also to a large extent a preliminary sketch of the nature and problems of Mark Rutherford.

Antoninus was engaged in a continuous wrestle to provide himself with thoughts which would overcome in the battle with life and death—thoughts which should make his existence tolerable and prevent anxiety about its termination. He was a man evidently beset with scepticisms. By constitution he was prone to reflection upon the imminence of the inevitable future, and he dwelt much in the

---

[1] *The Groombridge Diary*, p. 51.

[2] Volume and page numbers are not at present available for the quotations from these *Secular Review* articles. I used the copies in Hale White's Scrapbooks, and back in New York could find no issues of the magazine earlier than 1885.

gloom which the great shadow casts, more or less, over the career of all those who are endowed with the fatal tendency to reflectiveness. But he saw that the image of death, if continually present, was as a true Medusa's head, producing petrification of every power, and he unceasingly strove to rob it of its cruel and paralysing energy, so that he could walk and move, even with levity, in full sight of it. He was in the position in which many of us now are. He had no traditionary faith to which he could resort for oracular and unquestionable replies to all his doubts. The old Roman worship had decayed, and whatever help was necessary he had to obtain for himself. It is probable that all men who think at all about these things are compelled to work out their own salvation, even if born into the straitest sect from which they may never stray. Bunyan, for example, although orthodox, could not escape the universal destiny, and had an Apollyonic conflict lasting over years before he found peace. Nevertheless, it ever must be true that, when popular religions have all gone to dust, or when, as in our day they are half-way towards it—the most disgusting stage of all putrefaction—our difficulties are increased and the solitude is deepened.[1]

The crux of Antoninus's lesson is reconciliation with the inevitable process of nature, in which death is inextricably bound up with whatever makes life worth living. He suggests that it is absurd not to regard the time when we will cease to exist or be known with the same indifference as that with which we regard our nonexistence in the time before we were born. And he teaches us not to ask 'Why' in a spirit of rebellion, but to turn aside from painful reflections that can lead to no good. The consolation he offers may seem 'meagre' compared with 'the magnificent promises of the religions,' but it is 'based upon the everlasting adamant' and not to be shaken by any 'Higher Criticism.' His book, and the work of Epictetus, are 'the most nearly complete series of solutions which the world possesses of its most pressing problems.'

The last paragraph of the essay is worth quoting entire because it beautifully foreshadows the story of Mark Rutherford.

[1] This and the following quotations from W. H. White, 'Marcus Antoninus,' *Secular Review* (July 3, 1880).

There is assuredly no spectacle in the world of diviner interest to us than that of the hero who labours perpetually to fashion for himself a creed upon which he may lean; who does not content himself with shirking the duty imposed upon him, or with drugging himself into forgetfulness of it, but faces it. No obligation imposed upon man demands a more steadfast bravery. The blood is poured forth in secret, and there is no prospect of public triumph or applause. There is none of that fever of excitement and companionship which leads the soldier to an easy assault on the deadly battery. The enemy too, once slain, is not forever slain, but is endowed with an almost infinite faculty of resurrection. No rest is there from toils. By night and by day they recur under all conditions of melancholy and lack of strength. Heroism! Who that has been called upon to undertake this task, who that has had to fight this fight, will not say that even the Persians in the pass of Thermopylae exacted from the Lacedemonians an endurance and a courage less exalted.

'Ixion' analyzes and rejects as a kind of idolatry—or worse, as meaningless—the conception of God held by 'orthodox religious people': God as 'personal, perfect, omnipotent, omniscient, all-loving, and absolutely just.' [1] A personal God implies 'consciousness of separate self-hood . . . definition, limitation'; it is not a God embracing everything, in Whom, as St. Paul says, 'we live and move and have our being.' Then: 'Absolute perfection, like everything else which is absolute and unconditioned is an inanity—a nothing.' As for the Divine omnipotence, this too is a meaningless conception for it is obviously limited by God's other attributes. The God Hale White accepts—and it is all, he says, that is really essential and meaningful in the orthodox view—is the incessantly upward-climbing 'Destiny, or God of the World, inevitably accomplishing his will.' And again we get the lesson of Spinoza and the Stoics: The Universe of this God is 'a vast and equal republic, whose laws are never turned aside for [our] convenience.' His love is a source of health only 'when its conditions are duly observed.' It then 'pours

---

[1] This and the following quotations from W. H. White, 'Ixion,' *Secular Review* (November 11, 1880).

sunlight over the whole globe and returns affection for affection through human hearts.' We imagine lesser Gods because of our own weakness and selfishness, 'but when we come to look upon ourselves as part of the universal life, and cease to be careful about the "me" in which it happens at this moment to reveal itself, our God will no longer be a God who would reverse the rules of this great universe to gratify the whinings of foolish children, but will be the vitality and the purpose of the whole.'

This seems a stern rationalism which must entirely oppose the religion of Hale White's own heritage. Indeed, it will seem so in *The Autobiography*, where these ideas will be used by a certain character as weapons against Mark Rutherford's tottering faith. But that character, though 'sympathetic' on the whole, will not be spared his author's irony. And the work—all Hale White's work—will go on to show us that such ideas, in a mind of any complexity, do not in fact oppose the doctrines of religion, when these doctrines are understood in all their depth.

The Autobiography of Mark Rutherford appeared as a posthumous work edited by the author's friend, Reuben Shapcott, and it was with this disguise that all the other books were henceforth issued. The secret of Hale White's authorship was not kept from everyone. We know that he spoke of it freely in letters to George Jacob Holyoake, the reformer to whom his *Argument* on the franchise was addressed. But it is significant that Holyoake was not the kind of person with whom he could ever be intimate. The man's whole life was politics, and he was a simple enthusiast for Robert Owen's co-operative theories until he died. From those who were nearest him, however, Hale White did wish to keep the secret. In a letter to his good friend Mrs. Colenut he is guilty of what must be the only deliberately misleading statement in all his writings, 'I have never owned the book you name and should be quite justified in denying its authorship,'[1] he says, among other such remarks, referring obviously to *The Autobiography*. What is still more interesting, he did not tell even his own family. It was not till years later that he mentioned to his wife that he had written some books which their daughter could some day read to her. This seems strange, but the

---

[1] *Letters*, p. 11.

strangeness grows less when we consider what *The Autobiography* is. It is one of the most intimate confessional works in the history of literature, far more naked, for instance, than that of Rousseau. Hale White strips off what Rousseau would never go without: his spiritual pride. He confesses what it is most difficult to confess: weakness, need, pain and humiliation. Speaking to Holyoake, Hale White could regard Rutherford, as if from above, as a 'victim of the century,'[1] but those who really knew him would know that the victim was himself. Though his reticence was extreme (and calls perhaps for a kind of explanation outside the limits of the present study), it is not impossible to sympathize with a reluctance to bare oneself so far even to a wife.[2]

In this brief biography I have given mainly what seems important for our understanding of his work. We may at this point take a leap, therefore, over the next twenty-five years, mentioning only that in 1892, a year after the death of his wife, he retired from the civil service and his life became thereafter one of reading, writing, for a time that astronomy of which we have heard, and friendship. His books won the esteem, sometimes the grateful love, of a few, but never a large public, and though his authorship was at last an open

[1] Unpublished letter to Holyoake dated January 20, 1882, copy in the possession of Dr. R. Hale-White.

[2] Since writing the above, I have come across a letter by Hale White to William Dean Howells which makes explicit his desire for anonymity. It shows too that this did not mean an indifference to *recognition* by those who were not in his immediate circle and who understood him as he wished to be understood. The letter was written on February 25, 1886, in response to the Howells review in *Harper's New Monthly Magazine* which was quoted in Chapter I. It concludes: 'My reasons for publishing anonymously, or rather under an assumed name, were mainly that I did not desire praise, blame or in fact any talk about what I had done from anybody near me. I have felt too much and am too old to care for notoriety of any kind and wanted to be quiet. Consequently nobody who knows me ever says a word to me about the autobiography. This is what I like, but nevertheless I should be less than human did I not feel gladdened and exalted by such a criticism as that now before me from a man in your position and with such a name. Again I thank you, thank you with—to me—unaccustomed emotion; and as to such a friend I cannot wear a mask I beg to subscribe myself—devotedly yours—W. Hale White.' (Quoted by Stone, *op. cit.*, p. 124. The letter is in the Houghton Library, Howells Collection, MS. Am. 800.20.)

secret in the literary world, his absolute insistence on privacy kept that world always at a distance.

The most important single fact of his old age is a fact of temperament. It is that he remained to a remarkable degree what he had always been: it often seems, indeed, that no youth in his twenties could have exceeded the aging man in what we may call emotional potency. Until the end of his life he was as liable as he had ever been in his youth to the emotional extremes, as quiveringly alive to all he loved, as hungry for affection, as beset and troubled by inner contradictions. Such youth in age, resembling that of Yeats, is responsible, as we shall see, for the undiminished excellence of his later writings. His work remained a conquest of mind—and of style—over passion which nearly breaks through. The same youthfulness is responsible also for the continuing intensity of his friendships. Letters to other friends than the 'three' could now be collected, and they would form a volume as full of his characteristic thought and feeling, and often as beautiful, as any of his others. But it is to a result of that youthfulness more important than books or friendship that we now turn in concluding the story of his life. There came to him in 1907 a great love. And though he was seventy-six and she was thirty, nothing is stranger, among all its anomalies, than its power to overcome our surprise: the more we learn about it, the more surely it takes its place among the most beautiful love-stories in the history of literature. Our sanction for writing of this relationship comes from Hale White himself: 'I should like the world someday to know it,' he said, 'not to pry into it, Heaven forbid, but just to be aware that a wonderful thing has been on the earth.' [1]

The woman was Dorothy Vernon Horace Smith, daughter of a police magistrate for Westminster. For one who was to become a fine novelist, she was a singularly unliterary person. Until her meeting with Hale White, she had read very little. Her intellectual development had all taken place in the medium of the Anglican religion. During her teens, at an age when other talented youngsters are dreaming of fame or imitating favourite writers, she was struggling—by prayer—with a terrifying sense of sin. And her first published writing was not poetry or fiction but a pamphlet of four

[1] W. H. White, 'The 1910 MS.,' in the possession of Mrs. D. V. White.

sermons, printed when she was twenty-five at her own expense. At twenty-two, she tells us, 'I had passed through a dark cloud . . . but God had been with me in the cloud, and I came out of it with a desire for service. I had been delivered and I wanted to go forth and assure others that they would be delivered too.'[1] She began to teach a Bible class for boys of the poorer neighbourhood of her town (Beckenham), taking charge too of a week-day club and a cricket team—of cricket she was passionately fond. This work she continued right through the period of her relationship with Hale White (indeed, she has done religious work with young people almost to the present day), and it became for her, particularly in the early years, a most practical kind of education. For it brought the religion through which she looked at life and understood it into illuminating, enlarging contact with the problems of experience. She tells us:

My apprehensiveness, timidity and moral fussiness received so many salutary shocks that they died a natural death, leaving room for the true conscience to grow, as I was forced week by week to grapple with some plain and obvious question of right and wrong. . . . Let us fight real evils, not bogus ones.[2]

'Her methods are not those of the district visitor or Sunday School teacher,' Hale White wrote to a friend. 'She often reminds me of Tolstoy, whom, however, she had not read.'[3] The comparison with Tolstoy (perhaps he was thinking too of Tolstoy's school-teaching at Yasnaya Polyana) is apt, for she brought to her work the same absolute faith in a moral order as his, a similarly love-inspired psychological acuteness and the same rare electrifying honesty. ('There is a veracity which requires *genius* as distinctly as the versification of Shelley or Milton,' Hale White told her. 'This veracity you have.')[4]

It was her first novel, *Miss Mona*, which brought her to his attention. Though he was not perfectly satisfied with it as a work of art, he found in it qualities which were peculiarly congenial: an 'un-

---

[1] D. V. White, *Twelve Years with My Boys*, London, Methuen and Company, Ltd., 1912, p. 2.

[2] *Ibid.*, pp. 13-14.

[3] *Letters*, pp. 360-1.   [4] *The Groombridge Diary*, p. 295.

literary' freshness of vision, a subtle suggestiveness of technique, an English absolutely pure and simple. There was also an evident religiousness which contained elements both attractive and puzzling. And he invited her to visit him at Groombridge in Kent, where he lived with his unmarried daughter Mary ('Molly').

He met me at the station [she tells us], and took me for a long long walk; we walked for about two hours. He asked me many questions, none of which I minded answering. It is like being with a boy, he is so eager, shy and tender; his feelings so fresh and acute, as if he feels a thing now for the very first time. . . . He spoke sometimes with such fire. . . . He seemed to be very glad to know me, and when I said laughing, that I 'might very nearly never have come,' he said so earnestly, so youthfully, 'You *would* have come, you *would* have come; it was quite impossible you should not have come.' [1]

She then made a strange point of not returning for two months— was it to take stock of an overwhelming possibility?—but the interval over, she began to pay visits of increasing length and frequency. For the first time in his life Hale White had someone to talk to who not only did not mind his being 'serious' [2] but who looked where he looked, saw what he saw and responded as he did—or better still, did all these as he felt at once that he *should*. The description in *The Groombridge Diary* of their rich unimpeded conversations must be the envy of all those who have ever tried to share an inner life: their talk was a continuous feasting. It took only a few months for their love to become for them, miracle though they felt it to be, an accepted fact. 'I *flew* to you,' [3] he told her once, and again: 'He spoke of the "hunger and thirst and need" of his life, "an infinite need" which neither his books, nor his friends nor his religion had ever satisfied. I was to remember that I had satisfied that need.' [4] At last he went further: 'My love of God—I speak it with reverence—is my love of Dorothy.' [5]

He knew this was strange, and in 1910 he set down, as it were for

----

[1] *Ibid.*, pp. 1-2.   [2] *Ibid.*, p. 125.

[3] *Ibid.*, p. 124.   [4] *Ibid.*

[5] *Ibid.*, p. 127.

G

us, an explanation which he gave her to keep or not as she wished. This tells us in part:

Directly I saw Dorothy I felt that, although it was late, she was destined to be the fulfilment of my life. The conviction was as unhesitating as that which follows an axiom. Something was wrought in me instantaneously. It was spiritual regeneration answering to what is known as conversion in the language of religion. My creed it is true, so far as it was defined, did not change, but the aspect of the whole of life was altered. . . . For much that I have always felt indefinitely I had no words. She has given it articulation and consequently a new province has been marked out and added to my life. Love also appeared. Of this I shall say nothing except that it was the greater because it included reverence for genius more remarkable than any I have ever known in woman. It is a genius not only for this or that but for living, genius which shows itself in all the events of common existence as well as in her writing, her class and her music.[1]

The phrase, 'fulfilment of my life' is no mere flourish. His love for such a woman was a kind of confirmation and completion of his life's essential meanings. (It will be remembered that he said of Caleb Morris, 'He *made* me'; in the *Diary* we read: 'He told me that what he saw through Caleb Morris and had been looking for during these fifty years, he had seen again through me.' [2] Miss Smith had exactly the qualities of mind and temperament, exactly the attitudes to life, which had composed his private ideal from the beginning. This accounts for a remarkable similarity in the style and import of their writings, many of her insights having long since been dramatized in his books.[3] To say that she embodied his ideal, however, is not to say that they were simply alike. They were also strikingly different. But her different qualities were just those he had always prescribed for himself in vain; they were exactly the medicine, as it were, which he had always needed.

[1] '1910 MS.'

[2] *The Groombridge Diary*, p. 28.

[3] 'He said he was sometimes quite awestruck and frightened at our likeness to one another.' (*The Groombridge Diary*, p. 113.)

We learn what she was from that pamphlet of sermons; from her three novels, *Miss Mona* (1908), *Frank Burnet* (1909)—this one possibly a masterpiece—and *Isabel* (1911); from *Twelve Years with My Boys* (1912), an anonymous account of her 'Sunday School' work which is actually a profound essay on religion, life and the tangle of human relations; from *The Groombridge Diary* (1924), which her insight, that veracity he saw as requiring 'genius,' and the simple transparent style, make into a great portrait of Hale White and an essential part of his collected works; from her 'Occasional Note-books' a fascinating diary, full of life and wisdom which it is to be hoped she will continue and preserve; and finally, from the 'Dorothy Book,' a collection of paragraphs and sentences copied by him from her letters and conversation. This last work should some day be published, for it belongs among our precious volumes of meditations and is a revelation, like his own writings, of the deep 'secular' wisdom which religion can express.

It is, in fact, her religiousness that is the key to what she brought him: she was a living demonstration—'in all the events of common existence'—of that religion he had always sought. Being, moreover, an actual person, she was, as he had said, an extension of that religion into unexpected areas. For though she was a devout Anglican, she was one who could write:

We discussed creeds again. I said that if all creeds were done away with . . . my *religion* would still stand. This satisfied him; he said he knew it was so, and that it was so with him. He spoke of his absolute belief in those spiritual truths which the material forms embody. We are entirely at one, and I told him there will come a time when the 'form' no longer matters.[1]

That religion which lies beneath 'creeds' was the substance of his books and will be explored in the chapters to follow, but a prelim-inary definition now will perhaps shed light on her mind. It is an awareness of life's complexity, dwarfing our powers, and the ability —it is a gift of temperament—first to select out of the all-permitting

---

[1] *The Groombridge Diary*, pp. 139-40.

chaos those beliefs which 'save,' which are healthy, encouraging, ennobling, and then to rest on them faithfully.

As for her grasp of complexity, one observation from her youthful pamphlet of sermons will suggest what is meant. She points out that Christ, wishing us to be 'perfect,' says different things to different men. His perfection is balance, 'completeness,' not simply the possession of particular qualities, for every human quality has its way of being evil as well as good. 'How shall we be perfect? We must walk with open eyes. We must not blindly follow even virtue.'[1] From an insight like this into the other side of things can flow all the subtleties and ambiguities of a Gide or a Hale White.

But it was that second element in her religion—her temperament —which constituted her special value for him. She describes it herself in her *Twelve Years with My Boys*, where she tries to account for the success she had in spite of her shortcomings. She, too, we discover, had known 'a lively conflict between timid, melancholy and courageous hope, [but] the hope and the courage had conquered.... I had instinctively pursued and captured joy and held on to it as the best power with which to keep wretchedness at bay.'[2] And further on:

I cannot help knowing that there was a great deal of brightness in me, an immediate expansion of body, mind and spirit when touched by another human being, an instinct to love without criticism ... [a] breezy cheerfulness and robust common sense and downright justice.[3]

These are not random characteristics; they were the personal attributes that went with her 'faith,' the proof, as it were, that the faith came from deep and was secure. Hale White might have deduced them as necessary—indeed, he had often done so—but he knew them only as a hungry man knows the value of food, he himself, as we

[1] Dorothy V. Horace Smith (maiden name of Mrs. White), *Discourses on Character, Completeness, the Fatherhood of God, Life Everlasting*, Beckenham, Kent, 1902, pp. 21-2.

[2] *Twelve Years with My Boys*, p. 10.

[3] *Ibid.*, pp. 11-12.

have seen, spending most of his life in an atmosphere of self-created fear and gloom. It will be understood that Miss Smith entered such a life like a tonic burst of sunlight, answering its deepest 'need.' And what she taught him again and again, if only by bringing him joy, was how to *believe* (not in magic, but in the good possibilities of life) instead of fear. Thus in 1910 she writes:

He said that he was so liable to 'drop down at once to despondency, to despair, to fear—not base fears, though fears, that it was so hard to lift him at all.' 'Your love,' he said, 'is so powerful; it is the only thing that could ever have lifted me—that ever *will* lift me—that ever *has* lifted me.' He said that he did not think there could be anyone in the world to whom my love could have been of more help.[1]

They were happy, therefore, as few couples ever succeed in being. Nevertheless, until they were married in 1911, they also knew much painful trouble. There was the necessity they felt at first to accept the impossibility of marriage, which meant that she continued to be a visitor and he to suffer agonies at each farewell as she went home. There was his illness in 1908-09, leading to a dangerous operation and a slow recovery, an event made doubly distressing for her by her still anomalous position in the family. (A tendency existed to shut her out from a sorrow she longed to share with them openly as well as privately.) Above all, as may be guessed, there was his own temperament, which had now the great additional provocation of their difference in age.

We have seen that his love had always been uneasy and jealous. It was so once more; every outside interest that she had was a threat to his composure. Again and again between 1908 and 1911 they argued over 'her boys,' he refusing to understand why she continued to work among them. And reflecting on this in 1911, she comments:

I have since come to believe that the boys as boys were not the difficulty. It was his strange instinct for holding his possessions so tight that they run a risk of suffocation. He fears if they walk at liberty they are gone; so he holds them and chokes them, and then is

[1] *The Groombridge Diary*, p. 304.

disappointed to find them dead, though still of course in his grasp. Consequently, as I *moved* most in the direction of my boys, it was there he tried to stop me.[1]

He did not succeed, however, for her remarkable sensitivity and responsiveness were accompanied, as they rarely are, by the strength to call a halt to reasons when she felt herself right, and to stick to her guns. Sometimes she was hardly conscious of resisting: what she was simply would not brook distortion or dilution. And when arguments were over, he was glad.

I well remember in those early days [she continues the comment] how he once expressed a curious delight over the fact that with me if the reins tightened they snapped. I could neither understand the reins nor his delight. I was quite innocent of consciously pulling, of that I was sure.[2]

Another source of pain was the weakness of his faith in her love. Mistrustful as he was of life in general, it is not surprising that he could not steadily believe—especially during the time of his illness—that so young a woman could feel more for so old a man than an increasingly impatient pity. 'The more passionate my love,' he wrote to her in a letter of November 1909, 'the stronger the temptation to give way, to let myself break down, *to refuse to* summon up strength to believe—for it does need strength and effort. I have to struggle even to hope that it is possible you can love me.'[3] Mrs. White records a scene in the *Diary* which reveals well the unhappy drama to which this could lead. After a bad night, he had spent a morning of most complete and delightful communion with her, speaking of Milton, of Christ, of their love. What followed was a reversal (the fear of humiliation making love belie itself) reminiscent of Dostoevsky, though Mrs. White's account of it is deliberately 'toned down.'

[1] *The Groombridge Diary*, p. 84 *n.*
[2] *Ibid.*
[3] This is from an unpublished portion of the letter quoted in *The Groombridge Diary*, p. 287; it is taken from the MS. of *The Groombridge Diary*, in the possession of Mrs. D. V. White.

When I brought up his pudding after lunch, he asked me if I was leaving that afternoon. I said, no, I wanted to stay till Saturday. He said: 'I can't think why you are here at all,' and repeated it. I said: 'What do you mean?' He said: 'You know what I mean.' I told him my only happiness was here, and that he must give me all the happiness he could. As I turned to go he said: 'God still works miracles.'[1]

With their marriage, however, all troubles either vanished or grew easy to conquer, and the section of the *Diary* which follows is chiefly a description of happiness. Of happy families, it has been said, there is little to tell, and the entries grow less and less frequent. He died on March 14, 1913, and among his last words, uttered, we are told, with sudden distinctness after he had begun to wander, was: 'Dorothy, you have done me a lot of good.'[2]

[1] *Ibid.*, pp. 125-6.   [2] *Ibid.*, p. 438.

CHAPTER V

The Autobiography of
Mark Rutherford

I

THAT *The Autobiography of Mark Rutherford* (1881) and its sequel, *Mark Rutherford's Deliverance* (1885), are at many points an account of their author's own life no one would deny. Yet it is also true that there are certain discrepancies between Rutherford's history and that of his author. Along with 'a good deal' of fact 'under a semi-transparent disguise,' Hale White has told us, 'there is much added which is entirely fictitious.' [1] We know, too, that there is a constant irony levelled against Rutherford's character, not only by suggestion within the narrative, but directly by Rutherford's 'editor' Shapcott, who dwells on his defects and limitations: on his morbidity and the gulf, resulting in frequent pain, between his dreams and his capacities for realizing them. Finally, Hale White himself, it will be remembered, called him a 'victim of the century.' Does all this justify a separation between Hale White and his protagonist? I have already indicated my view that it does not.

To begin with Rutherford's character, it seems clear, in the light of what we know of his author's, that all criticism of this, direct or implied, is simply *self*-criticism. If the work does not give us every element of Hale White's personality, it does show those which he considered essential; and we may be sure that the self represented by Rutherford is a far more faithful picture of what he really was than, say, the Assistant Director of Naval Contracts he showed to the workaday world. The deeper self had been more or less concealed until the book, not only because of its sensitivity to rebuff but also as a matter of duty, for a living had to be made and complaint could

[1] *Early Life*, p. 5.

only give pain. But it was this self which had been the haunting remnant never told even in the fullest communion with friends, and which he had thirsted all his life to share, and it was precisely the excitement of uttering it at last that made the story of Mark Rutherford issue from him at such 'extra-ordinary high pressure,'[1] and in a style so charged and affecting. Indeed, it would be equally mistaken to separate Rutherford even from oneself, the reader. As often when a writer's self-criticism goes deep, Rutherford's limitations, failures and suffering are at last not those of *other* people but of humanity. For is not his 'morbidity' only a special vulnerability to those fears for which life gives all of us reasons enough? And that gulf between his dreams and his capacities—who has not known this? The man who is not aware of any Mark Rutherford inside himself, but who takes literally, so to speak, his own Assistant Directorship of Naval Contracts, is perhaps to be envied, but more for his happy temperament than for his wisdom.

Nor are the discrepancies between the histories of author and protagonist any proof that they are significantly different. Considering, once again, all we know of both, these discrepancies are seen to have two main causes. The first—and slightest—is Hale White's attempt at 'disguise,' a purpose understandable enough, as I have said in view of the work's embarrassing frankness as confession. On the whole this results only in trifling changes: changes in names, places and the order of events. The second and far more important reason for the work's fictional character is that it is the backward glance of a philosophic mind, concerned to present not a mere collection of personal anecdotes but a ripened insight into the quality and meaning of a life's experience. Such a guiding purpose, of course, is that of the novelist. To make detail the servant of mood and meaning, on behalf of which it is to be pruned, sharpened, rearranged and even, at times, invented, is to move straight in the direction of fiction. It is this that accounts for the work's power as art, for the fact that scene after scene has the economy, vividness and emotional persuasiveness of the actual novels to come. And it accounts, too, for the fact that what is apparently straightforward autobiography, where event follows event and people arrive and vanish merely

[1] *The Groombridge Diary*, p. 51.

because it happened so in life, has yet so much of a novel's unity and, like any novel of value, embodies a theme. The theme indeed—perhaps also as a result of the unity of the life—can be discovered at the bottom of far more of what happens than at first appears to be the case.

This theme is not often recognized, however, for while Hale White's first two books are his most widely read, they are read mainly for what lies on the surface. They are read as dramatized nineteenth-century history, history that has the advantage of a good style. They are considered to be a 'naturalistic' account of the chief problems of that century in England: the iniquities of the Industrial Revolution and the conflict between religion and science. Now this is true, but although it lends a certain 'importance,' it does not go deep enough. For Hale White, as for all permanently interesting writers, the problems of his own time are only the form in which that time has cast problems which belong to the human condition and are eternal. Though he looked *at* his world, as every good writer must, he also looked *through* it, which is equally necessary.

'We ought to endeavour to give our dreams reality,' reads one of his late 'notes,' 'but in reality we should preserve the dream.' [1] These two elements, brought together in human intention yet forever opposing each other, define the theme of Mark Rutherford's story and one of the major preoccupations of his author. That theme is the conflict between reality and the human 'dream.' For the latter, read all those ideas about reality by which we redeem it from chaos and —what is equally important to many—from indifference to ourselves. Now it may well be that Hale White's own time and place were peculiarly likely to bring this conflict to the foreground, for it was a time, as he says, of 'total chaos' when religions were changing or dissolving and 'hundreds of thousands of voices offer us pilotage.' [2] In such a time the individual who thinks must find himself frequently alone, and more aware than when protected by a concurring society or institution of the recalcitrance of the world to his ideas. Yet if the problem grew severe in the nineteenth century, it is also an inevitable

[1] W. H. White, *More Pages from a Journal*, London, Oxford University Press, 1910, p. 247.
[2] *Deliverance*, chap. v.

problem in human experience at any time. It is the essential formula, for instance, of all those works which show some particular ambition or vision of the self opposed by society. In Hale White it is precisely the essential formula, linking many such experiences, that keeps rising to the surface. And it is the varying solutions possible to the essential conflict which his work examines.

For the conflict between the dream—any dream—and reality can have a number of results. One, the perfect realization or validation of the dream in real life, is perhaps too rare a happiness to be considered. The reverse is more common: the failure to see any realization or validation at all, the gradual loss of hope and faith, and the capitulation to a reality altogether different from what was dreamed. Or else there is a compromise: the dream is modified to suit the reality and the reality is ennobled by the dream. Sometimes we do well to give up our dream—it may have been incapable of realization and have prevented us from doing justice to the life (the people, the wife) around us. Sometimes such 'wisdom' is an error of weakness, and to hold on to the dream stubbornly in *spite* of 'common sense,' and even of 'evidence,' is the truer wisdom. Either what seemed to oppose it may be destined to melt before persistence, or else the struggle to lift our lives toward it will at least raise them higher than they would otherwise have reached. These patterns of thought—of experience—recur not only in this first work but in all those which follow, and their formulation here may serve as clues to the underlying relatedness or identity of themes which may seem unconnected only because they are variously embodied.

Thus we meet at the outset the surprising affinity mentioned in Chapter I. For exactly the same conflict is at the bottom of that 'first novel' in which Gide presented his most complete image of life. Here is the theme of *The Counterfeiters* as it is stated by Gide's novelist Edouard: 'It is . . . the rivalry between the real world and the representation we make of it to ourselves. The manner in which the world of appearance imposes itself on us and the manner in which we try to impose on the outside world our own interpretation —this is the drama of our lives.' [1] In these words, however, we also

[1] André Gide, *The Counterfeiters*, translated by Dorothy Bussy, New York, Alfred A. Knopf, 1947, p. 189.

catch a glimpse of their difference. Gide is chiefly interested in the rise and fall, caused by this rivalry, of our ideas, and this can be regarded with something of the spectator's impersonal relish: as a 'drama.' But for Hale White the rivalry is less an intellectual problem —though it is that too—than a source of terrible difficulty in the business of living, and the word that occurs to him is not 'drama' but 'sorrow.' 'The sorrow of life is the rigidity of the material universe in which we are placed,' he says in a later essay on Spinoza, 'and there is a constant pressure of matter-of-fact evidence to prove that we are nothing but common and cheap products of the earth to which in a few moments or years we return.' [1] For him—for Mark Rutherford—a world in which he is an insignificant *thing* among identical millions is unbearable: when *his* dream of a meaning which gives the individual some importance is shattered, he suffers.

In Mark Rutherford's life there were two main sources of the kind of meaningfulness he needed so desperately: religion and love. Religion, relating the whole universe to man, is the greatest of those dreams by which man is given value, and one, moreover, which Rutherford's background and temperament made peculiarly congenial. But love, and especially the love between man and woman, is the most intense. And it is no accident that the two should come together in his story, as in so many of those which followed, for as Hale White views them they are profoundly related. A woman's love was for him exactly the same affirmation of a man's value as that of religion. It was 'a stream straight from the Highest,' a 'living witness . . . of an actuality in God which otherwise we should never know.' [2] Now, opposing the 'dream' of religion with which he began there were, beside the basic recalcitrance of life, the various industrial and intellectual developments of nineteenth-century England, and this was a 'reality' that could be formidable to the point of horror. Opposing him in his search for love were the difficulties of his own temperament and, for men like him, of human relationships in general. His story, then, is the story of his struggle to retain or rebuild a religion, and to find love, in the face of such opposition.

[1] *Pages*, pp. 33-4.
[2] *Deliverance*, chap. viii.

II

The Autobiography begins with a picture of the Calvinist community in which Mark Rutherford spent his childhood and youth. We are shown a world given over to a religion consisting chiefly of the mechanical observance of forms and the uninspired repetition of formulae. Of the once warmly felt meanings of those forms, meanings Rutherford was later to find especially attractive and illuminating, there was no trace. In his childhood he suffered from this religion chiefly on Sundays, days full of long, excruciatingly boring services and of leisure one dared not enliven. But having become a 'converted soul' at fourteen, he was taken several years later to a Dissenting college to prepare for the ministry, and there the dead formulae became his whole life. At this school the secular instruction was 'generally inefficient,' but worse still, the theological and Biblical training was 'a sham.' The Calvinist scheme was built up from manuals 'like a house of cards,' and the difficulties of belief were settled by a dozen tracts—settled all the more easily, indeed, because nothing was known of German literature save that the term German was a word of reproach. For all the failings and diseases of the soul, 'infinitely more complicated than those of the body,' this scheme was the one 'quack remedy.'[1]

The first seed of Rutherford's ultimate heresy was sown in the middle of his college career. It came from Wordsworth, whose *Lyrical Ballads* Rutherford likens, in its effect upon him, to the Divine apparition which changed Paul at Damascus. Without offering him a new doctrine, this work caused all mere system to decay, developed in him a habit of 'inner reference,'[2] and a dislike of occupying himself 'with what was not the embodiment or the illustration of some spiritual law,' and for 'the God of the Church' substituted a 'God of the hills, . . . in which literally I could live and move and have my being.' Like every religious reformer, Wordsworth recreated for his disciple his 'Supreme Divinity, substituting a new and living spirit for the old deity, once alive, but gradually hardened into an idol.'[3] It is to be noted that what thus liberated

---

[1] *The Autobiography*, chap. ii.   [2] *Ibid.*   [3] *Ibid.*

him from Calvinist orthodoxy, as it had done Hale White, was not
the opposition of 'reality' by way of science or sceptical thought but
rather a more satisfying religious idea: and that the tendency given
to, or strengthened in, his character was a tendency to absorption in
the 'dream,' the idea, the 'spiritual law.' This 'dream,' moreover,
was *personal*, it was an intellectual extension of his own most intimate
nature, a fact which determines many of its consequences. For it
could thus be at once true to the reality of the self and false to a
reality outside, a contradiction fertile in problems.

This expansion of his religion was the great experience of his
youth, and it is those whose youth also contained such an experience,
he tells us, who are most attractive to him; 'those who have had in
some form or other an enthusiastic stage in their history, when the
story of Genesis and of the Gospels has been rewritten, when God
has visibly walked in the garden, and the Son of God has drawn men
away from their daily occupations into the divinest of dreams.' The
experience ushered in the happiest time of his life. It was a time of
rich inner growth—wholly joyous because it was 'before all joy had
been darkened by the shadow of oncoming death'—a time 'when
books were read with tears in the eyes.' [1] The growth did not, however, result in any immediate formal heresy. 'Nearly every doctrine
in the college creed had once had a natural origin in the necessities
of human nature, and might be so interpreted as to become a
necessity again. To reach through to that original necessity . . .
became my object.' [2] Here is an example of the kind of sermon that
resulted. It is the type of that appropriation of religious symbols to
secular life, that process of making them '*intelligible*' (as he says),
which is one of the chief sources of Hale White's interest for us
today.

I remember . . . discoursing about the death of Christ. There was
not a single word which was ordinarily used in the pulpit which I
did not use—satisfaction for sin, penalty, redeeming blood, they were
all there—but I began by saying that in this world there was no
redemption for man but by blood; furthermore, the innocent had
everywhere and in all time to suffer for the guilty. It had been

[1] *The Autobiography*, chap. ii.   [2] *Ibid.*

objected that it was contrary to our notion of an all-loving Being that He should demand such a sacrifice; but, contrary or not, in this world it was true, quite apart from Jesus, that virtue was martyred every day, unknown and unconsoled, in order that the wicked might somehow be saved. This was part of the scheme of the world, and we might dislike it or not, we could not get rid of it. The consequences of my sin, moreover, are rendered less terrible by virtues not my own. I am literally saved from penalties because another pays the penalty for me. The Atonement, and what it accomplished for man, were therefore a sublime summing up as it were of what sublime men have to do for their race; an exemplification, rather than a contradiction, of Nature herself, as we know her in our own experience.[1]

But, of course, 'it was precisely this reaching after a meaning which constituted heresy,' for orthodoxy meant 'the acceptance of dogmas as communications from without, and not as born from within.'[2] The absorption of the young Rutherford in this 'divinest of dreams' was therefore followed by a characteristic punishment: isolation from the intellectual community in which he had grown up. And the first sign of this was the gentle but firm disapproval of his sermon by the College President, a response that fell on his enthusiasm 'like the hand of a corpse.'[3]

Along with the development which thus isolated him intellectually, moreover, there came another which isolated him in ways even more painful. As his mind filled and grew, he found it harder to get along with others. This was not lack of interest on his part. 'It was an excess of communicativeness, an eagerness to show what was most at my heart, and to ascertain what was at the heart of those to whom I talked, which made me incapable of mere fencing and trifling, and so often caused me to retreat into myself when I found absolute absence of response.'[4] He began to have 'a dream . . . of a perfect friendship'—the passage is quoted in Chapter I—a haunting ideal for which he searched 'as for the kingdom of heaven.'[5] To seek

[1] Ibid.
[2] Ibid.
[3] Ibid.
[4] Ibid.
[5] Ibid.

perfect ideas is less dangerous, however, than to seek perfect human relationships. This dream earned him much wounding disappointment. And trying people by his standard, he often 'prodigally wasted' the affection, less than ideal, perhaps, but *real*, which was available to him.

The basic conflict of his existence grew more painful after he had left college—unlike his author he does complete his training—and become an Independent minister in a small country town. The congregation is described with incisive irony: its deacons, like Mr. Catfield, whose religious beliefs, though not hypocritical, were never as sincere as the most trifling expression of pleasure or pain, its 'Dorcas meetings,' where the ladies gathered to sew for the poor, sip tea and gossip, while being read to by the stifling young minister from tracts he detested. Above all the other figures rises that of the deacon, Mr. Snale, a Dissenting Mr. Pecksniff, who would have been shocked to hear that meanness and selfishness were as much sins as breaking the Sabbath, and whose orthodoxy was a screen behind which these qualities were given free play. Rutherford's first sermon before this congregation, and what follows after it, are among Hale White's most beautiful and poignant pages,[1] and they contribute notably to the theme we are tracing out. He told them that every philosophy or religion was 'a remedy proposed to meet some extreme pressure' and that the special contribution of Jesus was that, confronted by two overpowering organizations, one political and the other ecclesiastical, 'He taught the doctrine of the kingdom of heaven; He trained Himself to have faith in the absolute monarchy of the soul, the absolute monarchy of His own; He tells us that each man should learn to find peace in his own thoughts and visions.' It is not surprising that the young minister should add next that Christianity was 'essentially the religion of the unknown and of the lonely, of those who are not a success. It was the religion of the man who goes through life thinking much, but who makes few friends and sees nothing come of his thoughts.' For between reality and our own ideas of it, as Gide was to point out, there is a 'rivalry'; faith in

[1] André Gide, in a conversation with the present writer shortly before his death and presumably long after he had last read *The Autobiography*, recalled this scene as especially moving.

one's own visions and worldly failure are therefore, as Rutherford's own life was showing, naturally connected.

But such faith is not easy to attain. This was what followed his impassioned first sermon:

> After the service was over I went down into the vestry. Nobody came near me but my landlord, the chapel-keeper, who said it was raining, and immediately went away to put out the lights and shut up the building. I had no umbrella, and there was nothing to be done but to walk out in the wet. When I got home I found that my supper, consisting of bread and cheese and a pint of beer, was on the table, but apparently it had been thought unnecessary to light the fire again at that time of night. I was overwrought, and paced about for hours in hysterics. All that I had been preaching seemed the merest vanity when I was brought face to face with the fact itself; and I reproached myself bitterly that my own creed would not stand the stress of an hour's actual trial. Towards morning I got into bed, but not to sleep; and when the dull daylight of Monday came, all support had vanished, and I seemed to be sinking into a bottomless abyss.[1]

It was at this time that Rutherford first became acquainted with 'that awful malady hypochondria,' and his melancholy took the fixed form of a suspicion that his brain was failing. For months his fear was so terrible that he could hardly conduct his affairs, and he prayed incessantly for death. Now the horrible two-day experience as a schoolmaster which introduced Hale White to *his* hypochondria will occur later in the book. Is there a significance in placing Rutherford's introduction to the malady here? I think there is: a significance which testifies to the 'Gidean' complexity of our author's insight, for it comes immediately after that affirmation of the monarchy of the soul and of faith in its visions, and we are thereby shown at once the other side of the coin. If the mind which remains independent of the fettering outside world can create the divinest dreams, it can also create things less creditable: for instance, a hell of groundless terrors. And freedom can mean merely lack of sympathy, of that sympathy

[1] *The Autobiography,* chap. iii.

H

from our fellows which is often necessary to keep us in healthy contact with reality.[1]

In the months that followed, the gulf between Rutherford and his congregation widened and he began to feel a certain dishonesty in continuing to use terms that meant different things to his hearers and himself—for 'truth lies in relation.'[2] Moreover, he was deeply distressed at his total failure, in the pulpit, to win the slightest response or to effect the slightest change. It was at this point that he met Edward Gibbon Mardon, who was to widen that gulf much further and who, though a good man and a true friend, caused him much suffering. Mardon, a compositor on the town paper, was an agnostic, a man of reason, 'who would not be satisfied with letting a half known thing alone and saying he believed it.'[3] The Higher Criticism was at his fingertips. He doubted that Christ ever lived, or, if he lived, was the man we know, nor would he accept Rutherford's defence that at least the Christ-idea has value. The story of Christ has value only as something that really happened, it inspires us only as an example of real, not poetically, imagined victory. The very idea of God as ordinarily entertained, Mardon called nonsense, 'and so are all these abstract, illimitable, self-annihilative attributes of which God is made up.'[4] To Rutherford it was literally agony to watch 'the dissolution of Jesus into mythologic vapour,' and even worse, to be gradually bereft of hope in a life beyond the grave. He realized later that such hope was merely an extension of 'the folly . . . of drawing from tomorrow only a reason for the joyfulness of today.'[5] But in this period 'Mardon's talk darkened my days and nights.' Now the view that Christ functions as a Great Example is

---

[1] It is here that Rutherford falls into that habit of taking a daily glass of wine, which, fearing to be enslaved by it, he breaks at the cost of much nervous anguish. 'I have never understood the maniacal craving, which is begotten by ardent spirits,' he says in Chapter III, 'but I understood enough to be convinced that the man who has once rescued himself from the dominion even of half a bottle, or three parts of a bottle of claret daily may assure himself that there is nothing more in life which he need dread.' And he goes on to give some advice on how to fight both the craving for drink and the malady hypochondria, advice which is all the more powerful in its 'literary' effect from being so purely, so earnestly, practical.

[2] *The Autobiography*, chap. iv.

[3] *Ibid.*   [4] *Ibid.*   [5] *Ibid.*, chap. v.

not only something Rutherford himself had recently preached; it is expressed by Hale White in his 'Letter on the death of Mrs. Street.' Moreover, exactly Mardon's opinion of the ordinary idea of God is in Hale White's essay 'Ixion.' When we remember this, the true, or at least highly probable, identity of Mardon becomes clear. This friend, whose 'sledge-hammer' [1] blows dealt so roughly with what Mark Rutherford cherished, is an example of the invented character who is more intimately revealing than many a real one. He is the voice of Hale White's own critical intelligence as it ruthlessly attacked in those days his remaining orthodox beliefs, and as perhaps it was also attacking, while he wrote, his still inextinguishable loyalty to the beautiful symbols.

One of the worst faults characteristic of men of thought like Rutherford is a tendency to slight people whose virtues are non-intellectual. In the mature Hale White, as we saw, an exactly opposite tendency was also at work, and it is what he *learned* from his guilt and the way he opposed it that ended by being far more characteristic of him. In the story of Rutherford we get several examples of this fault. But the most important for the 'plot' is the protagonist's treatment of his fiancée Ellen. Ellen was a girl he had loved before going to college for precisely those non-intellectual virtues—her cheerful active nature and her freedom from meanness and every 'vice of temper.' [2] But when a change in her circumstances forced her to hint that the time had come for them to be married, he suddenly realized that his feeling had changed. As a girl who never read books or was troubled by questions of orthodoxy or heresy, she seemed unlikely to give him the sympathy he had hoped for in marriage. In a painful scene he revealed his new attitude and the engagement was broken. Years later, in the *Deliverance*, it was to be precisely in this same Ellen, and in just these qualities he now ignored, that he would find the greatest happiness of his life, its very salvation.

There is, however, much more in this episode than an example of intellectual snobbery and self-obsession. It is one of the most Gidian episodes in the book, a lesson in the bottomless complexity of life and the relativity of every principle we draw from it as moral or as

---

[1] *Ibid.*, chap. iv.   [2] *Ibid.*, chap. v.

guide. For Rutherford's break with Ellen was less a decision than a
mindless plunge after an agony of vacillation among reasons equally
valid on both sides of the question. For instance, sympathy is necessary in a wife, and yet perfect sympathy is impossible, intellectual
sympathy is not the only kind, marriage to a good woman would be
a sufficient boon in his case because it would relieve him from 'the
insufferable solitude which was depressing me to death.' And so
forth. In this 'miserable condition' which preceded the break, he
visited the home of two spinsters, the Misses Arbour, who were as
orthodox as any other members of his congregation but whose
religion was also an expression of goodness and wisdom. One sister
was away, and the sympathy of the other with his evident distress
drew from him suddenly the whole story. In return, and to save him
from what she thought would be a terrible mistake, she told him the
story of her own marriage. For in fact she had been married, had
made the mistake, and it had ruined her life. Her story is the first
of the unhappy marriages in Hale White's work. I have said that
these fall roughly into two categories: one telling of the suffering of
one spouse through the general limitations and coarseness of the
other; the second of the cruel slighting of someone whose virtues
are not intellectual by an intellectual husband or wife—the fault
described above. Miss Arbour's is the former kind, and the tale of
what she endured at the hands of a dull, unimaginative and unfeeling
husband, who tortured her without the least awareness of guilt and
who was filled by her rebellion with righteous indignation, is re-
counted with masterful economy and brilliantly telling detail. It was
for the sake of its moral she now revealed her past, a moral she
insisted on passionately as a 'Divine message' for the young minister.
To argue himself into a marriage without sympathy was 'a parleying
with the Enemy of souls.'[1] This could have been true, of course, and
at this point in the story we are content to accept it. And yet this
moral, so right for her, is in fact to be contradicted in Rutherford's
own life by what happens much later in the *Deliverance*. The real
moral of the episode lies therefore much deeper than any partial one
derived from some individual's particular experience. Rutherford has
already formulated it: 'A general principle, a fine saying, is nothing

[1] *The Autobiography*, chap. v.

but a tool, and the wit of man is shown not in his possession of a well-furnished tool-chest, but in the ability to pick out the proper instrument and use it.'[1] It is just such upsetting reversals in attitude to people or acts, such contradiction of one moral or principle by another, and such an ultimate undercutting of them all by a reliance not on any fixed principle but on the flexibility of mind which can 'pick out the proper intruments' each case demands, that we find in Gide's work as a whole, and in *The Counterfeiters* most richly.

Life continued to strip Rutherford of all his inner supports, and the 'dream' of his religion went more and more to pieces. Though he became entirely unorthodox, however, he still could not accept man's total extinction—the thought of it obsessed him unto monomania. Death seemed the outside world's final victory in reducing man, with all his 'unquenchable longings,' to an insignificant bit of matter in a mindless universe.[2] He was amazed to see how calm Mardon remained when, struck down during an election by a Tory mob, he was for a while in danger of death. On Mardon's recovery they argued the matter. As usual, Rutherford had the worst of it, yet

---

[1] *Ibid.*

[2] It is interesting that just as religion and human love go together for Hale White, each being an affirmation of man's value, so death, which seems to cancel his value, brings up invariably the thought of the death of love, the thought of being forgotten. In the heartbreaking poem which serves as the motto for *The Autobiography*, beautiful in its hymn-like plainness and even awkwardness, a dying man reflects that in a little while

> 'Someone to my child will say,
> "You'll soon forget that you could play
> Beethoven; let us hear a strain
> From that slow movement once again."

> 'And so she'll play that melody,
> While I among the worms do lie;
> Dead to them all, forever dead;
> The churchyard clay dense overhead.'

In Chapter II, Mark Rutherford says, 'If I were to die not one of [my friends] would remember me for more than a week.' In Chapter VIII: 'If I were to drop into the grave, he [the common type of friend] would perhaps never give me another thought.' And in that short story about another Mark Rutherford character, 'A Mysterious Portrait,' the hero reflects, 'If I were to die, I should be forgotten a week after the burial.'

he remained convinced that the universe is informed with Mind to which our own minds answer—though he could not prove it, he felt it to be so. But what is the good, Mardon demanded, of affirming Intelligence about which nothing sensible can be said? And as for Rutherford's 'feeling,' Mardon could not follow him, he said, into the cloudy realm of sentiment. It is an interesting irony, directed this time *against* the voice of reason, that during this same visit, Mardon's daughter Mary, after denying that her father was as lacking in sentiment as he pretended, inadvertently proved it when she sang a song of Handel's that had been loved by her dead mother. Mardon was overcome by *feeling*, which made real for him a person *who did not exist*, and feeling was thus to some extent vindicated from his suggestion of its irrelevance. The episode of the song initiated Rutherford's overwhelming love for Mary Mardon, and this is another of those intense experiences in which the simplicity of Hale White's style grows beautiful with restrained passion.

Rutherford's unorthodoxy was not the shallow kind of a certain atheist he had once heard who had declared he would have made a better world than this one, in which death and unhappiness exist. He realizes that just as shadowless light is impossible, so is a happiness not defined by limits—by being distinct from what is not happiness —so is good without evil, and death without life. But though such ideas gave him comfort, they were not the proper equipment of an Independent minister. After a spiteful anonymous newspaper letter from Mr. Snale protesting his 'German gospel,' he finally quit the Independents, and he took instead a Unitarian pulpit. But this was no improvement, for the Unitarians turned out to be as 'petrified' in their own orthodoxy as any Calvinists. He was even more unhappy here than he had been before, and when he quit the Unitarians —since there was no place left to go—he had left the ministry for good.

The nature of his trouble is emphasized, and his ultimate 'deliverance' foreshadowed, by his encounters with two people who were of some help to him in this period. They both taught him, the first by implication and the second explicitly, the danger of unanchored 'dreaming' or speculating, and the health that lies in reality. One, an exception in his congregation, is Mrs. Lane. She is another of Hale

White's devoutly religious characters whose religion is also a mode
of wisdom. Her chief value for him, we are told, was that her
wisdom was not of books, which were now his only world. 'I
languished for lack of life. . . . Her world was the world of men and
women—more particularly of those she knew, and it was a world
in which it did me good to dwell.'[1] The other is a gentleman he
finds one day collecting butterflies. They became friends, and he
learns that the butterfly catcher once suffered a terrible unhappiness
that plunged him into the same kind of metaphysical speculation in
which Rutherford was now lost. His science had literally proved his
salvation, for it had fixed his mind on realities. His study was not
devoid of wonder, but his wonder was not 'a mere vacant profitless
stare.'[2] And he now shunned the other kind of thinking as he would
'a path which leads to madness.'[3] Rutherford was not yet, however,
fully ready to learn the lesson, which only life could teach.

The chapters telling of his movement away from all formal
religion are entitled, appropriately enough, 'Emancipation' and
'Progress in Emancipation.' But, as was previously suggested, such
emancipation meant, too, an increasing isolation from the only
community he knew. It is therefore by a kind of logic that these
chapters should have as a corollary theme the theme of loneliness.
The young minister has at this time been thrown entirely on the
resources available to him among the Unitarians by the rejection of
his offer of marriage to Mary Mardon: she felt it her duty to stay
with her father. He was entirely alone. But 'here, as amongst the
Independents, there was the same lack of personal affection, or even
the capability of it—excepting always Mrs. Lane.'[4] The page in
which he utters his longing must, however, be quoted entire. It is a
kind of thing to be found in the writings of nobody else.

The desire for something like sympathy and love absolutely
devoured me. I dwelt on all the instances in poetry and history in
which one human being had been bound to another human being,
and I reflected that my existence was of no earthly importance to
anybody. I could not altogether lay the blame on myself. God knows

---

[1] *The Autobiography*, chap. viii.
[2] *Ibid.*   [3] *Ibid.*   [4] *Ibid.*

that I would have stood against a wall and been shot for any man or woman whom I loved as cheerfully as I would have gone to bed, but nobody seemed to wish for such a love, or to know what to do with it. Oh the humiliations under which this weakness has bent me! Often and often I have thought that I have discovered somebody who could really comprehend the value of a passion which could tell everything and venture everything. I have overstepped all the bounds of etiquette in obtruding myself on him, and have opened my heart even to shame. I have then found that it was all on my side. For every dozen times I went to his house, he came to mine once, and only when pressed: I have languished in sickness for a month without his finding it out; and if I were to drop into the grave, he would perhaps never give me another thought. If I had been born a hundred years earlier, I should have transferred this burning longing to the unseen God and have become a devotee. But I was a hundred years too late, and I felt that it was mere cheating of myself and a mockery to think about love for the only God whom I knew the forces which maintain the universe. I am now getting old, and have altered in many things. The hunger and thirst of those years have abated, or rather, the fire has had ashes heaped on it, so that it is well nigh extinguished. I have been repulsed into self-reliance and reserve, having learned wisdom by experience; but still I know that the desire has not died, as so many other desires have died, by the natural evolution of age. It has been forcibly suppressed, and that is all. If anybody who reads these words of mine should be offered by any young dreamer such a devotion as I once had to offer, and had to take back again refused so often, let him in the name of all that is sacred accept it. It is simply the most precious thing in existence. Had I found anybody who would have thought so, my life would have been redeemed into something which I have often imagined, but now shall never know.[1]

Though Rutherford left the ministry, he found it hard to give up the ambition which had made it congenial to him in spite of all, the ambition which defines his 'dreamer's' nature. 'I clung to the hope that I might employ myself in some way which, however, feebly,

[1] *The Autobiography*, chap. viii.

would help mankind to the realization of some ideal.'[1] 'Fit for nothing,' however, he came to London to look for work. Here again the external facts of his life become identical with those of his author, his first job experience being the same as Hale White's after he left the college. It is that brief job as a schoolmaster already described, which taught Rutherford, too, by means of a loneliness which was a 'passion' and 'a kind of terror,' 'how thin is the floor on which we stand which separates us from the bottomless abyss.'[2]

A humiliating period of job-seeking followed, and then his 'emancipation' made it possible for him to get a job at last with a publisher of sceptical books. The man's name was Wollaston. Wollaston's friendliness to the young man was a great comfort, but from him Rutherford learned that 'emancipation' had its own kind of error, not to say fatuity. Wollaston examined him first for the scepticism he required. Did he believe in miracles? Rutherford believed in the ideas which the Biblical miracles expressed, but not in their historical reality; and though the first point was not understood, the second made him acceptable. Many of Wollaston's ideas resembled Mardon's—resembled, we may therefore say, Hale White's own—but the publisher 'differed entirely from [Mardon] in the process by which they had been brought about; and a mental comparison of the two told me what I had been told over and over again, that what we believe is not of so much importance as the path by which we travel to it.'[3]

Wollaston, as I have said, is a portrait of John Chapman, and the young George Eliot with whom Hale White worked at Chapman's is represented by Theresa, Wollaston's niece. The portrait of Theresa embodies all that Hale White ever noted in the original[4]: the unconventional intelligence, an intelligence which, in spite of her strong feelings, generally kept the upper hand; the perfect directness and honesty; above all, the genius for sympathy. The latter trait, needless to say, came to Rutherford now as water might come to a man dying of thirst. Though his love for Mary somehow remained, he responded to Theresa with a gratitude that was equally passionate. One of the most moving scenes in the book shows us how she met

[1] *Ibid.*
[2] *Ibid.*
[3] *Ibid.*, chap. ix.
[4] See pp. 41-42.

his need. He was not good at his job, being, he says, incapable of
thoroughness and accuracy. This inefficiency led to a climax of
humiliation, which, when Theresa's sympathy came to his aid, un-
manned him completely. Here is the passage which follows. For
those who care for Hale White, the observation with which it ends
is a kind of high water mark in his writing.

With a storm of tears, I laid open my heart. I told her how nothing
I had ever attempted had succeeded; that I had never even been able
to attain that degree of satisfaction with myself and my own conclusions without which a man cannot live; and that now I found I
was useless even to the best friends I had ever known, and that the
meanest clerk in the city would serve them better than I did. I was
beside myself, and I threw myself on my knees, burying my face in
Theresa's lap and sobbing convulsively. She did not repel me, but
she gently passed her fingers through my hair. Oh the transport of
that touch! It was as if water had been poured on a burnt hand, or
some miraculous Messiah had soothed the delirium of a fever-
stricken sufferer, and replaced his vision of torment with dreams of
Paradise. She gently lifted me up, and as I rose I saw her eyes too
were wet. 'My poor friend,' she said, 'I cannot talk to you now. You
are not strong enough, and for that matter, nor am I, but let me say
this to you, that you are altogether mistaken about yourself. The
meanest clerk in the city could not take your place here.' There was
just a slight emphasis I thought upon the word 'here.' 'Now,' she
said, 'you had better go, I will see about the pamphlet.' I went out
mechanically, and I anticipate my story so far as to say that, two days
after, another proof came in the proper form. I went to the printer
to offer to pay for the setting it up afresh, and was told that Miss
Wollaston had been there and had paid herself for the rectification
of the mistake, giving special injunctions that no notice of it was to
be given to her uncle. I should like to add one more beatitude to
those of the gospels and to say, Blessed are they who heal us of self-
despisings. Of all the services which can be done to man, I know of
none more precious.[1]

[1] *The Autobiography*, chap. ix.

The Autobiography closes appropriately enough on a consideration of the dreamer's ultimate refutation, as I have called it—death. It was Mardon who died, and his talk to Rutherford shortly before the end was again full of Hale White's own ideas as expressed in 'Ixion.' The dying man required no immortality except 'the survival of life and thought,' and he believed that our desire for personal immortality is only a form of that 'miserable egotism' which ought to be replaced by a care for 'the universal.' [1] The talk at his funeral by a former Unitarian minister who had been his friend made the same point: Mardon, it was said, would live 'as every force in nature lives —forever; transmuted into a thousand different forms. The original form utterly forgotten—but never perishing.' [2] But the comfort in such thoughts was for Mark Rutherford a limited comfort, and death remained for him a thing to be accepted in silence, 'as we accept the loss of youth and all other calamities.' [3]

In the note by Shapcott at the end of the book, the attentive reader will again find the one persistent theme emerging. Unable yet to find the rest of his late friend's manuscript, Shapcott gives us a glimpse of what it would contain. Though the death of Mary Mardon shortly after her father's was a terrible blow, the years that followed saw a change in Rutherford. He began gradually to substitute other pursuits for the depressing speculations which had kept him isolated from the world of ordinary men—he began to accept life as he found it. It was impossible and, he felt, even wrong, to suppress wholly the impulse to seek after meaning. 'Still . . . the long conflict died away gradually into a peace not formally concluded and with no specific stipulations, but nevertheless definite.' [4]

The conclusion of the story was found, however: it is *Mark Rutherford's Deliverance*. It will show us how that 'peace' was attained and what it meant.

[1] *Ibid.*   [2] *Ibid.*   [3] *Ibid.*   [4] *Ibid.*

CHAPTER VI

Mark Rutherford's Deliverance

IN Mark Rutherford, then, we have seen not merely a 'victim of the century,' but a permanent human type. He is the man given to 'inner reference,' and this is bound up with his desire for an ennobling meaning in life and for noble human relationships, since it is by these that the self is recognized and given value. He is one who wants, as he said, to live a life devoted to the realization of an ideal, and an ideal which grows from within. The first volume of his history has shown us this type with all its demands still youthfully absolute, and how such demands are necessarily and painfully disappointed. It will be the purpose of the second to show how such a 'dreamer' is saved from despair. In large part this means how he became resigned to things as they are. But that is not the whole story, for total capitulation to the mere brutal rushing chaos is not a tolerable state for men like Rutherford. What we see, rather, is how the absolute demands are modified, how the original dreams are brought closer to reality, not destroyed. In the end he has preserved or rediscovered certain crucial elements of his religion, adding to them certain lessons of life, and he has found love. Neither the religion nor the love are quite the same as originally dreamed, but based now on reality, they can stand against its pressure. And they can help him to live.

The *Deliverance*, therefore, has in the main two things to show. The first is the nature of that reality by which our dreamer was educated, and the second is the results of that education in his changed ideas and attitudes. It is in showing the first that Hale White presents that vivid and terrible picture of Victorian London which gives the work much of its value as history and accounts for much of its modest fame. What has already been said, however, should suggest that this picture is not merely history, any more than Mark Ruther-

110

ford is merely a nineteenth-century type. We can read it too as we would read 'history' in many good novels, as a particular illustration of a general law, that is, for its dramatic and philosophic contribution to the central meaning. Read so, the picture of the inferno of Victorian London becomes also a picture of reality at its most challenging—it presents the dreamer's problem in its extreme and most illuminating form. The insistence on Mark Rutherford's lack of special talents serves the same purpose. It enables us to see how reality is met by one unprovided with any unusual defences against it. The ideas and ideals which survive the battle as we see it here, therefore, will have nothing left to fear from life.

Rutherford's new direction is made evident in the first pages. When we take up his story again, we find that Theresa and Wollaston have dropped out of his life [1] and that he is writing columns for provincial newspapers about the House of Commons debates. The work is detestable as well as hard. He finds that it produces 'politic scepticism' [2] to watch grave issues being decided by men who are largely ignorant of what is involved and are driven by the mere 'lust' to be heard. His editors, moreover, keep demanding a kind of 'graphic and personal' [3] writing which he feels degrading. But a change has come over him: he no longer demands what is agreeable. He is now 'the better of what was half disease and half something healthy and good,' and this 'something' is clearly his old desire to live by and for an ideal.

In the first place, I had discovered that my appetite was far larger than my powers. Consumed by a longing for continuous intercourse with the best, I had no ability whatever to maintain it, and I had accepted as a fact, however mysterious it might be, that the human mind is created with the impulses of a seraph and the strength of a man. Furthermore, what was I that I should demand exceptional treatment? Thousands of men and women superior to myself, are

---

[1] In an Editor's Note to the first edition, taken out in subsequent ones but restored in that of 1936, we are told they emigrated to America and were never heard from again.

[2] *Deliverance*, chap. i.

[3] *Ibid.*

condemned, if that is the proper word to use, to almost total absence from themselves. The roar of the world for them is never lulled to rest, nor can silence ever be secured in which the voice of the divine can be heard.[1]

But hard unpleasant work, and the consequent self-exile, is not his only trouble. There is also his exile from those regions which Wordsworth had helped make a necessity for him—that is, from the country—to a city where 'hope, faith and God seemed impossible.' [2] Here is a description of that city, one of several, which helps us to accept so extreme a reaction.

As we walked over the Drury Lane gratings of the cellars a most foul stench came up, and one in particular I remember to this day. A man half dressed pushed open a broken window beneath us, just as we passed by, and there issued such a blast of corruption, made up of gases bred by filth, air breathed and rebreathed a hundred times, charged with odours of unnameable personal uncleanness and disease, that I staggered to the gutter with a qualm which I could scarcely conquer. At the doors of the houses stood grimy women with their arms folded and their hair disordered. Grimier boys and girls had tied a rope to broken railings and were swinging on it. The common door to a score of lodgings stood ever open, and the children swarmed up and down the stairs carrying with them patches of mud every time they came in from the street. The wholesome practice which amongst the decent poor marks off at least one day in the week as a day on which there is to be a change; when there is to be some attempt to procure order and cleanliness; a day to be preceded by soap and water, by shaving, and by as many clean clothes as can be procured, was unknown here. There was no break in the uniformity of squalor; nor was it even possible for any single family to emerge amidst such altogether oppressive surroundings. All self-respect, all effort to do anything more than to satisfy somehow the grossest wants, had departed. . . . The desire to decorate existence in some way or other with more or less care is nearly universal. The most sensual and the meanest almost always manifest

---

[1] *Deliverance*, chap. i.   [2] *Ibid.*

an indisposition to be content with mere material satisfaction. I have known selfish, gluttonous, drunken men to spend their leisure moments in trimming a bed of scarlet geraniums, and the vulgarest and most commonplace of mortals considers it a necessity to put a picture in the room or an ornament on the mantelpiece. The instinct, even in its lowest form, is divine. It is the commentary on the text that man shall not live by bread alone. It is evidence of an acknowledged compulsion—of which art is the highest manifestation—to *escape*. In the alleys behind Drury Lane this instinct, the very salt of life was dead. The only house in which it survived was in that of the undertaker, who displayed the willows, the black horses, and the coffin [in a picture in his window]. These may have been nothing more than an advertisement, but from the care with which it was made to resemble a natural piece of wood, I am inclined to believe that the man felt some pleasure in his work for its own sake, and that he was not utterly submerged. The cross in such dens as these, or, worse than dens, in such sewers! If it be anything, it is a symbol of victory, of power to triumph over resistance, and even death. Here was nothing but sullen subjugation, the most grovelling slavery, mitigated only by a tendency to mutiny. Here was a strength of circumstance to quell and dominate which neither Jesus nor Paul could have overcome—worse a thousand-fold than Scribes or Pharisees, or any form of persecution. The preaching of Jesus would have been powerless here; in fact, no known stimulus, nothing ever held up before men to stir the soul to activity, can do anything in the back streets of great cities, so long as they are the cesspools which they are now.[1]

I have quoted this at length for the additional reason that it conveys precisely the theme of the whole book. Drury Lane stands opposed to the impulse to transform life in accordance with a personal ideal, an impulse which is 'the very salt of life,' which is at the bottom of cleanliness, ornament and art, and of which religion—'the cross'— is the ultimate expression. And the horror of Drury Lane is that there the brute pressure of reality has triumphed and the impulse has been totally defeated.

[1] *Ibid.*, chap. ii.

Now in *The Autobiography* we had to be shown how Rutherford was deprived of the fragile comfort of beliefs that could not stand against a nineteenth-century critical intelligence. And for that intelligence—it was his own—he invented a Mardon, who showed chiefly what could *not* be believed. In the *Deliverance* the emphasis is to be on what *can* be believed. Instead of the voice of Hale White's reason, we must be given the voice of his faith. And in the place of a Mardon, we now get Rutherford's fellow journalist, M'Kay. As Mardon destroyed belief in the literal truth of religious symbols, so M'Kay will emphasize the permanent validity of their inner meanings, that in religion which is based on reality and can withstand the assault of Drury Lane. It is not only M'Kay who will do this, of course, any more than it was only Mardon in *The Autobiography* who conveyed that work's scepticism, for these are not quite novels, in which every detail is planned. The new emphasis will come into the narrative from many quarters. But M'Kay will be its chief dramatic embodiment.

In this friend of Rutherford's too, there is a great deal of the author, though most of it is carried to extremes. As was the case with Hale White, and will later be the case with Rutherford, M'Kay's working life is in striking contrast with his private life. In his columns, because the support of his family depends on it and politics seem to him futile anyway, he pretends to all the Tory opinions of his editors and lets loose the usual fireworks at party enemies. But in private, as if by reaction, 'his altogether outside vehemence and hypocrisy . . . produced a complete sincerity and transparency, extending even to the finest verbal distinctions.'[1] There is a further similarity, at least to the Rutherford type as he recurs in Hale White's work, and perhaps too, if my guesses have been right, to Hale White himself. In his relations with his wife, M'Kay is guilty of that classic fault of intellectuals described in the last chapter, and as Miss Arbour's is one of Hale White's two kinds of unhappy marriages, M'Kay's is the other. In M'Kay, as I said, this goes to extremes. His wife is a simple good woman whom he cannot help loving, for she worships him and is childishly affectionate. But he is irritated by her inability to follow his ideas and her tendency

[1] *Deliverance*, chap. i.

to echo what he says. His temper shortened by his hateful work, he is often cruel. He abruptly contradicts his own remarks when she repeats them, and keeps his talk to her pointedly on household affairs. 'She knew that these things were not what was on his mind, and she answered him in despairing tones which showed how much she felt the obtrusive condescension to her level.'[1] The description of this relationship and then of the change in M'Kay's behaviour when he learns she must die and 'a frightful pit came in view'[2] is another of the high-lights of these two volumes, where the most intense poignance is conveyed in language that remains flawlessly pure and modest. This passage is a good example, moreover, of how in Hale White rising emotion is evoked all the more intensely because of the generalizations which flow from it without transition, as if they too were symptoms of emotion.

It is M'Kay who takes up the ambition which Rutherford has relinquished with his career as a minister, the ambition to 'help mankind a little to the realization of an ideal.'[3] He is a man who has 'a passionate desire to reform the world.'[4] The spectacle of Drury Lane poisons all his pleasures. It is not merely a place of suffering but a place of moral degradation. Brought up on the Bible and on Bunyan, he is convinced 'that it was possible even now to touch depraved men and women with an idea which should recast their lives.'[5] M'Kay is to utter much of Hale White's insight, but this does not exempt him from his author's criticism. Like Gide, Hale White is always alert to the possibilities of error in his own attitudes. And on M'Kay's recurrence to the apostles and to Bunyan he makes the very Protestant comment:

So it is that the main obstacle to our success is a success which has preceded us. We instinctively follow the antecedent form, consequently we either pass by, or deny altogether, the life of our own time, because its expression has changed. We never do practically believe that the Messiah is not incarnated twice in the same flesh. He came as Jesus, and we look for Him as Jesus now, overlooking the manifestation of today, and dying, perhaps, without recognizing it.[6]

[1] Ibid., chap. ii.   [2] Ibid.   [3] The Autobiography, chap. i.
[4] Deliverance, chap. ii.   [5] Ibid.   [6] Ibid.

I

He decides to rent a room in Drury Lane 'as a place to which those who wished might resort at different times and find some quietude and what fortifying thoughts he could collect to enable men to endure their almost unendurable sufferings.' [1] The episode of his first talk at this room is characteristic of Hale White in its union of passionate idealism and irony, an irony based on his unfailing awareness of the complicating mocking realities of existence. The talk—it is really a sermon, as the little room is a kind of ultimate Protestant chapel—is a profound analysis of the function of religion and of the way it 'saves.' Religion, M'Kay says, is 'a controlling influence' to bind our scattered energies together 'without which we do not know what we are doing.' We cannot limit ourselves to 'a certain defined course.'

But still it is an enormous, an incalculable advantage for us to have some irreversible standard set up in us by which everything we meet is to be judged. That is the meaning of the prophecy—whether it will ever be fulfilled God only knows—that Christ shall judge the world. All religions have been this. They have said that in the midst of the infinitely possible—infinitely possible evil and infinitely possible good too—we become distracted. A thousand forces good and bad act upon us. It is necessary, if we are to be men, if we are to be saved, that we should be rescued from this tumult, and that our feet should be planted upon a path. [2]

For M'Kay it is Christ who was best fitted to be this 'central shaping force' and 'he would try to get them to see things with the eyes of Christ, to love with His love, to judge with His judgment.' [3]

Thus the idealism. But idealism does not, as I say, go unopposed, unmocked. First, four out of six of his listeners begin to whistle with all their might, and as Mr. and Mrs. M'Kay and Mark Rutherford leave the room, push each other upon them and kick after them an old kettle which splashes them with mud. Nor is this all—the enemy of the ideal is also within. When they reach home, Mrs. M'Kay tries to say something about what she has heard. Christian love dissolves instantly before the irritation of the intellectual. The face of this new

---

[1] *Deliverance*, chap. ii.   [2] *Ibid.*   [3] *Ibid.*

apostle of Christ clouds over at once. After a minute of silence, M'Kay observes that the window ought to be cleaned—he can hardly see through it—and his wife, in distress, leaves the room.

It is to be noted that poor Rutherford, who is the embodiment of his author's characteristic feelings, and not, till his education is complete, of his judgment, tends to represent the view which requires correction. In *The Autobiography* he insists on a personal immortality and a Mind for the universe which is like our own and to which our minds respond. It is thus he opposes Mardon. In the *Deliverance*, on the other hand, his 'emancipation' leads him at first to almost total scepticism, the classic excess of the disappointed. To M'Kay's dream of 'saving' the squalid victims of Drury Lane through the power of an 'idea' he replies that he himself would have no ideas to offer, and that in any case, without the support of a belief in hell-fire, religious or moral ideas would have no power at all. Well, the fact is that with Drury Lane as a whole they can do nothing. Its denizens are so 'immersed in the selfishness naturally begotten of their incessant struggle for existence and the incessant warfare with society,' it is such a mass of 'dark impenetrable subterranean blackguardism,' that 'our civilization seemed nothing but a thin film or crust lying over a volcanic pit, and I often wondered whether some day the pit would not break up through it and destroy us all.' [1] But he goes on:

M'Kay's dreams were therefore not realized, and yet it would be a mistake to say that they ended in nothing. It often happens that a grand attempt, although it may fail—miserably fail—is fruitful in the end and leaves a result, not the hoped-for result it is true, but one which would never have been attained without it. A youth strives after the impossible, and he is apt to break his heart because he has never even touched it, but nevertheless his whole life is the sweeter for the striving; and the archer who aims at a mark a hundred yards away will send his arrow further than he who sets his bow and his arm for fifty yards. So it was with M'Kay. He did not convert Drury Lane, but he saved two or three.[2]

Again Hale White, like Gide, is to be found not behind one or

[1] *Ibid.*, chap. v.   [2] *Ibid.*

another of two opposing principles but deeper than both, where opposites join hands and work together.

The 'two or three' whom they save are described in detail: they are examples of defeat and suffering so painful that they seem provided as a kind of basic test of the relevance and power to help of Rutherford's final ideas. Their problems are the ignoble thorny problems of real life—rhetoric, poetry, the wealth of associations that attract so many to traditional beliefs, will not help them in their 'great gaping needs.'[1] One of these victims resembles Rutherford—and Hale White—so obviously that he seems a deliberate replica in miniature, and Rutherford himself notes the resemblance. This is Clark, a lapsed Calvinist, obsessed with metaphysical problems he is unable to solve, in love with books which only 'served to sharpen the contrast between himself and his lot'[2] and also—exactly what is soon to happen to Rutherford—a copying clerk tormented by the monotony of his work and the obscenity of his colleagues. But what is interesting is that *all* the victims resemble their author. It is as though he had, whether consciously or not, embodied his own characteristic troubles to be the test of his final affirmations. Even the phrases used to describe them are often familiar. Taylor is a coal-porter in Somerset House, who might have been happy in the country at a congenial trade but who is good for little in the city and must become a 'servant of servants.' 'He was not eminent for any-thing in particular, and an educated man, selecting as his friends those only who stood for something, would not have taken the slightest notice of him.' (The same thing is later said of Rutherford.) But 'although commonplace, he had demands made upon him for an endurance by no means commonplace, and he had sorrows as exquisite as those of his betters.'[3] His worst trouble is the brutally contemptuous treatment of his superiors, which he dare not resent. Precisely this trouble is literally to kill Rutherford and keeps recur-ring in Hale White's pictures of work or job-seeking. 'Suffering of any kind,' Rutherford observes, 'is hard to bear, but the suffering which especially damages character is that which is caused by the neglect or oppression of man.'[4]

[1] *Deliverance*, chap. vi.
[2] *Ibid.*
[3] *Ibid.*, chap. v.
[4] *Ibid.*

Then there is John, the waiter, whom 'the world had well-nigh overpowered . . . entirely [and] crushed . . . out of all shape, so that what he was originally, or might have been, it was almost impossible to tell.'[1] *His* worst sorrow is his wife.

A man may endure much, provided he knows that he will be well supported when his day's toil is over; but if the help for which he looks fails, he falls. Oh, those weary days in that dark back dining-room from which not a square inch of sky was visible! Weary days haunted by a fear that while he was there unknown mischief was being done! weary days, whose close nevertheless he dreaded![2]

The trouble with his wife is that she is a drunkard. Any fears that haunted his author's working day would, of course, have been different. Yet fundamental similarities obviously remain.

And finally there is Cardinal. He too is a lapsed Dissenter, and he too has trouble with his wife (she is insanely jealous, though they care little for each other). But the trouble we are shown is that he is a man of ideas and ideals which he has not the wit to apply judiciously but which 'take hold' of him, as we have been told ideas do to Rutherford. Even M'Kay is exasperated when he quits a job merely because his employers have decided to sell a slightly cheaper line of goods. He thinks it dishonest—and so becomes a burden on his friends. Of him we are told:

He was an honest, affectionate soul, and his peculiarities were a necessary result of the total chaos of a time without any moral guidance. With no church, no philosophy, no religion, the wonder is that anybody on whom use and wont relax their hold should ever do anything. Cardinal was adrift, like thousands and hundreds of thousands of others, and amidst the storm and pitchy darkness of the night, thousands and hundreds of thousands of voices offer us pilotage.[3]

Cardinal clearly shares with Rutherford, as well as with Miriam of the later *Miriam's Schooling*, the function of symbolizing their

---

[1] *Ibid.*   [2] *Ibid.*   [3] *Ibid.*

author's major problem: that of finding a tenable substitute for that greatest of 'dreams,' the 'central shaping force' of a lost religion.

W. D. Taylor, as we have seen, thought that all of Hale White's work was written in response to certain violent sneers at the working class by the reactionary Member of Parliament, Robert Lowe. If a single motive is to be found, however, it would be truer to say that it was written to express and to suggest a way to alleviate sorrows like those of the above victims of Drury Lane. To some extent they could be—and had to be—helped by certain practical changes. Clark is taken away from that office; Taylor is found a job as an outdoor porter where his bosses were more human. But troubles remain for all of them less easily solved—inner unrest, the painful mixture of human relations, death. In the chapter entitled 'Drury Lane Theology' we are given some of the 'fortifying' thoughts which M'Kay and Rutherford offered their 'disciples.' These thoughts are secular, but it appears that they are also religious. The most important lesson they teach, and the key to all their endeavours, is the lesson of contentment with one's lot, and even some joy in it, for in mere insurrection and scepticism—that is, scepticism not of the supernatural but of values, ideals, hopes—man cannot abide. What is this but the doctrine taught by all religions of reconciliation with God, acceptance of His will as somehow good and compatible with man's upward strivings? Reality authorizes despair as little as it does simple optimism. If reasoning leads to the former, we can remember what all religions have taught: that in the face of infinity, of God—'the sphere of our understanding, whose function it seems to be to imprison us, is limited.' [1] Never halt in despair, therefore, but go on till you have found some faith which will 'anchor' you. They teach further that if Nature is Rhadamanthine in her exaction of penalties down to the uttermost farthing, yet there is in her also 'an infinite Pity, healing all wounds, softening all calamities, ever hastening to alleviate and repair.' And this is exactly the meaning of Christianity, which is 'an expression of nature, a projection of her into a biography and a creed.' [2] They teach finally the absolute necessity, also a lesson of their religion, of maintaining the distinction between 'the higher and the lower, heaven and hell.' Today, Rutherford says, the words

[1] *Deliverance*, chap. vi.   [2] *Ibid.*

right and wrong shade off into each other, and we laugh at the notion of a personal devil. 'But the horror at evil which could find no other expression than in the creation of a devil is no subject for laughter, and if it does not in some shape or other survive, the race itself will not survive. Its [Christianity's] doctrine and its sacred story are fixtures in concrete form of precious thoughts, purchased by blood and tears.'[1]

To theologians the talks of M'Kay and Rutherford might sound like 'feeble wandering,' the doctrines pitifully paltry. But they seemed to wander, Rutherford suggests, only if one had not the 'key,' which was their desire to say to each individual what *he* required to bring him to 'contentment,' rather than to remain faithful to some ambitious and consistent set of dogmas. And as for the charge that they had so little to offer: 'We said all we knew, and we would most thankfully have said more, had we been sure that it must be true.'[2] Their theology, in short, was a 'Drury Lane theology'—the religious 'dream' as modified by reality and shaped to help us to endure it.

The continuity of story and meaning I have here maintained is interrupted in the book by a return to the past and to Rutherford's home town, in which we are reintroduced to the girl Ellen, whom he had jilted in the previous volume. Before we come to her, however, we learn a good deal about Mrs. Butts, *née* Leroy, whose son became Ellen's first husband. As a child Rutherford had loved Miss Leroy. She was the daughter of a French republican and a person whose intensely devout religion did not prevent her from disturbing her small-town neighbours, for it did not narrow her in any way. She could turn from Thomas à Kempis to the most shocking novels, believed more in personal cleanliness and fresh air than in neatness and dusting, and—blessed virtue for the young Mark—was not afraid of 'spoiling children.' To the surprise of all she had married a simple miller named Butts, good but dull. Their son Clem was an early friend of Rutherford. His type was that of the dilettante who does many things rather well and none perfectly, and who uses his gifts only to make the world share his admiration and fondness for himself. Ellen had married him. He had had a brief period of prosperity

---

[1] *Ibid.*   [2] *Ibid.*

during which, by his neglect, he had intensified Rutherford's painful feeling of his own insignificance. Then he had ruined himself by a flirtation with the squire's wife. Ellen, to whom the squire wrote the story, never reproached her husband, though her feeling for him changed. 'She had a divine disposition, not infrequent among women, to seek in herself the reason for any wrong which was done to her.'[1] She accompanied him to Australia, and there he died, leaving her with a baby daughter. Thus Rutherford's account of her past. After an interval of two years he reads an advertisement that is clearly hers, in which a widow lady asks for work with children. His old love for her, though he does not recognize it at first, begins to revive; he meets her again (in a scene of great beauty), and they marry.

Ellen, too, has a contribution to make to the work's meanings. She is there to 'oppose,' to complicate, the meaning of Rutherford. She is the type of those whom reality, i.e. life and suffering, has taught not to reject their original faith but rather to cling to it with a deeper sincerity as the one unshakeable support. In her the phenomenon of a wise *and* a literal faith, of which we have already glimpsed examples, is explained, and we are shown, too, the common ground that an 'emancipated' mind like Rutherford's can find with one which never felt the need of emancipation at all. To attain that common ground, as I say, *both* have had to be educated by life. He has passed beyond a simple rejection of religious forms to a grasp of their inner human meaning, the feelings and experiences to which they correspond. For her this has not been necessary. She is not an intellectual: that is, her mind is not perpetually invaded by new ideas with which the old forms must be made consistent. But what makes the old forms her *own*, what gives her faith its personal character, is the real feelings life has taught her to fill them with, feelings which they help her to articulate and to which they give direction. One may say, indeed, that unless these do embody the believer's personal experience, he rather assents, to use William White's distinction, than believes. As a Calvinist, Ellen believes in an all-foreknowing God, in the unique 'calling' or duty by which each man must stand fast, and above all, in the duty for each of us of

[1] *Deliverance*, chap. iv.

that selfless love and mercy taught by Jesus. All these beliefs, for Rutherford, embody a 'secular' meaning with which he can agree. And while she does not mind his slight differences from her, 'for it is only when feeling has ceased to accompany a creed that it becomes fixed and verbal departures from it are counted heresy,' he does not mind expressing himself in her forms. 'It even gave me pleasure to talk in her dialect, so familiar to me, but for so many years unused.' [1]

It is with regard to the last of the beliefs mentioned above that Hale White makes explicit his view of the meaning of faith, a view which is of central importance in his work. Jesus' lesson of a love that demands no return, he says, is 'the idea' in morality, and His greatness lay in the fact that He taught this idea, and not any limitation of it, relying on it to the uttermost. 'This has always seemed to me to be the real meaning of the word faith,' he comments. 'It is permanent confidence in the idea, a confidence never to be broken down by apparent failure, or by examples by which ordinary people prove that qualification is necessary.' [2] It is not necessarily, we see, a belief in the supernatural. Rather, it is a crucial weapon in the 'secular' struggle at the heart of this work and of its author's thinking, man's struggle to realize his ideals in the face of resisting reality. This is the notion of faith in our author's mind when, through Shapcott, he remarks that Rutherford never sank into 'absolute denial,' [3] or when he calls God, affirming His confidence in Job (in the essay on that Biblical character) a 'believer.' [4] It is such faith that is the defining quality of Goethe's Faust, as scepticism is that of his Mephistopheles.

But the insights of religion are not the only lessons Rutherford is to learn. There are others less lofty and general—'not book lessons,' he tells us. 'They have been taught me by my own experience, and as a rule, I have always found that in my own most special perplexities, I get but little help from books or other persons.' [5] His 'deliverance,' in short, must be a deliverance from the actual pressures of life which reach us in intimate ignoble ways that religion, or philosophy, or literature, rarely stoop to consider. There is the lack of friends, for instance, to enliven the humble home he has now set up with his

---

[1] Ibid., chap. viii.
[2] Ibid., chap. iv.
[3] The Autobiography, chap. ix.
[4] 'Notes on the Book of Job,' Deliverance.
[5] Deliverance, chap. viii.

wife and step-daughter. For his irritability, due to incessant fatigue, and his impatience with trivial chatter repel the commonplace, while clever people feel that 'I stood for nothing. "There was nothing in me." '[1] There is his ill-health, especially the 'hypochondriacal' fears, which the responsibility of a family have increased. But worse than all else, there is his job. Needing more money, he has taken a job as a clerk, which keeps him writing what 'called forth no single faculty of the mind'[2] from ten to seven. With the time he has to travel added, he is away from home eleven hours a day, and often the cry rises in him: 'Is this life?' His colleagues, moreover, break the killing monotony with a constant obscenity which torments him; and there is a boss, 'the terror of the place,'[3] who rages and swears at the men till he spits blood and whose brutal criticism is all the more galling because he is always in the right. 'How I watched that clock!'[4] Rutherford exclaims in another of the many passages in Hale White which, though perfectly written, it seems an impertinence to call 'literature.'

His greatest support is his wife's love. He has longed for a perfect love all his life, and had once rejected Ellen's because she did not match his youthful dreams. Finding her again, after having grown acquainted with the ordeal of life, he knew that 'my many wanderings were over.'[5] She is not a dream woman embodying an ideal combination of ideal virtues; she is only a real one. But in the valley of the shadow of reality where he now wanders, he learns what she is worth.

If a man wants to know what the potency of love is, he must be a menial; he must be despised . . . God's mercy be praised ever more for it! . . . 'What is there in me?' I have said, 'is she not the victim of some self-created delusion?' and I was wretched till I considered that in her I saw the Divine Nature itself, and that her passion was a stream straight from the Highest. The love of woman is, in other words, a living witness never failing of an actuality in God which otherwise we should never know. This led me on to connect it with Christianity; but I am getting incoherent and must stop.

[1] *Deliverance*, chap. viii.   [2] *Ibid.*   [3] *Ibid.*
[4] *Ibid.*   [5] *Ibid.*, chap. vii.

And he goes on to share with us, in simple earnestness, the other life-taught lessons that have brought about his 'deliverance.' There are two 'stratagems' that help him endure his job. He vows never to 'answer back' his boss, though the effort to be still is sometimes tremendous. And he keeps his job and his 'true self' entirely separate; his thoughts, even his family, remain a secret from his office colleagues, while at home he never utters a word about his work. Other lessons are perhaps of wider application. There is 'the blessed lesson which is taught by familiarity with sorrow, that the greater part of what is dreadful in it lies in the imagination.'[1] He tells us never to dwell on the merely insoluble or tragic, not to complain, not to waste the present in continual anticipation of the future, not to argue, but to leave proof or disproof to time. He tells us that love, life's greatest comfort, must be deliberately tended and estranging trifles ejected at once, lest the once exalted become the vulgar and mean. And he tells us to 'cease the trick of contrast,' which sometimes stimulates progress, but which is also a great danger. When he realized one day (like the Carlyle of *Sartor Resartus*) that he had no special right to so much happiness, or even to so much virtue, 'straightway it seemed as if the centre of a whole system of dissatisfaction were removed, and as if the system collapsed.'[2] These lessons are perhaps 'commonplaces,' though in the text they are supported by much just and illuminating observation. But if they are commonplace, it is not because they are easy to learn truly, but rather because the wise are forever arriving at them. What they combine to teach is the same thing taught by Rutherford's Drury Lane theology, namely, reconciliation with that outer reality which began as the young dreamer's enemy. For youth, perhaps, claiming bliss and triumph as a right, this must generally have the look of an ignoble acceptance of defeat. But in time we learn that such defeat is the lot of life, and that even the successful have avoided it only in appearance.

Rutherford must still know pain. At one time his wife grows

---

[1] *Ibid.*, chap. viii. He goes on: 'The true Gorgon head is seldom seen in reality. That it exists I do not doubt, but it is not so commonly visible as we think.'

[2] *Ibid.* The reader will recall, from *Sartor Resartus*, Carlyle's 'Make thy claim of wages a zero.'

dangerously ill and he is not given leave from his job for a single day to take care of her. But even in the account of this terrible distress a positive note is now struck. His struggle toward the 'dream' in Drury Lane produces, as such struggle often will, an unexpected reward. The wife of a 'disciple,' flighty only until *weight* is placed on her, becomes their invaluable nurse. And he learns yet again how merit exists in real people to which his intellectual's addiction to formulae blinds him. His little step-daughter Marie, who had seemed to him insignificant, also becomes a wonderful nurse. Their trouble is the key needed to unlock what is in her. His new remorseful love for her is almost wild in its intensity, and teaches him, as half a lifetime had failed to do, what Jesus must have felt when He spoke of little children. The holiday at the seaside which follows this episode and closes the book is one of his most beautiful descriptions of nature, as passionate and precise as a scene in *The Prelude*. And though it is late autumn:

The season of the year, which is usually supposed to make men pensive, had no such effect upon us. Everything in the future, even the winter in London, was painted by Hope, and the death of the summer brought no sadness. Rather did summer dying in such fashion fill our hearts with repose, and even more than repose—with actual joy.[1]

On this note of a joy which is a conquest of reality, not a blindness to it, the autobiography ends. The remarks by Shapcott which follow tell us that a month later, after an unusually violent outburst by his boss, Rutherford, who had remained silent, turned white and died. Out of 'a mass of odds and ends' apparently written by Rutherford for publication but rejected, Shapcott adds 'one or two' to the present volume. And the way is opened for the gradual issuance of others.

I have tried to disengage the theme which has lifted this very personal confession to the universal and the timeless. But the work has also a vivid narrative life which has perhaps been insufficiently emphasized. Though there is an even greater variety of explicit

[1] *Deliverance*, chap. ix.

reflections than I have shown—much of it of a wisdom it was hard to resist quoting—characterization and dramatic development worthy of his best fiction lend everywhere their irreplaceable interest.

One point more. We have seen that these first two books show Hale White's own progress from the absolute dreaming of youth to maturity's reconciliation with reality, and that this was attended by a change from literal faith in a supernatural religion to a grasp of its permanent human meanings, meanings for which the supernatural elements were a symbolic language. It is not quite right, however, to suggest that the meanings of religious symbols are perfectly separable from them. The insights of religion, while human and discoverable outside it, are a certain *kind* of insight, they refer to certain *kinds* of experience, and they make certain *kinds* of suggestions. Though these can be put into one's own language—and must be, indeed, if they are to be of real value to us—it is religion which, in response to a powerful need, placed them in the foreground and gave them their most appropriate, coherent, forceful and beautiful expression. (Just so the characteristic insights of any great writer can be abstracted and used by others, and were to be found elsewhere before him, and yet they are also uniquely *his*, because he felt them strongest and expressed them most vividly.) Because the experience and insight peculiar to religion were especially congenial to Hale White, it is not surprising that he found congenial, too, the symbols in which they had been thus embodied. His first two books may therefore be said to serve the additional purpose of defining the vocabulary which he was to use in those to follow and which remained all his life a language natural to his thought.[1]

[1] Hale White left no record of the origin of the name Mark Rutherford, and it has been taken as invented and without special significance. There was, however, an eighteenth-century poet of considerable merit whose name was Mark Akenside. And if Hale White knew him, he must have found the resemblance between this man's life and thought and his own positively uncanny. Akenside, who was born in 1721 and died in 1770, was the son of a Nonconformist butcher. At eighteen he began to study for the Dissenting Ministry at the University of Edinburgh, but shortly afterward he gave this up for the study of medicine. He became a doctor, but would have starved if not for the patronage won him by his poetry, for though he was said to be enchanting as a friend, he was always offending patients who differed from his religious views or his republican principles. At seventeen he

Three short pieces were included in the volume containing the *Deliverance*: the essays 'Notes on the Book of Job' and 'Principles' and a story entitled 'A Mysterious Portrait.' With these, too, as with so much else hereafter, the temptation will have to be resisted to discuss their rich contents in detail. It must suffice to make clear that all three deal with the same problems as those which lie at the bottom of the history of Mark Rutherford, and indeed, in one form or another, of the rest of Hale White's work.

The story of Job is analysed, not as a story of miracle, nor yet as the statement of a consistent philosophy, but as the 'record of an experience,' a point of view underlying, as we shall see, all of its author's writings on the Bible. Its main idea is that the universe is 'constructed on no plan or theory which the intellect of man can grasp.'[1] *This* is God's answer to Job, and 'the secret, if there be one, of the poem,' no simple reassuring miraculous solution to his

wrote a 'Hymn to Science'—a remarkable poem for a boy—in which the entire universe, including man's mind and his society, is declared to be governed by laws which the wise man seeks to learn in order to 'cool [his] passion's fires' and become 'the judge of [his] desires.' His most ambitious work, a long philosophical poem in blank verse entitled 'The Pleasures of Imagination,' is an affirmation of Deism, or the Religion of Nature. Nature's beauty, we are told, not only serves 'to brighten the dull glooms of care, and make the destined road of life Delightful to the feet' (Bk. III, 505-7); it is also the token of 'Truth' and 'Good,' and its lovely and majestic order shapes the appreciative mind to a similar order, ennobling it. In Nature we behold and love what God beholds and loves.

> Thus the men
> Whom Nature's works can charm with God himself
> Hold converse, grow familiar day by day
> With his conceptions, act upon his plan
> And form to his the relish of their souls.
>
> (Bk. III, 629-33)

Having read so much of Mark Rutherford's most passionate beliefs, derived, it is true, from Wordsworth, we are hardly surprised to come upon a 'Hymn to Cheerfulness' which bids that goddess brighten the heart of the poet, depressed by night, by winter, by 'yon deep death-bell,' which 'Renew my mind's oppressive gloom, Till starting Horror shakes the room.' In the same way poem after poem has the strangest air of introducing us again to the mind of Mark Rutherford. It is tempting to suppose that Hale White felt this too and that he tells us so, though guardedly, in the name he selected for his hero.

[1] 'Notes on the Book of Job,' *Deliverance*.

problems. It requires him to save *himself*—just as Mark Rutherford did—by looking about him with understanding, and by accepting the universe as he finds it.

As the Job essay is about our need to accept 'reality,' 'A Mysterious Portrait' is about that faith in the 'dream' by which we oppose it. This enigmatic and beautifully written story tells how a melancholy man of thought (exactly the same character as Mark Rutherford) loves a woman who vanishes for years after a first glimpse and forever after a second. A scarf she leaves behind, and clear footprints, one day, in the wet, seem to make it impossible that she be a hallucination, though a portrait of her which he accidentally discovers—it is called Stella—turns out to be a figment of the artist's imagination. He clings to his memory of the vision all his life, and it keeps him from degradation, from accepting less from life than it had seemed to promise. At the same time it keeps him lonely. In the end he says frankly that he cannot explain what happened, and he is ready to admit that he may have suffered from 'some passing disorder of the brain, although that theory is not sound at all points and there are circumstances inconsistent with it.' [1] This is almost an echo of the definition of faith given us by Mark Rutherford, and what the story dramatizes is the basic faith-situation. For the reality of Stella—the hero's star-like ideal—there is some evidence, we see, but not enough *if one is disposed to doubt.* And the results of that faith are equally ambiguous: if he is uplifted by it, he is also deprived and made lonely. Just so Mark Rutherford's capacity to 'dream' was 'half disease, and half something healthy and good,' while *The Revolution in Tanner's Lane* is to tell us that man's tendency to get excited by flags and other such symbols (products of the 'dream') is no doubt 'evidence of the weakness of human nature, but like much more evidence of the same order, it is double-voiced, and testifies also to our strength.' [2]

'Principles,' which comes between the other two, faces directly the problem raised by their 'conflicting' ideas. Principles, we are told, are often dangerously misleading, because life itself is too concrete and complex for them to be perfectly appropriate. And yet it is also

[1] 'A Mysterious Portrait,' *Deliverance.*
[2] *The Revolution,* chap. xxv.

true that man's greatest gift—his 'divinity'—is his power of 'actualizing the abstract,' [1] that is, of realizing his principles. How do we know, then, when resignation to reality is the sensible course and when it is a premature acceptance of defeat? Hale White has nowhere concentrated more wisdom into fewer or fitter words than in his answer to that question, an answer which, needless to say, is not simple or single. This makes paraphrase or synopsis more inadequate than usual, and the reader is referred, for a glimpse of what is perhaps the essay's main idea, to the passage already examined in Chapter I.

[1] 'Principles,' *Deliverance.*

CHAPTER VII

The Revolution in Tanner's Lane

AS autobiography—and as history—Hale White's first two books have been spared a kind of formal criticism which has dealt pretty harshly with his novels. Calling themselves 'true,' they could be excused for their neglect of certain narrative proprieties; the novels, we are told, also neglected them—and without the excuse. E. A. Baker, otherwise finely appreciative of Hale White's merits, sums up most of the charges against him as a writer of fiction. Mr. Baker tells us that he 'had no structural ability whatever. He dispenses with anything of the nature of a plot, and even the outlines of his stories are broken and discrepant. . . . Hardy was clumsy enough in his transitions; Mark Rutherford ignores the art entirely and rambles on from one striking incident to the next in the most fortuitous way.'[1] Mr. Baker omits only to censure his freedom in commenting on his characters and events, another usual criticism. It will, I hope, become clear as I describe the novels that these common charges are altogether wrong. But it may be useful first to examine them directly.

Of Hale White's interspersed remarks I have already said that, as a kind of irresistible reaction to what has taken place, they most often increase reality and intensity. It seems, moreover, a mere pedantry to wish away comments which are relevant, wise and beautifully expressed. One can surely admire Flaubert without raising his esthetic of impersonality to an absolute law. In the actual experience of novel reading I think that only two sorts of author's interruption

---

[1] E. A. Baker, *The History of the English Novel*, IX, pp. 103-4. Mr. Baker does mention the two autobiographical works in this connection, but he clearly implies that what he says is true of all the longer fictions as well.

necessarily damage a work. These are the explicit repetition of what
has already been conveyed by the narrative, which blunts effective-
ness; and the psychologizing or philosophizing by which a writer
tries—always in vain—to reason into existence what he has failed to
create dramatically. Hale White is guilty of neither fault. His tendency to comment goes along with the severest reticence in the
handling of his story, a reticence which requires, in much the same
way as that of Gide, the constant collaboration of the reader's own
intelligence. And character and story in his novels are always distinct
from his comments; everything essential is dramatized. (The comments of George Eliot, also traditionally deprecated, can as a rule
be defended on exactly the same grounds.)

It is true that his people sometimes die or fall in love rather
suddenly, that he will overleap years in a sentence and spend a page
on a single moment, that *The Revolution in Tanner's Lane* seems to be
two novels with only accidental connection, *Catherine Furze* seems
interrupted by an irrelevant story, and *Clara Hopgood* seems to
continue for a page or so after its real drama is over. But on the
whole, these are flaws only to readers who have not quite grasped
what the novels are about. For it need hardly be said that it is a
novel's meaning that determines its proper form, that determines
what belongs, what should be skipped over or emphasized, where a
development properly begins, reaches a climax and comes to an end.
When a reader is surprised by what happens or by how it is told,
there is at least a possibility that his interpretation is at fault, that he
is being challenged to deepen or alter it until the discrepancy is
explained. Such challenging surprises are, indeed, the special pleasure
of reading the work of an original and penetrating mind, and it is a
rather self-defeating confidence to insist at once, when we are
puzzled by a writer entitled to respect, that the fault is his and not
our own. In the main, as I say, Hale White's 'flaws' are of just this
kind: they are the procedure of an original artist, frankly slighting,
not truth, nor logic of development, nor real novelistic tact, but
conventions irrelevant to his purpose. When that purpose is grasped,
the 'flaws' disappear. Or, if any remain, they are of no importance.

Something else happens when his meanings are grasped: we see
that his stories do not 'ramble' but that the actions composing them

are linked, complete each other and make a unified whole which embodies an idea. And if the word plot is not to be applied only to a chain of obvious actions, of violent actions, of actions which get their significance, not from the new context but from an old melo- dramatic tradition, then this means that he has plot.

The Revolution in Tanner's Lane, first published in 1887, seems divided, as I have said, into two novels only slightly connected. But if it is 'inartistic' on that account, one wonders how it could ever be called plotless, even by those for whom plot necessarily involves melodrama. Each of its halves tells a story composed of actions which are not only meaningfully related but exciting, and which one need hardly be interested in character to understand. Since these stories are also of obvious and 'progressive' social significance (their chief character won Ralph Fox's 'leftist' approval as one of the few working-class revolutionaries truly depicted in fiction) [1] it is easy to see why this novel has always been his most popular, the safest to recommend first in making converts to Hale White.

It is certainly among the work's merits that it is exciting for obvious as well as other reasons, and that it dramatizes, to a greater degree than those which follow, much important social history. But the novel's distinction comes chiefly from something else. It comes from the quality of the author's mind and temperament. It comes from his delicate and intense awareness of the intimate emotions: friendship, the thirst for sympathy, the complicated mutual guilt in unsuitable marriages, parental love, the see-saw conflict between feeling and reason. It comes, above all, from the fact that in situations and with characters which would hurry a lesser intelligence into 'black and white' social protest or satire, our author resists every temptation to simplify. His chief character, the revolutionary Calvinist printer, Zachariah Coleman, becomes at last a man wholly and finally 'committed to nothing . . . and not subsidized by his reputation to defend a system.'

He was not, in fact, despite all his love of logic, the 'yes *or* no' from which most people cannot escape, but a 'yes *and* no'; not

---

[1] Ralph Fox, *The Novel and the People*, New York, International Publishers, 1945, pp. 93-4.

immorally and through lack of resolution, but by reason of an original receptivity and the circumstances of his training. If he had been merely a student the case would have been different; but he was not a student. He was a journeyman printer; and hard work has a tendency to demolish the distinctions of dialectics. He had also been to school outside his shop, and had learned many lessons, often confusing and apparently contradictory. Blanketeer marches; his first wife; the workhouse; imprisonment; his second wife; the little Pauline, had each come to him with its own special message, and the net result was a character, but a character disappointing to persons who prefer men and women of linear magnitude to those of three dimensions.[1]

Now it is from such awareness of ambiguity, of complexity, that the theme issues which will be embodied in the way the story is told. This indicates that it will probably not lie on the surface of the narrative but in its deeper implications, and that when the surface narrative breaks in two, it may well be on behalf of a chain of meanings which continues unbroken. Indeed, this is precisely the case. And though some dissatisfaction may still be legitimate that a story was not contrived to duplicate exactly the unity of the theme (a reasonable fictional ideal), the scrupulous critic ought really to be mollified by the fact that on the level of meaning the two halves come together and that they are in every other respect beautifully done.

The Revolution in Tanner's Lane is a historical novel, and its unifying subject is the Puritan religion as it functioned—and decayed—in the two generations preceding that of the author. We see it first in 1814-16, when, along with the inevitable shallow and formal believers, there were still many for whom their faith was an explanation of life which had room for the deepest, most realistic insight and the strongest feeling. And we see it next a generation later, when it had fallen almost completely into the hands of the shallow formalists, and among others had been replaced either by glib philosophy without roots in feeling or by nothing at all. The political and the human dramas are, of course, of great interest to the author, and to us. But what constitutes their deeper, their unifying interest is that they

---

[1] *The Revolution*, chap. xxiv.

provide the ordeal of experience by which the religious faith of the characters is tested and its power to help made known.

In the first half the theme is carried by Zachariah Coleman, as he was at the beginning of that education described above, and by his wife of three months. They are both strictly orthodox Independents, and yet they differ as people of any faith—or none—might differ. Zachariah is a man of thought and of passionate responsiveness, ardently radical, like many Puritans of that epoch, and even capable of intoxication with the poetry of Byron, which fills his mind with images of romantic love. He is a man aware of the realities of his own inner life as well as of the complications introduced from outside, and by these his religious beliefs are forever being challenged. Mrs. Coleman, on the other hand, is one of those who are not concerned with realities, inner or outer, but who accept in all simplicity the forms and clichés of their milieu. She can contradict her beliefs with a good conscience as long as she is careful to observe their letter. Her life is therefore, as a rule, more comfortable than his. But doubting, painful thought can deepen a religion till it becomes a form of insight into the way things really go, and how they are to be borne, and this is a help in trouble denied to the mere acceptance of verbal formulae. It is this we are to see in the story of Mr. and Mrs. Coleman.

When the story opens, Zachariah has already become aware of his wife's total incapacity to give him the love and sympathy he craves. She is not only unintelligent, but cold, and she seems to care about nothing but her endless domestic war on dirt and disorder, or the mechanical observance of her religious duties. Even his return home one day with a bloody head—he had been struck down by a Tory drayman for refusing to lift his hat to the detestable Prince Regent—excites annoyance at the mess, sooner than sympathy. This does not mean she is the simple villain of the piece. We are later told that she might have been a better woman with someone else, that Zachariah's type brought out the worst in her. And once, hot with a grievance, her husband is visited by the disturbing thought that she too, in her prayers, was in direct contact with the Almighty. But this cannot mitigate the anguish of his mistake; for a man like him the vista of a life without love is horrible. 'His religion was a part of himself,'[1] however, and with the sense of trouble comes always the conviction of his duty to bear it without despair. To this he has been 'called.'

By an irony which is to bring him much inner conflict—and instruction—his growing estrangement from his wife, who ostensibly shares his all-important beliefs, is accompanied by a growing closeness to three friends who are practically infidels. He had been helped in that fight with the drayman by a radical young aristocrat, Major Maitland, and the Major had introduced him to an underground political club called The Friends of the People. Here he had been disgusted at the loud foolish beery discussion in which the struggle to redress real grievances was swamped. But he had met at least one more like the Major, a French republican named Caillaud, whose radicalism was also intelligent as well as ardent. The third friend was Caillaud's daughter Pauline, a young woman surprisingly alive to all her father's ideas. Among the ladies of Pike Street Chapel, she would have been 'like a wild sea gull in a farmyard of peaceful clucking brown-speckled fowls.'[2] Strange people for an orthodox Calvinist to be drawn to! The Major is a handsome young man of the world, not at all profligate but entirely free and secular in all his ideas; while the Caillauds believe in some sort of a 'Supreme,' but one who has the sense to share their own enlightened views of social justice and morality. All three are surely damned, and Zachariah's great-grandfather would have denounced them without hesitation.

In a chapter entitled 'The Horizon Widens,' Zachariah's beliefs confront those of the two heirs of French enlightenment. The result is not the Puritan's total discomfiture. When Pauline mocks the idea that God could also be responsible for the present contemptible rulers of England, Zachariah answers with a quotation: 'I form the light and create darkness: I make peace and create evil; I the Lord do all these things.' And for the reader not too 'enlightened' himself to take a hint, it is she who seems shallow. For, as every suggestion of the reality in Puritanism has been preparing us to understand, the idea of a single Author of both good and evil is the same as the idea, profoundly true, of their necessary interdependence, a point also

---

[1] *The Revolution*, chap. i.

[2] *Ibid.*, chap. vi.

made in *The Autobiography*. Zachariah's thinking may have begun with the Biblical statement, but the nature of life is the proof.

After the talk, Caillaud tells his daughter to show their guest her art. She puts on a short black velvet dress and red stockings and sticks a red artificial flower in her hair and a guazy shawl on her shoulders. Then, accompanied by her father on the oboe, she goes into a series of graceful evolutions 'designed apparently to show the capacity of a beautiful figure for poetic expression. . . . There was no definite character in the dance beyond mere beauty.' This is not to be the last time that Hale White makes the Puritan opposition between the sense of beauty and the sense of moral responsibility. It is indeed a source of his inner wealth that he can at the same time see them opposed and see the claims of both. Zachariah, however, has so far learned to honour only the claims of the moral life, and he is terribly confused by the pleasure he takes in the performance. For the matter of that, he is not far wrong in his sense of its danger—later he cannot get the performer's body out of his thoughts. But when he fails to commend Pauline as her father expects, she, remembering, exclaims:

'Ah, of course you are Puritans. I am a—what do you call it? a daughter—no, that isn't it—a child of the devil. I won't have that though. My father isn't the devil. Even *you* wouldn't say that, Mr. Coleman. Ah, I have no business to joke, you look so solemn; you think my tricks are satanic; but what was it in your book. "*C'est moi, l'Eternel, qui fais toutes les choses là*"?' [1]

Thus, by his own religion, he is invited to accept what appears to contradict it.

Meanwhile, Mrs. Coleman too is being introduced to certain difficulties—difficulties, however, which her type is able to avoid facing squarely. The Major's gallantries, though innocent to him, are not so in their effect on the Puritan lady—for 'the symbolism of an act varies much.' [2] Once, when he has persuaded the Colemans to come with him to a performance of *Othello*, Zachariah is separated from them and it is necessary for her to go and return with the hand-

---

[1] *Ibid.*, chap. v.

[2] *Ibid.*, chap. iii.

some Major. The next morning, talking over the play with her husband—

She was even affectionate—affectionate for her—and playfully patted his shoulder as he went out, warning him not to be so late again. What was the cause of her gaiety? Was she thinking improperly of the Major? No. If she had gone with Zachariah alone to the theatre would she have been so cheerful? No. Did she really think she loved her husband better? Yes. The human heart, even the heart of Mrs. Coleman, is beyond our analysis.[1]

We come next to a half-ironic, half-pathetic contrast between Puritanism as wisdom and Puritanism as a structure of language and symbol in which even intelligent believers must sometimes be constricted and cut off from their fellows. Zachariah invites his friends to Sunday tea and chapel afterwards, with their ultimate conversion his hidden motive. (Significantly, it is his wife who instigated this. *He* has been suffering real guilt at his failure to make the attempt, but she, interested in the Major, is unhindered by any awareness of difficulties.) The scene of the 'tea' and the sermon at the chapel which follows are among Hale White's finest pages. While his wife presides with demure satisfaction over the teapot and his friends engage in political chat (Pauline reposing blithely on her 'Supreme'), Zachariah, tense, awaits his moment, and then pours out the beliefs he desperately wants them to share. They are moved and drawn by his emotion, but of course the attempt is a failure. For he has simply recited the Calvinist scheme of redemption, and, what is fatal, done it largely in St. Paul's words. 'How clear it all seemed to him, how indisputable! Childish association and years of unquestioning repetition gave an absolute certainty to what was almost unmeaning to other people.'[2] Moreover, 'he was a century and a half too late' not only to reach others with such words but even to apply them himself with the necessary singlemindedness. He ought to have 'looked straight into their eyes and told them, each one there and then, that they were in bonds of iniquity, sold unto Satan, and in danger of hell-fire.' But he could not. 'The system was still the same, even to

[1] *The Revolution*, chap. iii.   [2] *Ibid.*, chap. vi.

its smallest details, but the application had become difficult. The application, indeed, was a good deal left to the sinner himself. That was the difference.'[1]

Thus the merely intelligent Puritan. We meet next a Puritan genius. This is the Reverend Thomas Bradshaw, of Pike Street Meeting-house, a minister who drew from far crowds of *men*, as well as women, but who, being given to hypochondria (there had been tragedy in his life), sometimes turned 'combative or melancholy' and sent them away with the briefest of sermons. He was an outspoken radical, '*claiming*' descent from Bradshaw the regicide, and actually supporting the execution of a traitor to The Friends of the People— of which more in a moment. In Mr. Bradshaw, Hale White pays the debt he was always conscious of owing to the great ministers he had known; particularly, no doubt, to Caleb Morris. Among his gifts is not only wisdom but a poet's power to feel and articulate justly the exact human context of his ideas. Where great passions are in question, of course, we know to what just expression can rise. We see it in Mr. Bradshaw's sermon on 'Jephthah,' which is not only profound but electric at every point with the heart's eloquence, terribly moving—a masterpiece. It is, moreover, far from 'rambling' from our story as a careless reader might suppose, absolutely central to it. It is an elucidation of the basic tenets of that Puritanism which is the story's subject.

Without notes (which he never used), Mr. Bradshaw interpreted for his people the beautiful tale of the harlot's son. Jephthah has been 'elected' by God, though others are more respectable, to lead Israel against Ammon, and he has vowed to sacrifice to the Lord whoever meets him at his threshold if he returns victorious. Here are some extracts from the sermon, which is worth quoting at length:

'Jephthah's rash vow—this is sometimes called. I say it is not a rash vow. It may be rash to those who have never been brought to extremity by the children of Ammon—to those who have not cared whether Ammon or Christ wins. Men and women sitting here in comfortable pews'—this was said with a kind of snarl—'may talk of Jephthah's rash vow. God be with them, what do they know of the

[1] *Ibid.*

struggles of such a soul? It does not say so directly in the Bible, but we are led to infer it, that Jephthah was successful because of his vow. "The Lord delivered them into his hands." He would not have done it if he had been displeased with the "rash vow" ' (another snarl). ' "He smote them from Aroer even till thou come to Minith." Ah, but what follows? . . . Jephthah had played for a great stake. Ought the Almighty—let us speak it with reverence—to have let him off with an ox, or even with a serf? I say that if we are to conquer Ammon, we must pay for it, and we ought to pay for it . . . Jephthah comes back in triumph. Let me read the passage to you:—"Behold his daughter came out to meet him with timbrels and with dances: *and she was his only child: beside her he had neither son nor daughter*. And it came to pass, when he saw her, that he rent his clothes and said, 'Alas, my daughter! thou hast brought me very low, and thou art one of them that trouble me: for I have opened my mouth unto the Lord, and I cannot go back." ' Now, you read poetry, I dare say— what you call poetry. I say in all of it—all, at least, I have seen— nothing comes up to that. *"She was his only child: beside her he had neither son nor daughter"* '—(Mr. Bradshaw's voice broke a little as he went over the words again with great deliberation and infinite pathos.)—'There is no thought in Jephthah of recantation, nor in the maiden of revolt, but nevertheless he has his own sorrow. *He is brought very low.* She asks for two months by herself upon the mountains before her death. What a time for him! At the end of the two months God held him still to his vow; he did not shrink; she submitted, and was slain. But you will want me to tell you in con- clusion where the gospel is in all this. I say the gospel is to be found in the Old Testament as well as in the New. I say the Word of God is one, and His message is here this night for you and me as distinctly as it is at the end of the sacred volume. Observe, as I have told you before, that Jephthah is the son of the harlot. He hath mercy on whom He will have mercy. He calls them His people who are not His people; and He calls her beloved which was not beloved. God at any rate is no stickler for hereditary rights. Moreover, it does not follow because you, my hearers, have God-fearing parents, that God has elected you. He may have chosen, instead of you, instead of me, the wretchedest creature outside, whose rags we will not touch. But to what did God elect Jephthah? To a respectable, easy, decent existence, with money at interest, regular meals, sleep after them, and unbroken rest at night? He elected him to that tremendous oath and that tremendous penalty. He elected him to the agony he endured while she was away upon the hills! That is God's election; an election to the cross and to the cry, "Eli, Eli, lama Sabachthani." "Yes," you will say, "but he elected him to the victory over Ammon." Doubtless He did; but what cared Jephthah for his victory over Ammon when she came to meet him, or, indeed, for the rest of his life? What is a victory, what are triumphal arches and the praise of all creation, to a lonely man? Be sure, if God elects you, He elects you to suffering. Whom He loveth He chasteneth, and His stripes are not play-work. Ammon will not be conquered unless your heart be well nigh broken. I tell you, too, as Christ's minister, that you are not to direct your course according to your own desires. You are not to say, "I will give up this and that so that I may be saved." Did not St. Paul wish himself accursed from Christ for his brethren? If God should command you to go down to the bottomless pit in fulfilment of His blessed designs, it is your place to go. Out with self—I was about to say this damned self; and if Israel calls, if Christ calls, take not a sheep or an ox—that is easy enough—but take your choicest possession, take your own heart, your own blood, your very self, to the altar.'[1]

The word God has been rendered unusable for many of us today because of the sentimental magical notions traditionally associated with it. We are heirs, moreover, to another tradition, a kind of 'village atheist' tradition which has made the total rejection of our religious heritage seem a guarantee of intelligence. But is the orthodox Puritanism of such a sermon really a less accurate view of the way life goes and what it demands of us than that implied in certain political attitudes, say, in which slogans are regarded as realities, good intentions are expected to lead automatically to their proper rewards, and a transference in the ownership of the means of production is supposed to ensure forever the simple virtue of leaders and followers alike? This is an extreme case, of course: most sensible

[1] *The Revolution*, chap. vii.

people have by now passed beyond it. But it can stand forever as
an example of the type of superstition, amounting to a positive faith
in magic, which can even pass itself off as 'scientific' because it
repeats current axioms in current lingo.

Immediately after the sermon we are shown how Zachariah
struggles to apply it to the pain *he* has been 'elected' to endure.
Though Mr. Bradshaw had gone to the Major's heart, 'a rather difficult passage in the case of a man about town like me,'[1] he had left
Mrs. Coleman quite self-possessed, and when they are alone she
primly reproves her husband's earlier outburst. The day's events
have roused in Zachariah a strange mass of inarticulate feeling (it is
Hale White's genius that he can thus evoke what cannot be formulated)—and *this* is what meets him at home. The sense of his trouble
rises within him now as never before. Jephthah had at least saved
Israel. But what was the good of his cold and loveless life? He
remembered that Mr. Bradshaw had said it was not for us to
question God's designs, and he believed this, and yet the 'why'
tormented him. This protest of his reason seemed a sin. 'Poor wretch!
he thought he was struggling against his weakness; but he was in
reality struggling against his strength.'[2] Does this mean that Hale
White thinks his reason is more to be relied on here than his faith—
than what faith teaches him (as wisdom teaches others) of the folly
of trying to reduce *everything* to a plan we can grasp and the necessity
of accepting what cannot be altered? No, for after much agonized
pacing, Zachariah 'fell upon his knees and poured himself out before
his Maker, entreating him for light.' And as at dawn he crept into
bed ('light was coming to the world in obedience to the Divine
command, but not to him'),[3] he thought he would never sleep again
except in his grave. 'But an unseen Hand presently touched him,
and he knew nothing till he was awakened by the broad day stream-
ing over him.'[4] Thus, as reason (though it *is* a strength) yields before
that infinitely complex reality which Zachariah calls God, healing
comes from it in ways the reason cannot foresee, a development one
need not be religious to find convincing.

Meanwhile, Zachariah's political activities are moving him toward

---

[1] *The Revolution*, chap. vii.   [2] *Ibid.*
[3] *Ibid.*   [4] *Ibid.*

trials of his faith even more severe. In December 1814 the muddle-headed majority of The Friends of the People are demanding 'action,' though they don't really know what kind, they are not properly organized and they are opposed not only by the middle class but by their own. (Our three friends are called traitors for pointing all this out.) The club's boozing secretary, moreover, has been half frightened, half bribed, into turning police informer. On the eve of an important meeting, to which the police would have followed him, he is shot dead by someone unknown. The Major and the Caillauds flee to Paris, and the Colemans, she warned by Mr. Brad-shaw, who had apparently known all in advance, head for Man-chester. It is in the two chapters which follow, significantly entitled 'A Strain on the Cable' and 'Disintegration by Degrees,' that the religious development of Zachariah takes its next steps.

The first chapter does not so much carry him away from his religion as *stretch* that religion to accommodate still more of reality. For us it is a demonstration of the nature of faith, as Hale White has already defined it in the *Deliverance*, faith as 'permanent confidence in the idea, a confidence never to be broken down by apparent failure, or by examples by which ordinary people prove that quali-fication is necessary.'[1] The 'idea' of his religion, in its essence, is the idea that human existence, the whole universe, can be trusted to proceed as they *ought* to: neither rebellion nor despair are ever in order. Hale White shows us that a faith which has not become a kind of repose on this is no more than a mechanical assent to verbal formulae. During the first frightening days of Zachariah's joblessness in Manchester, Mrs. Coleman's faith, which has never been troubled by contact with reality, shows its true mettle. 'I'm sure we shall starve!'[2] is her contribution to their struggle. Zachariah reminds her of Mr. Bradshaw's sermon on the passage through the Red Sea—he had pointed out how the very time and place of worst distress became the time and place of deliverance. And at this the cruel-fanged 'reptile' lurking in her inner darkness completely reveals itself —and she bursts into shrill ugly resentment and hysteria.

Life has arguments, however, before which even the strongest faith turns shaky. One of these is the experience of suing for a job

[1] *Deliverance*, chap. iv.   [2] *The Revolution*, chap. ix.

from bosses who treat you with contempt. Though Zachariah 'had some self-respect' because he knew 'he was cared for by God . . . these men treated him as if he were not a person, an individual soul, but as an atom of a mass, to be swept out anywhere, into the gutter—into the river.' [1] After a terrible day of this, the worst—the ultimate—doubt rises in him. 'Does God really know anything about me?' And the secular reader is prevented from rejecting the religious question as outside his own experience—for its secular form comes next: 'Are we not born by the millions, like spawn, and crushed out of existence like spawn?' [2] We see that the Puritan's worst doubt is exactly the same as our own—that sweeping doubt of the value of our efforts, of ourselves, which cripples the mind. The Puritan, however, had an advantage over us, as Hale White suggests. Thoughts 'not in harmony' with our natures, with life, bewilder us because we do not know 'the degree of authority which (our) thoughts and impulses possess.' [3] Zachariah did—he repelled the crippling doubt as a temptation of Satan. And later, when he is attacked by something still more horrible, a 'nameless terror' which seized him when he was tired and depressed and which readers of Hale White will recognize, then too 'he had his precedent.' He remembered how Christian had also walked on a quagmire 'into which, if even a good man falls, he can find no bottom; he remembered that gloom so profound "that oftentimes, when he lifted up his foot to set it forward, he knew not where or upon what he should set it next." ' Other wonderful sentences from 'the immortal Progress' are quoted here, where their human meaning leaps into light. And the passage ends:

Lastly, he remembered that by-and-by the day broke, and Christian cried, '*He hath turned the shadow of death into the morning.*' He remembered all this; he could give it a place in the dispensation of things, and could therefore lift himself above it. [4]

Soon afterward he meets a friend who thinks he might get him a job. He comes home rejoicing, not only at this hope but at the proof that his trust in God has been justified. He asks his wife to kneel

---

[1] *The Revolution*, chap. ix.   [2] *Ibid.*
[3] *Ibid.*   [4] *Ibid.*

down with him and give thanks. But it is life and feeling in a religion which now do more and now do less than is formally required. Life and feeling have no place in hers, and she is therefore never impelled to do either more or less. She now chills him by asking him to wait till she gets off her things, pointing out, too, that they are not yet sure of the job; and when she returns it is time for regular prayers anyway. The next day he gets a job as good and as permanent as the one in London. Thus the faith of 'doubting' Zachariah is justified against the actual faithlessness of his merely orthodox wife. And if it is true that he might *not* have got the job, his faith is still justified. For it would have made him struggle on until something else came along—he would always, in the long run, be more right than the doubter.

The next chapter's 'disintegrating' lesson is the story of Pauline's life which the Colemans hear during a reunion with all three of the old friends in Manchester. She is the daughter of a woman who lived unmarried first with one man and then with another, and who is yet shown (by Caillaud) to be good and honourable, a mother to be proud of. Caillaud had adopted the girl. So far has Zachariah come that when his wife later declares that they are not to be invited again, he actually answers, 'Why not?' And by a fine irony, Mrs. Coleman's intensest heat against the daughter of adultery springs into being from something very close to the sin she is condemning. That same night she wonders, during a revery, whether the Major will ever again take her to the theatre, and suddenly she realizes that Pauline is attractive. The thought is like burning acid, and never leaves her again.

It is not necessary to dwell on the rest of the story by which the theme is further varied and developed. Zachariah and his friends become involved in the march of the desperate 'Blanketeers,' whose unreasoning heat they try in vain to control, the Major is killed by a member of the militia and Caillaud, shooting his assailant, is condemned to execution. Zachariah flees to Liverpool, leaving his wife ill in the hands of a poor neighbour, and there he too falls ill. In a terrible chapter called 'The School of Adversity: the Sixth Form Thereof,' he awakens from a coma to find himself in the workhouse, where inmates are treated like vermin by vicious irresponsible

doctors and superintendents. It was then a place, we are told, calculated to induce something worse than atheism—a conviction that
Satan ruled the world. Rescued and rejoined by his wife, he decides
one day, against her will, to pay a farewell visit to Caillaud. He is
retained as a prisoner for two years. His wife dies after three months,
and in one of those abrupt paragraphs so annoying to some, the
story ends with the information that, on release, he married Pauline,
that they had a daughter, and that a year later Pauline was dead.
Though the information is so ruthlessly compressed, it is conveyed
with a peculiar and moving beauty. And in the compression itself
a meaning can be found. 'Zachariah's first wife is an incidental
victim to the imperious command of his loyalty,' one critic finely
observes. 'We feel him so dutiful that it is natural not to be detained
either in the Cimmerian dark of his captivity or in the Elysian field
of his second marriage. We enter and are dismissed from both in
half a page.'[1]

The second story of the novel takes place in Cowfold (Bedford)
about the time of Hale White's childhood, and the reader acquainted
with the author's life is therefore partly aware of what to expect.
Some years before Cowfold had had a minister of Mr. Bradshaw's
type, but now, instead of Mr. Bradshaw's religion, we get the kind
Hale White himself encountered at Bunyan's Meeting. We get that
of the present minister of Tanner's Lane Chapel, the Reverend Mr.
John Broad. Broad is a heavy man, who eats like a horse and whose
religion often seems regarded as a career in which his chief duty is to
keep his food supplies uninterrupted. To his son, who is studying for
the ministry, he writes, for instance, of the importance of being
invited to speak from a 'metropolitan pulpit,' and he warns him to
choose his sermon texts with care.

A young minister, I need hardly say, my dear Thomas, ought to
confine himself to what is generally accepted, and not to particular-
ize. For this reason he should avoid not only all disputed topics, but,
as far as possible, all reference to particular offences. I always myself
doubted the wisdom, for example, of sermons against covetousness,
or worldliness, or hypocrisy. Let us follow our Lord and Master, and

---

[1] 'C,' 'The Art of Mark Rutherford,' *Academy*, LVI (February 4, 1899), p. 162

warn our hearers against sin, and leave the application to the Holy Spirit. I only mention this matter now because I have found two or three young students err in this direction, and the error, I am sure, militates against their usefulness.[1]

Broad's continual blurring of the selfish note by the pious (as in that 'usefulness'), we are not, however, permitted to call simply hypocritical. For—

He was . . . not a hypocrite, that is to say, not an ordinary novel or stage hypocrite. There is no such thing as a human being simply hypocritical or simply sincere. We are all hypocrites, more or less, in every word and every action, and what is more, in every thought. Furthermore, there are degrees of natural capacity for sincerity, and Mr. Broad was probably as sincere as his build of soul and body allowed him to be. Certainly no doubt of the truth of what he preached ever crossed his mind.[2]

No, in his case, as everywhere in Hale White (even, for instance, in that of the traitorous Secretary of The Friends of the People), evil is due 'not so much to a distinct determination to do wrong under a full sense of the enormity of the offence, as to a drowsy inapprehension that any great violation of the law is being committed.'[3] This insight into the source of crime was that of the twenty-seven-year-old Hale White in his essay 'Births, Deaths and Marriages,' but it perfectly explains the 'villains' he was to create over two decades later, villains in whom evil and mental fuzziness always go together. Thus, Isaac Allan, an intelligent member of Broad's congregation, can say of Broad: 'He never seems to me to see anything clearly; at least he never makes me see anything clearly; the whole world is in a fog to him.'[4]

As Zachariah tested Mr. Bradshaw's religion, we now have

[1] *The Revolution*, chap. xxiv.
[2] *Ibid.*, chap. xvii.
[3] W. H. White, 'Births, Deaths and Marriages,' *Chambers's Journal*, IX (March 6, 1858), p. 155.
[4] *The Revolution*, chap. xxiv.

George Allan, Isaac's son, to test Broad's. George is a simple decent young man, not a thinker like Zachariah, but one driven to thought at certain moments by trouble. The difference between Mr. Bradshaw and Broad, and that too between Zachariah and George, account for a difference in the quality of the second half of the novel. There is an inevitable lessening of intellectual richness and emotional intensity. Vivid, and even poignant, as characterization and drama often remain, the chief merit of this second story lies in its depiction not of individual experience but of a society. In this too, however, triumphs are possible. They are achieved, and in its own way the second story is also first rate. It is social satire: incisive, subtle and funny.

Not only is Broad's religion a contrast to that of Mr. Bradshaw, so is his attitude to politics. He is surrounded by deacons whose influence on him is in direct proportion to the size of their subscription to the chapel. For this reason, in spite of the traditional liberalism of the Independents and of Tanner's Lane, he becomes the pious tool of the well-to-do Tory farmers. In the fierce political conflict dividing the town—the Whigs demanding the abolition of the duty on foreign corn which permits English farmers to keep their prices high—Broad preserves a neutrality which is so obvious a defection from what might have been expected that it helps the Tories. To the requests of the Allans that he take a stand, he replies that though we should be wise as serpents we must also be harmless as doves, and he must beware of making his politics a stumbling-block to his congregation.

The Allans are his opposition in the story. George's parents are both friends of Zachariah's, and though devout are as deep and sincere in their religious thinking and as ardently liberal in their politics. Broad's hatred of them, not only for what they do but also, inevitably, for what they are, is his warmest emotion, and when the course of events gives him a chance to do them harm (in a holy way) he seizes it.

First, however, they are brought closer together. George Allan and Broad's daughter, Priscilla, fall in love, and worldly advantage induces the minister, and their son's feelings, the Allans, to permit the young people to marry. This is another marriage of the kind that tries the husband's soul. It differs from Zachariah's in that Priscilla is merely stupid, and George's pain is mitigated—and complicated—by the fact that she truly loves him. Nevertheless, it is no joke—though we smile—when the young man tries to explain to her the iniquity of the Corn Law, to which he is passionately opposed. And his exasperation deepens into misery as the honeymoon fades and the gulf opened between them by her silliness continues to widen. One night, indeed, which he spends with his parents, his mother's silent sympathy unmans him completely, and he weeps in her arms—the first time since childhood.

Nothing ever heard in Tanner's Lane Chapel connects itself with his trouble, or for that matter with any actual experience. But one Sunday, on a visit to the Colemans in London, he gets a glimpse of the reality which religion can contain. They go to hear the aged Mr. Bradshaw, who speaks on the text, 'Take heed to thyself that thou offer not thy burnt offering in any place thou seest.' Mr. Bradshaw begins by saying that it is not enough for a religion to help one to a knowledge of the future life and the way to heaven. If it does not help one to endure one's own private difficulties, it is not really one's religion. 'You must make your own religion, and it is only what you make yourself which will be of any use to you.'[1] Still, there are truths in the Bible which are wonderful in being at once universal and peculiarly adapted to each individual's inmost wants. One of these was the day's text. Its meaning is, we learn, that we should make our offerings only to the highest, the best. The punishment for dis-obeying this 'Divine law' is *disappointment*, lack of response and perhaps the recoil into angry cynicism. 'My young friends, young men and young women, you are particularly prone to go wrong in this matter. You not only lay your possessions but yourselves on altars by the wayside.'[2] This was the first sermon that ever 'came home' to George. And on another occasion the glimpse of what religion can mean is widened, when Zachariah, who knows the young man's trouble, gives him an *Imitation of Christ*. 'Other people may write about science or philosophy,' Zachariah remarks, 'but this man writes about *me*.' He reads and explains certain sentences

[1] *The Revolution*, chap. xxiv.
[2] *Ibid*.

from the little book—which, indeed, the secular reader may still find quite as pertinent to life as he says. And—

As the exposition grew George's heart dilated, and he was carried beyond his troubles. It was the birth in him—even in him, a Cowfold ironmonger, not a scholar by any means—of what philosophers call *the idea*, that Incarnation which has ever been our Redemption.[1]

But, as George is soon to discover, it is too late in the day for him to find the same comfort in religion as Zachariah. The political excitement increases in Cowfold, and with it increases the animosity between Broad and the Allans. The climax of both comes at once on the night of the voting, when the Whigs lose and a drunken mob of them makes for Broad's house. George, hurrying there to stop them, is accused by his father-in-law of having been their leader. And before the heat between them has begun to cool, poor Priscilla suddenly dies of a fever, another victim of her author's plotting impatience.

In the three months of self-accusing grief that follow for George 'the gospel according to Tanner's Lane' receives its chief test, and fails completely. Not only does he find it impossible to believe in its supernatural consolations—and this is strange, we are told, for he had never read a sceptical work—but he finds it in every way irrelevant and useless. 'He is cast forth to wrestle with his sufferings alone,' and help when it comes, comes from elsewhere.

It is surely [Hale White remarks] a terrible charge to bring against a religious system, that in the conflict which has to be waged by every son of Adam with disease, misfortune, death, the believers in it are provided with neither armour nor weapons. Surely a real religion, handed down from century to century, ought to have accumulated a store of consolatory truths which will be of some help to us in time of need. If it can tell us nothing, if we cannot face a single disaster any the better for it, and if we never dream of turning to it when we are in distress, of what value is it? There is one religious teacher, however, which seldom fails those who are in

---

[1] *The Revolution*, chap. xxiv.

health, and, at last did not fail him. He was helped by no priest and by no philosophy; but Nature helped him, the beneficent Power which heals the burn or scar and covers it with new skin.[1]

And note that it is religion Nature teaches, another hint that for Hale White, religious and secular thinking, when each is deep, are only different forms of the same thing.

His daughter's death does not, of course, alter Broad's feelings toward the Allans, and shortly thereafter the minister springs his mine. His nasty and foolish son Thomas had been set to spy on the Allans in London and had collected 'evidence.' After some amusing deliberations between the piously spiteful Broad and his more frankly vindictive deacons, it is decided to call the Allans to account at a public meeting. Disturbing political activities, absence from services, are only minor charges: the chief one is George's improper conduct with Zachariah Coleman's daughter Pauline. (This is false, of course.) Now it happens that Tom Broad had once all but attacked Pauline, and in deliberate revenge the high-spirited girl had scored a cross on his wrist with a pair of scissors. At the meeting, when Tom has virtuously offered his evidence, George's father rises and asks how he came by that scar on his wrist. Tom faints and the meeting ends in confusion.

The story and its theme conclude together when Broad (struck down by paralysis) is replaced at Tanner's Lane by a young M.A. from the University of London brought in by the more emancipated members of the congregation. (It is this, by the way, which the author actually names as 'the revolution in Tanner's Lane,' and yet, coming so late in the novel, it can hardly be the only revolution referred to in the title. One must suppose it to be the last step in the revolution long in progress, which we have here traced out.) The first sermon of the new minister, who is soon to drop the afternoon services, give weekday lectures—and write essays—on secular subjects, and bring home a wife who reads German, is on the Atonement. And in this sermon Hale White's irony reaches even to himself. For the minister's idea that 'salvation meant perfect sympathy with Christ—"Not I, but Christ liveth in me," '[2] is Hale White's

---

[1] *Ibid.*, chap. xxvi.   [2] *Ibid.*, chap. xxvii.

own. When it is ironically described as being uttered by this product of enlightenment 'with fluent self-confidence,' the inference is clear that such religion, though it may sound the same, is not the religion of Zachariah Coleman. It has come too easily, it has not been made part of men by a lifetime's thought and emotion, and while it can be understood as Plato is understood, it can no longer help men to live. Thus, though Hale White has tried to show the permanent truth in Zachariah's beliefs, he recognizes too that something belonged to them—and something of great value—which we who come later can never share.

CHAPTER VIII

Miriam's Schooling

AFTER an interval of three years—in 1890—Reuben Shapcott issued another book by his late friend, containing the novelette *Miriam's Schooling* and four shorter pieces. *Miriam's Schooling*, a little *Bildungsroman*, is a masterpiece, but it is done with such simplicity, clarity and compression, and its tone and (ostensible) subject matter are so modest, that its distinction might be easy to overlook. The reader may think he sees a 'Victorian' tale of a country girl's life, amusing, touching, 'true,' but a trifle. This modest tale, however, dramatizes a very modern complexity of insight, and indeed is the most Gidian of Hale White's works. Its theme is the same as that of the story of Mark Rutherford, which, it will be remembered, was also that of *The Counterfeiters*: 'the rivalry between the real world and the representation we make of it to ourselves.' And it is brought even closer to the French novel, which, beneath the surface, it amazingly resembles, by the fact that its protagonist engages in that rivalry without the help or hindrance of a religion. Like *The Counterfeiters*, it is a study of the problem—the dangers—of moral freedom, the very freedom which has, we know, its author's own allegiance.

The story begins in Cowfold about the middle of the century, and its heroine is Miriam Tacci, the daughter of a clockmaker. Her father, her world and she are described with trenchancy and humour. But there are very few of Hale White's 'objective' details, often so similar to those of other Victorian novels, which have not a deeper relation to the theme than meets the eye. So with the description of Miriam. She was clean, but disorderly; good in history (human and particular) and weak in arithmetic (abstract); liked to sing, but would not do exercises or subordinate herself in groups; was tender to pets, but took no care of them. Her best quality was a 'certain originality in her criticisms on Cowfold men, women and events, a certain

153

rectification which she always gave to the conventional mode of regarding them.'[1] The final revealing touch in her introduction is an episode of her girlhood, when, out of sympathy for a decent old man accused of arson, and resentment at Cowfold's lack of sympathy, she is ready to commit perjury to save him.

What we have been shown is a nature possessing excellent qualities—above all emotional responsiveness and the ability to see things for herself—but lacking in the self-discipline, the power to entertain and live by well-grounded abstractions which is required to prevent such qualities from turning into defects. And this lack is not made up from outside—by training, culture, religion—as in other epochs it might partly have been. Thus, though she is truthful, it is only because she has the directness of all fearless temperaments.

Her veracity rested on no principle. She was not like Jeanie Deans, that triumph of culture, in whom a generalization had so far prevailed that it was able to overcome the strongest of passions and prevent a lie even to save a sister's life. Miriam had been brought up in no such divine school. She had heard that lying was wrong, but she had no religion, although she listened to a sermon once every Sunday, and consequently the relation in which the several duties and impulses stood to one another was totally different from that which was established in Sir Walter's heroine. By some strange chance, too, tradition, which often takes the place of religion, had no power over her; and although hatred of oppression and of harsh dealing is a very estimable quality, and one which will go a long way toward constructing an ethical system for us, it will not do everything.[2]

Miriam is at the other end from Jeanie Deans, she is at culture's starting-point. Exactly this is the source of her interest.

For the questions the book is designed to ask and answer are, first, what are the dangers faced by one abandoned, as she is, to her own

[1] W. H. White, *Miriam's Schooling and Other Papers*, London, Oxford University Press, 1936, p. 53. (In the footnotes to this work I must cite page numbers, since it is not divided into chapters.)

[2] *Ibid.*, p. 62.

passionate unschooled desires; and second, what reliable principles, what 'religion,' can such a person achieve through the lessons of experience alone. Interesting questions—and fundamental in Hale White—for if the troubles of his protagonists are partly due to the religionless nineteenth century, they are also due, as I have said, to the human condition. In any time there are problems—there are extremes of suffering—beyond the power of most formal intellectual or religious consolations. And therefore what he asks with regard to Miriam we all must ask with regard to ourselves. What Miriam learns, we all must learn. It is, as it were, the basic minium needed for life. With such questions at its heart, of course, *Miriam's Schooling* becomes a kind of sequel to *The Revolution in Tanner's Lane*: the next step after the decline of Puritanism there described. And what is that 'basic minimum' she acquires so painfully from contact with experience alone? The tale has two epigraphs, a sentence of Scott's showing an example of courage and another from Euripides calling wisdom the acquaintance with necessity,[1] which suggests that it is the lesson of the Stoics. But her story will remind us too that it is something more. We shall see that it is precisely the essential lessons of the religion—Stoical too—which she had never been taught—Zachariah Coleman's religion, of which only the forms decay, but never their deeper meanings.

Before turning to Miriam's story itself, however, it will be of interest to examine some of its strangely exact parallels with the audacious modern work to which I have compared it. We note first —and this is a key to all the work of Gide and Hale White—that the poles between which characters move in both novels are those of self-indulgence and self-sacrifice. Miriam is Hale White's Bernard; like him she begins in a moral freedom that grows ambiguous in its possibilities, capable of leading to evil as well as to good; and like him she learns at last that mere self-aggrandizement is self-defeating, that a concern with self must, for inner health and happiness, be

---

[1] From Scott's *The Monastery*: 'He wrung the water from his dress, and plunging into the moors, directed his course to the north-east by the assistance of the polar star.' And from Euripedes: 'The man amongst mortals who is acquainted with necessity is wise, and is acquainted with divine things.' Quoted on p. 47 of *Miriam's Schooling*.

replaced by a concern with that which is other. The problem of life is not, however, as simple as this sounds. For as Gide's novel gradually reveals, all our ideas, however they pretend to flow un-distorted from 'objective' reality, *must* contain that element of self which makes them different from what they pretend to describe. This self, in fact, is the devil, and because of it our ideas cannot help being counterfeit: it is thus Gide's two basic symbols come together. Hence the underlying theme of *The Counterfeiters*, as Gide's novelist Edouard formulates it: 'the rivalry between reality and our own re-presentation of it.' This is also, as I say, the underlying theme of *Miriam's Schooling*. And the insight of the 'counterfeit' from which it rises—those endless counterfeits produced by the clever devil of our selfishness—appears not only in the English novel's dramatic structure but scattered throughout in explicit comment.

We have, for instance, a cynic—like Strouvilhou, but not, of course, so finished a monster—to suggest the darkest side of this truth: that all 'fine words' are merely lies. This is Montgomery, Miriam's faithless lover, who, himself corrupt, can believe in nothing noble, mocks his own incipient decent impulses and declares that all of life is based on cheating. '"Illusion, delusion—delusion, illusion," he hummed it as if it were the refrain of a ballad; "it is nothing but that from the day we are born till the day we die."'[1] And his view is often confirmed by the aptness of characters to take self-justifying reasons for truth and self-gratifying words for things. 'There is no person whom we can more easily deceive—no, not even the silliest gull—than ourselves,' Hale White remarks. 'We are always perfectly willing to deny ourselves to any extent, or even to ruin ourselves, but unfortunately it does not seem right that we should do so. It is not selfishness, but a moral obligation which intervenes.'[2] To provide such 'legitimizing' reasons for self-indulgence is exactly the devil's function in *The Counterfeiters*. And now behold how in Hale White too the very symbol of the counterfeit coin issues from this. Miriam finds it pleasant to her self-esteem one day to replace the complex reality of her kind landlady with the word 'conventional.' 'It was really not coin of the realm,' we are told, 'but gilded brass—a

---

[1] *Miriam's Schooling*, pp. 101-2.
[2] *Ibid.*, p. 90.

forgery; and the language is full of such forgeries, which we continually circulate, and worst of all, pass off upon ourselves.'[1]

That, as I say, is in both novels the truth's darker side. But there is another. From Gide we learn at last that if all our ideas are counterfeit, yet the gilt on our forgeries—like that on Bernard's false coin—is 'worth more than two sous,'[2] may give them some value, value enough for human purposes. Social conventions, for instance, though counterfeit, may be good as well as bad: 'What a fine convention it would be,' cries Bernard, 'that rested on the bona fides of every individual!'[3] Our counterfeits can have the value *which they elicit from us*. In *Miriam's Schooling* Hale White, using, like Gide, that same word 'gilt' for good, as well as pejoratively, makes exactly the same affirmation. When Miriam and her brother come to London for the first time, their youthful hopes transform its ugly chaos.

Dingy Clerkenwell and Aldersgate Street were gilded with a plentiful and radiant deposit of that precious metal of which youth has such an infinite store—actual metal, not the 'delusive ray' by any means, for it is the most real thing in existence, more real than the bullion forks and spoons which we buy later on, when we feel we can afford them, and far more real than the silver tea-service with which, still later, we are presented amidst cheers by our admiring friends in the Common Council, for our increasing efforts to uphold their interests.[4]

What their minds make of London may be another 'forgery,' since the real London is different, but their feelings are real and set them to work with real energy. Such feelings, enlisted on behalf of a mere idea, can go a long way to making its realization possible; whereas that silver tea-service represents a life of lies in which even the liars don't believe. It is our real feelings, in short, which put the gilt of reality on our mind's forgeries. And this is so even though that gilt must rub off at last (as it will from Bernard's coin) and another set of forgeries require gilding by the feelings of another time.

Further parallels with Gide could be cited, but I will close this list

---

[1] *Ibid.*, p. 80.   [3] André Gide, *The Counterfeiters*, p. 177.
[2] *Ibid.*, p. 185.   [4] *Miriam's Schooling*, pp. 70-1.

with one: the book even contains a sample of an 'acte gratuit.' The concept of the motiveless act recurs in *The Counterfeiters*, but of course, Gide's most spectacular example of it is in *The Cellars of the Vatican*. And it is perhaps significant that Gide's *acte gratuit* is a murder, while Hale White's is a good deed. It is Miriam's attempt to save by perjury a man accused of arson, an attempt which is pure impulse, for she has no connection with him and has not been asked. In rejecting the useless lie, the man's lawyers wonder why she did it, and one calls her act ' "perfectly motiveless . . . a noteworthy instance," for he was a bit of a philosopher, "of an action performed without any motive whatever. I have always maintained the possibility of such actions." ' [1] Not to open the question of whether a truly motiveless act is conceivable, her deed, like Lafcadio's, is a dramatization of the mind's freedom at least from ordinary notions of causation, its capacity for the new, the surprising, by which it can always break out of any theory which pretends to describe it with final accuracy—that is, in effect, to limit it. This native human freedom to do *otherwise*—perhaps worse, perhaps better—than is expected is the necessary foundation from which grow the characteristic problems and solutions of our two authors.

Let us turn now to the particular adventures by which Miriam is schooled. These are initiated by an aunt, Mrs. Dabbs. Mrs. Dabbs is one who perpetually transforms the realities of her life into the clichés of a second-rate romance with herself as heroine, for she is 'literary' and owns volumes of poetry by people like Mrs. Hemans. ('Into these she occasionally looked, and refreshed herself by comparing her intellect with that of the female kind generally.') [2] Suggesting that a girl of Miriam's talents is 'vegetating' in the country, she causes her and her brother, Andrew, to come to London, where they take a dingy lodging in a slum and the boy is given a job in the butcher-shop of Mr. Dabbs.

We have seen how their youthful dreams gilded the city as they entered it the first time, and how their author insisted the gilt was real. Yet Hale White proceeds to 'contradict' himself in what follows, just as Gide does continually in his novel, to the 'irritation'

---

[1] *Miriam's Schooling*, p. 64.
[2] *Ibid.*, p. 66.

of the reader in search of the theme. For the dreams rapidly fade and the reality which replaces them is not merely the depressing ugliness of the actual city but, for Andrew, a hateful job which he endures only with the help of increasing amounts of liquor, and, for Miriam, a futile torturing passion for a dissipated weakling.

In the story of her passion we are shown the consequences of absorption in the self and the self's desires alone. One I have already mentioned. Her potentialities for good, which we have discovered in her spontaneous sympathy for Mr. Cutts, accused of arson, are swallowed up in a selfishness that can even be cruel. This we see first in her impatience at having to attend an hour at her landlady's sickbed when her lover is waiting. 'Was the Miriam who chafed at her disappointment,' asks her author, himself relating the two events, '. . . the same Miriam who walked over to see Mortimer, Wake and Collins on behalf of Mr. Cutts? Precisely the same.'[1] She is even worse when her brother loses his job through drunkenness and then is laid up by a drunken accident. Her single concern is lest she be forced to leave London, and even the fact that her brother might be dying disturbs her only so far as it interferes with her relationship with her beloved Montgomery.

But moral decay is not the only penalty for total domination by one's own desires. Far worse is the fact that there is nothing left to support one in the event of their total defeat. This she learns one day when she sees Montgomery staggering drunk into the home of a prostitute, his arm about her waist. 'Every interest which she had in life had been allowed to die under the shadow of this one. Every thought had taken one direction—everything had been bitter or sweet by reference to one object alone; and this gone, there followed utter collapse.'[2]

As we have already been told, she belonged to a time when trouble had to be faced alone, 'with no weapons and with no armour save those which Nature provides. . . . She was no better protected than if Socrates, Epictetus, and all ecclesiastical establishments from the time of Moses had never existed.'[3] She sinks into a despair that,

[1] *Ibid.*, p. 91.
[2] *Ibid.*, p. 110.
[3] *Ibid.*, p. 98.

during a walk through a particularly depressing part of London, on a particularly gloomy day, leads her to the brink of suicide.

> When she reached the dock the temptation presented itself to her with fearful force to throw herself in it [the water] and be at rest. Usually in our troubles there is a prospect of an untried resource which may afford relief, or a glimmer of a distance which we may possibly reach, and where we may find peace, but for Miriam there was no distance, no reserve: this was her first acquaintance with an experience not rare, alas! but below it humanity cannot go, when all life ebbs from us, when we stretch out our arms in vain, when there is no God—nothing but a brazen Moloch, worse than the Satan of theology ten thousand times, because it is dead. A Satan we might conquer, or at least we should feel the delight of combat in resisting him; but what can we do against this leaden 'order of things' which makes our nerves ministers of madness?[1]

That day's walk ends in an illness, during which she awakens from a coma to find that her voluntary nurse is none other than the 'conventional' Miss Tippit, the landlady whose own illness Miriam had regarded simply as a nuisance.

This descent into the very depths of the valley of the shadow proves for Miriam, as it does for other Hale White characters, to be a turning-point. It leads her to her first glimpse of the lesson that is to be her salvation. Recuperating from her illness at the home of family friends in Salisbury, she pays a visit to Stonehenge, that cluster of great stones arranged in a circle by a forgotten culture for an unknown purpose. There she is 'oppressed with the sense of her own nothingness and the nothingness of man.'[2] At this, 'suddenly, and without any apparent connection with what had gone before,

---

[1] *Miriam's Schooling*, p. 113.

[2] *Ibid.*, p. 117. This experience was her author's. In an unpublished letter to Jack, dated July 13, 1888 (copy in the possession of Dr. R. Hale-White), he writes: 'Stonehenge, and more especially its vast plain, struck me *harder* than anything I have ever seen, but these hoary stones, about which nothing is known, gave rise to thoughts not particularly profitable. A monument like this so easily lends itself to the very simple, but perfectly worthless depression begotten by the transitory passage of the generations across the planet.'

and indeed, in contrast with it, it came into Miriam's mind that she must do something for her fellow creatures. How came it there? Who can tell?'[1] And she decides to become a nurse.

'Who can tell?' the author asks, but of course, it is the reader's business at least to make the attempt. Hale White helps us a little in a paragraph in which he recurs to the question, admitting his heroine's 'inadequacy' of motive.

But what brought Paul to the disciples at Damascus? A light in the sky and a vision. . . . Miriam had a vitality, a susceptibility or fluidity of character—call it what you will—which do not need great provocation. There are some mortals on this earth to whom nothing more than a certain summer morning very early, or a certain glance from a fellow-creature dead for years, has been the Incarnation, the Crucifixion, the Resurrection, or the Descent of the Holy Ghost.[2]

What Miriam has glimpsed is that Infinity of which we are a part and which, because it reduces the self's importance, lessens the force not only of personal trouble but also of what divides us from each other. A perfectly realistic insight, and granting her character, an adequate realistic motive, and yet might not Zachariah Coleman have called it a glimpse of God—that God whose Fatherhood makes all men small and all men brothers? There can surely be no conception of God, at any rate, of which this will not be one of the elements. And that Hale White intends us to link the idea of infinity with that of the Creator his religious parallels in the quoted passage make clear. So much of God at least, Miriam's story tells us, we can all come to at last, whatever we name it.

But it is characteristic of the story's wonderful closeness to life as lived, rather than as played with in the mind, that Miriam's first response to this true lesson should be wrong—should carry her too far for her own strength—and that she should need to learn it again and apply it more modestly. In Hale White the simple heroic solution is generally unattainable, or rather a heroism even greater is

[1] *Miriam's Schooling*, p. 117.
[2] *Ibid.*, p. 170.

required of his characters: that which struggles on forever amid the endless complications of ordinary daily life. So Miriam's dramatic self-sacrifice as a nurse becomes an exacting drudgery at which she proves incompetent, and though she struggles long, she is dismissed. Since she has seen her lover die in the hospital of a drunken accident, nothing is left to keep her in London, and she returns to Cowfold. And it is there, in the home she had left out of the common vanity of supposing that elsewhere life's problems would be easier, that she finds the modest deliverance that is allotted her. As so often in Hale White, the crucial lesson in her schooling is marriage. And it is a man of God, introducing her to the laws of 'heaven,' who helps her to understand it.

Her marriage, which (like a typical Hale White character) she drifts into rather than chooses, is to a good man named Didymus Farrow, who loves her 'in his way' but whose temperament is very different from hers. He is a cheerful placid basket-maker, contented with his life and his work—at which his skill is great—and entirely unable to supply her with the romance for which her heart still stubbornly yearns. While he spends happy evenings whittling and whistling, Miriam turns to books for the first time in her life. It must already have become clear that Miriam's basic feelings and basic problems, like those of all his protagonists, are her author's. And now, though she is not an intellectual, as Mark Rutherford was, she is to share in certain of the intellectual's troubles too. The reading she comes to love as an 'escape' from reality—a use of art rightly honoured in the *Deliverance*—augments her misery, for it increases the self-absorbed dreaming which cuts her off from the life she must live. She is everywhere withdrawn, unable to share in the town's distractions or the simple chatter of visiting ladies, and herself feels that she casts a hateful 'cold shadow' on those about her. This shadow might be called the Intellectual's Shadow. Its essential characteristic is not the mere possession of ideas but the repellent, though inevitable, self-absorption which results from an active inner life.

The effect of reading is shown vividly in her encounter with the particularly harmful *Romeo and Juliet*. In that rapturous vicarious experience, 'she saw . . . the possibilities of love.'[1] 'Ah God!' her

[1] *Miriam's Schooling*, p. 129.

author comments in sympathy, 'what is the count of all the men and women whom, since it was first "plaid publiquely with great applause," this tragedy has reminded of the *what might have been!*'[1] She has been imagining herself Juliet: here is how the real husband replaces the ideal.

Mr. Didymus Farrow, during his wife's absence in Verona, had been very much engaged in whittling a monkey which toppled over on a long pole, but being dissatisfied with its performance he had taken his accordion out of the box, and, just as Lady Capulet called, he struck up 'Down amongst the dead men,' which, whatever its merit may be, is not particularly adapted to that instrument. Verona and Romeo were straightway replaced by Cowfold and the Cowfold consort. He was in the best of spirits, and he stooped down just as his wife was waking, took the cat—which was lying before the fire—and threw it on her lap.

'Oh, please do not!' she exclaimed, a little angry, shocked and sad.[2]

And as the days pass, she becomes aware, with a sense of actual danger, for marriage was then forever, that she might be growing to hate her husband.

In her London adventure we saw a first collapse due to excessive self-absorption and a recoil into the opposite too extreme to be maintained. The crisis that comes to her now is exactly the same, but, as with a spiral rather than a circle, it repeats itself on a higher level. It has come to a Miriam less simply passionate, more mature, more capable of accepting a solution which is real—that is, limited. Her salvation this time will go deep. And it will last.

The man who is to help her grasp her final lesson enters the narrative at exactly this moment of danger: it is Mr. Armstrong, the vicar of a near-by parish, whom she meets on a walk. And it need not be supposed that I am pushing the parallel with *The Counterfeiters* too far when I suggest that Mr. Armstrong is Miriam's version of the angel that appeared to Bernard. It is true that Gide's angel symbolizes something internal, but his purpose is to dislodge the self from the

---

[1] *Ibid.*, p. 130. [2] *Ibid.*

M

centre of the young protagonist's universe. And this is exactly the role of the good vicar. Bernard's problem is, in a sense, that of a worthwhile career: Miriam's is more generally human. And so Mr. Armstrong is to substitute for self (it is only, of course, a matter of emphasis) not merely other people but the whole of outer reality which contains them, the universe, in short, and its ineluctable laws, in obedience to which alone man can find true freedom and lasting peace. This is the lesson of reality—but it is also religious: 'In His will,' said Dante, 'is our peace.'

For though Mr. Armstrong is an ordinary parson in most respects, he is distinguished by a passion for astronomy, and has even turned his church tower into an observatory. This scandalizes one pious soul, who complains to the vicar's servant that a church is 'consecrated to the service of God.' The simple man replies: 'Ah! how do you know? Very likely o' nights—for he's up there when you're abed and asleep —he's looking into heaven through that there glass, and sees God and the blessed angels.'[1] The good woman is astonished at the ignorance of the lower classes, who do not know God is a 'Spirit,' but it happens that the servant is more right than she. For, as Spinoza taught, the study of Nature is precisely the study of God, and Mr. Armstrong's most certain knowledge of His character and His will is gained precisely at his telescope.

To this mode of knowledge Miriam is now introduced by a peep through a little telescope which Mr. Armstrong is carrying. And it is significant that he introduces her at the same time to her husband, of whom—as an individual in his own right rather than as an appendage to her—she still knows nothing. Mr. Farrow has made the telescope's case, and the vicar surprises her by the fervour of his admiration for her husband's craftsmanship. There were no short-cuts in the work which would later show up as invalidating defects. With this modest observation is revealed the true basis of her husband's 'unromantic' cheerfulness and placidity. His skill at his work is a willingness to abide by the laws of reality rather than to grasp at satisfactions in defiance of them. Thus solidly based, he is not tormented like Miriam by yearnings impossible to fulfil. All that we see of him—and his skill—hereafter will bear out this first hint.

[1] *Miriam's Schooling*, p. 137.

On the vicar's invitation, Miriam and her husband visit his observatory one evening. And as the observatory is in a church, and its telescope is to teach them the lessons of heaven, is not the preliminary lecture he gives them with the ardour of an enthusiast a sermon—and perhaps a more truly 'religious' one than the uninterested mechanical sermons he delivers on Sundays? His ardour is all for the sufficiently marvellous realities of the stars, not their poetic associations or the dreams they evoke of 'what is beyond and beyond and beyond and all that nonsense.'[1] For: 'To understand is the great thing, not to gape,'[2] he says in a speech reminiscent of the butterfly-catcher of *The Autobiography*. And: 'The great beauty of astronomy is not what is incomprehensible in it, but its comprehensibility—its geometrical exactitude.'[3]

Didymus, who grasps the vicar's first lesson at once, though Miriam does not, constructs for her a model solar system, and when he shows it to her, all grows suddenly clear. 'Really, how clever you are!'[4] she exclaims, while her husband is surprised at the praise, so much involved in doing that he had never paused to regard himself. Henceforth, 'the firmament, instead of being a mere muddle—beautiful, indeed, she had always thought it—had a plan in it.'[5] That the Reverend Mr. Bradshaw thought the same need hardly be emphasized. The lesson's ultimate implications are later also made clear to her. She learns 'that the earth . . . was the merest speck of dust in the universe.'[6] Did not Job hear much the same thing out of the whirlwind: that he and his desires are not the sole preoccupation of the Divine, who makes it rain 'where no man is'? And we are told that Miriam 'owed her initiation to Mr. Armstrong, but also to her husband.'[7]

At the vicar's request Didymus next begins to build a large orrery, which will show the stars and the earth in motion. Miriam is interested in the work, but wants no rehearsals which will diminish her pleasure in its first dramatic start into life. She is one of those who seek to enjoy results without the labour which must precede. Her

[1] *Ibid.*, p. 141.   [2] *Ibid.*, p. 140.
[3] *Ibid.*, p. 141.   [4] *Ibid.*, p. 143.
[5] *Ibid.*, pp. 143-4.   [6] *Ibid.*, p. 148.
[7] *Ibid.*, p. 144.

husband, however, spends as much time in perfecting the orrery with sandpaper and file as he has done in building it.

Miriam learned something when she saw that a wheel whose revolution was not in a perfect plane could give rise to so much annoyance, and she learned something also when she saw how her husband, in the true spirit of a genuine craftsman, remained discontented if there was the slightest looseness in a bearing.

'Do you think it matters?' said she.

'Matters! Don't you see that if it goes on it gets worse? Every wobble increases the next, and not only so, it sets the whole thing wobbling.'[1]

When it is done, the orrery works perfectly—except for a moment when a harder lesson still is presented them: that danger lies everywhere, even in the struggle for perfect safety. The machine stops because of a tiny shaving caught in a cog. 'The nicety of his own handicraft was the cause of the disaster.'[2] It is soon removed, and all is well. 'Strange,' says her husband with a smile, 'that such a chip as that should upset the whole solar system.'[3]

Needless to say, such remarks, like every detail of this episode, are far less innocent than they seem. What Miriam is being taught—and by science itself, religion's supposed enemy—is the great truth at the heart of religion, that of the interrelationship of man and the universe, and the necessity of accepting one's place as an element in that whole, whose laws we must obey or be punished. Moreover, does not the final detail of the chip suggest the Calvinist idea—which is perhaps a 'contradiction' of the other—that without 'grace' even virtue will be unavailing, that though it is best to do right, life is so complex that we must be ready to find that sometimes all our virtue makes no difference?

It is not to be supposed that Miriam is instantly 'saved' by these lessons. The process is gradual and the gap between her inner life and reality continues to bring her pain. One wet and dreary day she has a talk with the town man of all work, Mr. Fitchew, an ignorant

---

[1] *Miriam's Schooling*, p. 146.   [2] *Ibid.*, p. 147.
[3] *Ibid.*

stubborn man, 'one of the honestest souls in the place. . . . His literature was Cowfold, the people, the animals, the inanimate objects of which it was made up, and his criticism on these was often just.' [1] He attends neither church nor chapel, and the Dissenting Sunday School superintendent compares this to a refusal to take orders on a ship from the captain who understands navigation. But, as we easily gather, that 'literature' he has studied has taught him navigation enough for his own needs. We are further informed that 'he was afflicted with a kind of nervous dyspepsia, not infrequent even among the poor, and it kept him awake at night and gave him the "horrors."' [2] Miriam's talk with him is her final lesson within the compass of the story. He tells her of his terrible nights, and how his 'missis' lay stolidly sleeping, while 'I could have druv my head agin the door-post.' [3] His missis is a person who knows nothing of 'horrors,' but who does what must be done in their life unemotionally and without palaver. Looking thus from outside at a situation much like her own, Miriam can see that it is just as well his wife is what she is. And after a moment's thought, he too agrees. 'If she was allus aslaverin' on me and apityin' me it wouldn't do me no good; and then we are as we are, and we must make the best of it.' A simple statement, but comment should no longer be needed to indicate how much Hale White's simplicity contains. Though it continued to rain all night, the rain was over when she rose at four the next morning, and instead there streamed through her window a fresh south-west wind, 'the bearer inland even as far as Cowfold of Atlantic vitality, dissipating fogs, disinfecting poisons—the Life-Giver.' And here is the end of *Miriam's Schooling*:

She put on her clothes silently, went downstairs and opened the back-door. . . . Not a soul was to be seen, and she went on undisturbed till she came to her favourite spot where she had first met Mr. Armstrong. She paced about for a little while, and then sat down and . . . watched the dawn. It was not a clear sky but barred toward the east with cloud, the rain-cloud of the night. She watched and watched and thought after her fashion, mostly with incoherence, but

[1] *Ibid.*, pp. 149-50.   [2] *Ibid.*, p. 151.
[3] *Ibid.*

with rapidity and intensity. At last came the first flush of scarlet upon the bars, and *the dead storm contributed its own share to the growing beauty.* [Italics mine.] The rooks were now astir, and flew, one after the other, in an irregular line eastwards black against the sky. Still the colour spread, until at last it began to rise into pure light, and in a moment more the first glowing point of the disc was above the horizon. Miriam fell on her knees against the little seat and sobbed, and [her] dog, wondering, came and sat by her and licked her face with tender pity. Presently she recovered, rose, went home, let herself in softly before her husband was downstairs, and prepared the breakfast. He soon appeared, was in the best of spirits, and laughed at her being able to leave the room without waking him. She looked happy, but was rather quiet at their meal; and after he had caressed the cat for a little while, he pitched her, as he had done before, on Miriam's lap. She was about to get up to cut some bread and butter, and she went behind him and kissed the top of his head. He turned round, his eyes sparkling, and tried to lay hold of her, but she stepped backward and eluded him. He mused a little, and when she sat down he said in a tone which for him was strangely serious—

'Thank you, my dear; that was very, very sweet.'[1]

What Miriam's schooling has taught her is the price of living among counterfeits fashioned by selfish desire and the reward of accepting reality. That price is constant disappointment as the real breaks through and a freezing isolation from others who remain stubbornly themselves. This reward is not the imagined bliss of absolute fulfilment of desire—which calls for a Heaven—it is freedom from suffering, and then the gradual awakening to the value of the real, a value, which, because it is other than ourselves, is full of that novelty which teaches us and helps us grow. It is a reward not easy to retain. Being actual, it involves constant struggle: oneself must change, for the problem never does. So, at the very end, her husband again throws that cat into her lap, a playfulness that had made her once 'a little angry, shocked and sad.' This time, however, her focus has changed from self and its dreams to him, and the kiss with which she now responds, another 'slight' detail like so many of

[1] *Miriam's Schooling*, pp. 153-4.

those of which her story is made, is yet its fitting close. It is the final sign of Miriam's reconciliation with reality—that is, with God.

The volume containing *Miriam's Schooling* opens with three monologues based on the Bible, whose wealth of meaning is veiled by their author's characteristic modesty and reticence of treatment. In the first, Jotham tells his children of the achievements of their grandfather, Gideon; in the second we hear from Samuel an expanded version of the self-justification he offered at Ramah; and in the third, Saul's Horite wife, Rizpah, passionately justifies her husband against his two enemies, Samuel, the priest, and David, the leaping dancing adulterer, who 'turned everything into songs.'[1] Each monologue sticks to the Biblical tale with the same self-effacing fidelity to the subject that Hale White was later to show in his critical writings. As a result, certain readers have asked, with regard to both, what the writer has himself contributed. These readers have been too hasty. For in fact Hale White's gifts are as evident in such work as in his own stories; but they are exerted not in covert self-glorification but in 'bringing out' what lies at the bottom of his subject. This means often a kind of recapitulation, but one full of those slight emphases, expansions, arrangements which suddenly fill with meaning what had been opaque. And where passion is involved, that same passion is evoked again, and the result, as everywhere in Hale White, is beauty, however modest its dress.

Before we take our necessarily brief glance at these stories (a whole chapter could be spent on them with profit), it will be useful to make clear how their author read the Bible and what he found in it. For, as I have said, it remained for him, as for so many in the nineteenth century who were equally 'emancipated' from dogma, almost as important as it had been for their devout forebears. He read and re-read it all his life, finding it always richer, and the effect of such reading is naturally to be found everywhere in his work. But he has himself explained how he read it and what he found in it. 'The reason why the Bible remains outside us,' he once remarked to his wife, 'and has so little effect on us is that we do not translate or adapt it. . . . It is a mistake to suppose that the Bible is exclusively a religious book.'[2] It is not a 'religious' book in the sense that it is not a mere anthology

[1] *Ibid.*, p. 43.   [2] *The Groombridge Diary*, p. 313.

of dogmas, of supernatural rewards and punishments and of miraculous history requiring simple unintelligent acceptance. On the contrary, as he has said elsewhere, those who can 'translate' will find that 'the surviving vitality of the Old Testament [and we know he means also the New] lies in the continual recurrence in our own lives of its histories and circumstances';[1] and that 'the symbolism of many of [its] stories . . . is natural, not arbitrary or accidental. They are the vesture of ideas.'[2] Here is a passage from a letter written in 1898 which beautifully explains his relationship to the Bible and what he felt to be most important in it, and which will shed light on all he ever wrote of it.

I told you I was reading the Bible, with the invaluable help of Kautsch's translation. I have now finished the Old Testament. Nothing for years has been so profitable to me, or perhaps it would be more correct to say, has so quickened me. Association has much to do with this. Brought up on the Bible as I was, and as you were, its words are the accredited messengers of so much, which, if it has been revealed to others, has not been revealed in that way, and lacks the peculiar authority and sacredness with which we invest it. If you ask me whether the O.T. is a religious book, I hardly know what to answer. In its absolute, terrible sincerity—yes; in the astonishing purity of the prophetic morality—yes; in the equally astonishing conception of a *one* God to whom justice and all that we call right are dear—yes. Chemosh, it is true, is acknowledged as the God of the Moabites; Jehovah's power does not extend beyond Palestine, but yet he is superior to all his rivals and 'he made the heavens.' This thought, for which we have to thank the Hebrews, that He who 'made the heavens' is just and demands justice between men; that He also demands the supremacy of the best in us and not the worst, is perhaps the greatest that ever entered the human brain. 'Seek him' (says Amos) 'that maketh the Pleiades and Orion.' Is not that magnificent? But the series of treatises which we bind together as the O.T. is certainly not religious in the sense that it contains any answer what-

---

[1] *Last Pages*, p. 114.
[2] W. H. White, *John Bunyan*, London, Edinburgh, and New York, Thomas Nelson and Sons, Ltd., undated, p. 25.

ever to the questions which most disturb us modern folk. The immortality of the soul is not only not taught, but its necessity is not
felt. The Psalmist cries:

> I am a sojourner in the earth;
> Hide not thy commandments from me.

Man desires to live according to God's law, although in a few short
years he will be with the dead who praise not God. No doubt the
Jew believed that Jehovah rewarded obedience by temporal prosperity, but it is quite impossible to read the Bible fairly and assign
temporal prosperity as the sole motive for piety. This attitude is
completely strange and foreign to us. . . .[1]

   The three Biblical characters, then, whose stories he illuminat-
ingly retells, emerge as far more than themselves. He shows them
to be representative of three eternally recurring human types.
Gideon, who was called from his father's humble farm to lead the
overthrow of the Midianites, who forever doubted his election,
demanding signs to confirm it (the sheepskin, dry and wet, etc.),
who made a monument out of the gold of captured Midianite ear-
rings which was to be a record of what God had done, but which
came instead to be worshipped as an idol, and who, now that he has
been dead a generation, seems to his son to have lived in vain—this
Gideon should not be hard to recognize. He is the 'hero' who leads
forward the race by means of a gift which must struggle against his
own fears and weakness. His milestones and records become idols
to the foolish multitude (their very meaning thus contradicted) and
he may often seem to have lived in vain because his immediate goals
are not reached. Such immediate 'futility,' however, has frequently
proved to be something else—for God's time is not ours. Thus the
monologue, which concludes in a burst of despair that Gideon's effort
should 'end in nothing,' is followed without comment by two brief
quotations. The first is headed 'Fourteen Hundred Years Later' and
comes from the Epistle to the Romans: 'The time would fail me to
tell of Gideon . . . who through faith . . . out of weakness was made
strong, waxed valiant in fight, turned to flight the armies of the

---

[1] *Letters*, pp. 176-8.

aliens.' And the second is headed 'Three Thousand Years Later' and comes from Scott's *Old Mortality*: '"The sword of the Lord, and of Gideon," answered Balfour as he parried and returned the blow.' [1] So living has been Gideon's struggle and his son's despair that this sudden vista of a glory extending even to three thousand years is thrilling.

Samuel and Saul represent types eternally opposed. The first is the priest of God, whose function it is to perceive and preserve God's Law. This Law, maintained by Samuel in all its 'astonishing purity,' seems a burden to the Jews; but it is their safeguard: 'it was the Law which marked them off from the heathen, who were doomed to fall by their sins.' [2] For Law, may we not read any principles (though the justice of the Jews is the highest) by which the man who is faithful to them outwits the weaknesses and temptations of his humanity and accomplishes his higher purposes? Saul, on the other hand, for all his respect for the Law, is always ready, at the crucial moment, to place 'human' considerations—convenience, kindness—before it. For instance, in a time of danger he does not wait for Samuel to give the pre-battle sacrifice, though it is the office of the priest, but does it himself, so he can attack the enemy. And when God, through Samuel, demands the enemy's total slaughter, he is too soft-hearted and leaves some alive. For such transgressions, Samuel dooms him and gives his crown to David, and in spite of all Saul's victories, Samuel is right. For 'if Israel is to live, it will not be because Saul overcame the Amalekites and the Philistines, but because the lamp of God in my hands has not been extinguished.' [3] That is, it is not a few victories that count in a long struggle but the ability to abide by principles. The crown goes to David because, though he is a sinner, he 'belongs to us; he fears the Lord and his prophets; he may go a-whoring, but it will not be after Baal.' [4] He may break some rules that are *humanly* important, in other words, but he will be faithful to the essential principles of the great task, the Law of God and his prophets, which is the peculiar burden and glory of the Jews, which distinguishes them from the heathen, and which will preserve them.

It is a wonderful stroke that Saul is defended in the last monologue

---

[1] 'Gideon,' *Miriam's Schooling*.
[2] 'Samuel,' *Miriam's Schooling*.
[3] *Ibid.*
[4] *Ibid.*

by his heathen wife. For to be a heathen is to be outside the Law, that is, to be a creature of passion, of 'humanity,' neither constrained nor ennobled by allegiance to principles. Sure enough, her monologue is a cry of passion, of sensuality, even, which she places above all laws, and with which Hale White clearly and strikingly sympathizes.

Rizpah resents the inflexibility of the Jewish God. 'Would you or I deal so with our friends?' she asks, '. . . would we let the penalty endure when the heart is changed and forgiveness is sought?'[1] Here, perhaps, some of us will have no difficulty in calling her wholly wrong, for the divine, the *real*, is not humane. But she is perhaps less wholly wrong when she hints that Samuel's zeal for the Law is only jealousy for his own authority as priest. For Hale White—like Gide—is sufficiently aware of the mixture of human motives to have intended this accusation to be heard with respect. It may be partly true. The fact remains, however, that only a 'heathen' would be so eager to discredit the noble motive, to reduce it entirely to its 'human' ingredient, for she is herself incapable of that aspiration by which the human transcends itself.

I have sketched the basic types delineated in these Bible stories, but it should be mentioned, too, that every one of the familiar Biblical details is shown in meaningful relation with character and fate and therefore contribute to the underlying themes. The reader will perhaps be reminded by this of Gide's treatment of such material. For here, indeed, is another similarity between our two writers. Both see myth as complex many sided symbol and both rewrite it with such continuous meaningfulness and such economy (content merely to present the symbolic detail—not to explain it), that every reading teaches one more.

A word, in conclusion, about the fourth short item in the volume. This is a story called 'Michael Trevanion'—another study of Puritanism like that of *The Revolution in Tanner's Lane*. An intensely devout father consents to lie—and thereby to damn himself eternally—in order to save his beloved son from marriage to a girl who is not, he feels, among the Lord's chosen. (His passion for his son is such, moreover, that we are led to suspect a less noble motive, that is, simple

[1] 'Saul,' *Miriam's Schooling*.

jealous possessiveness.) Having slandered the girl, he finds that he was wrong, that in fact she is good and at least as surely the Lord's as he himself had been. He has been guilty of sin, not only in slandering her but in presuming to know God's judgment of another. He ends in a new uncertainty and humility. The story's intellectual interest lies in its vivid and subtle picture of the Puritan mind, of which *every* impulse—evil as well as good—can find expression in its religion. That religion is shown to be a rich symbolic language, not really more limiting than any other; what it will express, as is the case with every language, is limited only by the user's character and intelligence. And the story's beauty and power, which are considerable, come from its nakedly direct account of two passions, that of the father for the son and that of the son for his sweetheart. Where the concern with Puritanism might for some readers slow the story down or cool it off—for it is often analysed explicitly—the passion, which is evoked with all Hale White's usual intensity, beautifully restores speed and heat—and leaves the final impression.

CHAPTER IX

Catherine Furze

Catherine Furze, published in 1893, is perhaps the loveliest of Hale White's novels. It has a quality of summer noon, of ripeness and ease. It is leisurely, but never slow, full, but without superfluity. The author seems not only to be following out his theme but to be sharing deliberately a rich harvest of memories and reflections. Hence the solidity of Catherine's world: the society of Easthorpe (which is another version of Bedford at the time of Hale White's youth), and the beautiful countryside round about. Hence, too, something newly relaxed and complete in his comments on what takes place, these providing more than ever an atmosphere of wisdom, grave or ironic, which strengthens every other effect and adds a beauty of its own.

The novel is about love. But once again it must be said that Hale White's exploration of his subject goes far deeper than meets the casual eye, that his directness, clarity and readability are deceptive, and that his comments, explaining so much, never explain the whole. For this the whole novel must be kept in mind and alertness maintained to the most delicate hints. That such requirements have not often been met is indicated by the frequency with which a certain climactic scene has been regarded as a *non sequitur* and patronized accordingly. What has puzzled is the sudden break through the narrative surface of the novel's chief meanings, which were intended by then to be familiar. Indeed, they might have been familiar for the additional reason that they have occurred in Hale White before, his earlier works being full of clues to what is now for the first time in the centre of the picture. Let us take a preliminary glance at these meanings, then, in order that we may proceed through the novel itself with open eyes.

To say that the novel is about love is only a beginning. It is actually about love as an agent, as an agent of spiritual awakening. It is a story of 'conversion,' as it used to be called in the Christian sects—and the reader will find that for all its 'modern' psychological realism the heroine's adventure duplicates every essential feature of those old-fashioned religious transformations. For what were they in essence? They were a sudden awakening to the reality of that division preached by St. Paul between the higher and lower, spirit and flesh, good and evil, a division which Hale White in the *Deliverance* called 'the world's salvation.'[1] And the convert is saved by rejecting the evil, which meant above all his own selfish sinful self, and passionately embracing, in the person of Christ, the good. This describes exactly, though some of the terms must be taken as symbolic, what happens in the novel. That Hale White does indeed want us to relate his heroine's spiritual awakening through love to the religious experience is indicated by a real old-fashioned conversion which the book also contains. The sudden transformation of 'Orkid' Jim has seemed melodramatic and unconvincing to many 'realists' among Hale White's readers, in spite of the author's insistence that such things did used to happen, but what they have failed to notice is that it is a deliberate repetition, on a different level, of the change of Catherine, which constitutes, in a way, its proof. It is true, of course, that conversions like Jim's have been made rare by the weakening hold on men's minds of formal religion; but this means only that the process now takes place in other ways. 'Be sure,' says the Reverend Mr. Cardew, 'that He will come to you in a shape in which it will not be easy to recognize Him.'[2] And when the drama has been fulfilled—in that scene regarded as a *non sequitur*— this beautiful sentence formulates what has happened: 'The disguises are manifold which the Immortal Son assumes in the work of our redemption.'[3]

It is not due to any exigency of story-telling that the novel combines the subject of spiritual awakening with that of human love. Hale White has told us elsewhere that it is in love that the process of conversion is to be most clearly seen—proved there to be a reality

[1] *Deliverance*, chap. vi.
[2] W. H. White, *Catherine Furze*, London, T. Fisher Unwin, 1894, chap. vi.
[3] *Ibid.*, chap. xxi.

and not, as the simple materialist might think, a bit of religious magic or hypocrisy. The love for each other of man and woman is essentially physical, which means lawless and selfish. Yet, drawn by the physical, lovers tend to rise to something which is higher and to find easier than ever before the difficult moral act of denying themselves for another's happiness. And this link in the novel between human love and spiritual awakening carries us deeper still. For the mixture of spirit and flesh, of the divine and the human, which is found in love is also the distinguishing character of Christianity; it is in Christianity that love—love not for God as pure spirit but precisely for a flesh-and-blood embodiment of Him—came to the aid of a humanity engaged in the terribly difficult struggle to live by the Law. And thus we come finally to rock bottom: the novel's basic subject is the nature of Christianity.

Now the parallel between human love and Christianity extends itself to a certain ambiguity which they share. For the mixture that exists in each between spirit and flesh, between the law of righteousness and the claims of the human, means not only that the human in them is uplifted to the divine but that the divine is lowered to the human. Though love, for instance, can lead to spiritual-moral awakening, these are not necessarily the steps in a comfortable upward progress. In the human heart both aspects will generally coexist, will interpenetrate each other, so that the most earthly passion will contain that which lifts it 'above' the physical, and the most spiritual that which drags it 'down.' The novel dares to suggest that this latter possibility exists also in Christianity, that certain of its elements can lead to, or sanction, what is dangerous. To emphasize these elements is heresy, but it is a heresy that had actually occurred in England a generation before Hale White: the minister guilty of it was removed from his pulpit, and we shall come to evidence that Hale White had him in mind in creating the minister of the novel. But there will be even more conclusive evidence that this link between Christianity and human love, and the ambiguity they share, is its basic theme. It will be found in a little interpolated story written by the minister, a 'Gidian' device by which the novel's theme is repeated and made unmistakable.

The reader may already have recognized the novel of Gide which this resembles. Does not his *Symphonie Pastorale* also expose the dangerous sanctions which can be found in the Christian religion? The resemblance between the two novels is indeed strangely close: in both these sanctions are sought by Protestant ministers drunk with a forbidden love which they do not acknowledge even to themselves. So repulsive does this self-indulgent religion become to the pastor's son in Gide that the young man turns to Catholicism—that is, Gide implies, to another excess—to restrain himself by external authority. In Hale White's novel salvation, as well as danger, will come from within.

The lovers of the story are happily chosen to dramatize the tangle of spirit and flesh. First there is the girl of the title, the daughter of an Easthorpe ironmonger. The story opens with a picture of Easthorpe society, and then of the girl's parents: the father a simple-minded, easily bewildered man, the mother snobbish and selfish but apt at disguising these qualities, at least to herself, as virtues; and against such a background of honest and dishonest simplicity the figure of Catherine stands out in vivid contrast. For she is spiritual sister to all the other Hale White protagonists, met like the others before the test that will awaken and school her, and her sincerity, directness and intensity are rather a thorn in the flesh of her genteel mother.

Mrs. Furze, for instance, wants to move from their rooms behind the shop to a neighbourhood called the Terrace. The move is expensive and will be inconvenient for Mr. Furze, but, on the other hand, among the stucco homes of the Terrace dwell the brewer's family and other lights of Easthorpe society. Luckily for Mrs. Furze, their home burns down. In order to accomplish the move to the Terrace without Catherine's opposition, Mrs. Furze sends her away on a visit with a false idea of what is to be done in her absence. Her dishonesty, Hale White ironically remarks, is perhaps not quite lying, since in society we all agree to say things nobody believes, and a strict standard must not be applied. But:

Every now and then at rarest intervals a creature is introduced to us who speaks the veritable reality and wakes in us the slumbering conviction of universal imposture. We know that he is not as other men are; we look into his eyes and see that they penetrate us through and through, but we cannot help ourselves, and we jabber to him as we jabber to the rest of the world. It was ridiculous that her mother should talk as she did to Catherine. Mrs. Furze was perfectly aware that she was not deluding her daughter; but she assumed that the delusion was complete.[1]

Nor was it only the girl's honesty that was a nuisance. She had a lively sympathy for the suffering of others, and it was she who forced her father to assume responsibility when a workman was blinded at his forge and to hire the man's son Tom.

So far she is much like Miriam. But she has another quality which introduces a vital difference. She has strength—that is, she has a natural gift for self-discipline, for responding, at whatever cost to herself, to the call of a principle which has won her allegiance. This is so deeply inherent that it can operate without the intervention of the reason: she sometimes responds, as we shall see, without knowing why, and even against her will. On the whole, however, this quality is bound up with the inability to deceive herself—that is, with clarity of mind. And it is interesting that her record at school is exactly the reverse of Miriam's, for she is weak in history and exceptional in arithmetic and geometry.

Now Catherine has had no contact with books or with a religion that touched her personally, those two sources in Hale White of aspiration and trouble. It is therefore no restlessness of her own, but rather her mother's impatience with her irritating virtues, that sends her out to meet her fate. One day, having lured the brewer's wife— a detestable snob—to visit her at the new house, Mrs. Furze is dismayed to see that Catherine treats the woman coldly, but jumps up in delight to welcome a certain much-loved farmer's wife who drops in at the same time. This is the last straw, and Catherine is sent away to school to be 'finished.'

The school, run by two Calvinist spinsters, is an innocuous place, but it has one distinction: the religious instruction is given by a remarkably talented minister. On her first Sunday there Catherine attends Mr. Cardew's service with the rest of the school, and she finds him a man of about thirty-five, 'with curved lips, which were, how-

[1] *Catherine Furze*, chap. iii.

ever, compressed as if with determination or downright resolution.'[1]
He resembled a portrait she had once seen of Edward Irving. Each
of these details is a hint, though one may not fully know of what
until the story is told. Curving lips, of course, traditionally suggest a
temperament which is passionate and self-indulgent, their compression the struggle against such tendencies by conscious principles.
But the resemblance to Irving is even more revealing. For Irving was
a Scottish minister who was unusually eloquent and popular but who
in 1830, four years before his death, was expelled from the ministry.
Among his dangerous views was that of Christ's identity with man
in all his characteristics, even—or so ran the accusation—in His
liability to sin. Nor is this all. There was, besides, a painful romantic
episode in Irving's life, an episode in which the 'human,' not to say
the sinful, rose up against the law, in the form of a binding obligation to another. At a time when he was engaged to someone else, he
fell in love with Jane Welch, later Mrs. Carlyle. He asked his fiancée's
family for a release, but was refused. Was there a connection between
such a tendency to the inconvenient surge of passion and such
religious heresies? With regard to the real minister we cannot be
certain, but we will be in no doubt with regard to the fictional.

The reader has seen enough of Hale White's conscious artistry to
need no assurance that Mr. Cardew's first sermon, given almost
entire as it is, will bear a significant relation to the novel's theme. The
minister presents the girl with her first experience of religion as a
language for truths that touch the inmost heart, that can change one's
view of self and the world, and thereby one's whole life. And still
firm and untempted, he is still inwardly free to emphasize the great
law in his religion which draws man 'upward,' rather than the
human indulgence it has for unlawful weakness. His text is from
Luke xviii, 18 to 22, the words of Jesus to the 'ruler' that he sell all
he has, give the money to the poor and follow Him. And like
another Mr. Bradshaw showing us how exciting and meaningful a
sermon can be, 'Mr. Cardew did not approach his theme circuitously
or indifferently, but seemed in haste to be on close terms with it, as
if it had dwelt with him and he was eager to deliver his message.'[2]
His message will be familiar to us: it is Hale White's view of the

---

[1] *Catherine Furze*, chap. vi.   [2] *Ibid.*

essential saving truth of Christianity. Christ, he says, is the supreme standard offered to man to save him from the chaos of possibilities suggested from within him and without. But if we would be saved by Christ, if we would really live by His standard, we must 'sell all.' 'The surrender must be absolute. . . . Sell not only your property, but your very self. Part with all your preferences, your loves, your thoughts, your very soul, if only you can gain Him.'[1] Thus we see Mr. Cardew expounding as *idea* that self-surrender which his fate will soon make a real anguish, and far more difficult than he knows. And his closing words also contain a meaning which will be directed ironically against himself. 'Be sure too that He will come to you in a shape in which it will not be easy to recognize Him.'[2]

But now, here is the effect of the sermon on Catherine:

Whether it was the preacher's personality, or what he said, Catherine could hardly distinguish, but she was profoundly moved. [Note again the 'mixture,' which continually recurs.] Such speaking was altogether new to her; the world in which Mr. Cardew moved was one which she had never entered, and yet it seemed to her as if something necessary and familiar to her, but long lost, had been restored. She began now to look forward to Sunday with intense expectation; a new motive for life was supplied to her, and a new force urged her through each day. It was with her as we can imagine it to be with some bud long folded in darkness which, silently in the dewy May night, loosens its leaves, and, as the sun rises, bares itself to the depths of its cup to the blue sky and the light.[3]

Her awakening, the 'conversion' by which she is to be 'saved,' has begun.

Mr. Cardew notices Catherine for the first time a month later during one of the regular Monday morning examinations on his sermon of the day before. He has again preached on that 'dualism.' His text has been: 'So then with the mind I myself serve the law of God, but with the flesh the law of sin.' Now he asks the class to remember how he interpreted 'the body of this death,' from which Paul had longed to be delivered. One student (speaking, one may

---

[1] *Ibid.*   [2] *Ibid.*   [3] *Ibid.*

suppose, for worldliness) is significantly wrong: she says, 'The death of this body.' But his teaching has not been lost on Catherine. She says: 'This body of death.' And, her voice trembling (as the voice does when an intimate thought is made public), she explains, 'He opposes the two natures in him by the strongest words at his command—death and life. One *is* death, the other *is* life, and he prays to be delivered from death, not the death of the body, but from death-in-life.'[1] This is the definition of salvation which must be remembered when her fate is achieved.

It is an irony which is at the heart of the theme, that though they are brought together by such a revelation of the moral law, the very sensibility that makes it live for them also sweeps them rapidly to a state of danger. They meet again when Mr. and Mrs. Cardew come to tea at the school. He asks her about her reading and they talk of Dr. Johnson. Their words are few, but they contain that electricity of self-revelation and mutual recognition which so often makes thrilling the most casual exchange between articulate people of mind. Mrs. Cardew, alas, is not one of these. She thinks and feels—and deeply, too—but not quickly, and not in ways she can easily express. There is no trace of the *artist* in her make-up, and for this her husband cannot forgive her, in spite of all her virtues. At tea, her plain, though really sensible remarks (remarks offered, moreover, to help him through an awkward silence which followed one of his), only irritate him. For he, it becomes clear, is one of Hale White's dream-rapt intellectuals, so lost in his book-nourished inner life that the claims and values of reality have grown dim. He can be as cruel to his wife as M'Kay was to his, cruel enough to bring tears. 'He pitied her but he pitied himself more, and though her tears wrought on him sufficiently to prevent any further cruelty, he did not repent.'[2] When later, at her husband's suggestion, she tries to read *Paradise Lost*, asking Catherine to help her because she has heard him praise the girl's mind, he is vexed at her very obedience. And the poetry serves only to awaken the minister and Catherine even more to their exciting affinity.

It is on this occasion that danger first appears. After the talk about Milton, he takes advantage of an intoxicating moment alone with

[1] *Catherine Furze*, chap. vii.   [2] *Ibid.*

Catherine in the garden to confess his longing for intellectual sympathy, something for which he has in Eastthorpe been starved. As they stroll, she stumbles, and he holds her hand a second longer than necessary. 'To Catherine it seemed as if she were being sucked in by a whirlpool and carried she knew not whither.'[1] There is a moment when she returns his hand's tightening pressure. Then: 'Suddenly something passed through her brain, swift as the flash of the swiftest blazing meteor.'[2] Instantly she drops his hand and goes back to the house. And when Mrs. Cardew asks for her a moment later, he answers, 'I suppose she is indoors.'

Two and a half pages of comment follow on the behaviour of each, comment which is not only of the most wonderful wisdom but of the utmost relevance to the theme. 'A canting hypocritical parson type not uncommon,' Hale White supposes the reader to be saying, 'described over and over again in novels and thoroughly familiar to theatregoers.'[3] But the sincerity of David's psalms, for instance, need not be discredited because of his adultery.

The man was inconsistent, it is true, inconsistent exactly because there was so much in him that was great, for which let us be thankful. Let us take notice, too, of what lies side by side quietly in our own souls. God help us if all that is good in us is to be invalidated by the presence of the most contradictory evil.[4]

Moreover, the virtues themselves derive their energy from what can also lead to crime, for 'it is a fact that vitality means passion.'[5]

As for Catherine's escape, the author is vexed that a complicated process should offer so little to show. But:

The antagonistic and fiercely combatant forces did *so* issue in that deed, and the present historian has no intention to attempt an anlysis. One thing is clear to him, that the quick stride up the garden path was urged not by any single, easily predominating impulse which had been enabled to annihilate all others. Do not those of us, who have been mercifully prevented from damning ourselves before the whole world, who have succeeded and triumphed—do we not

[1] *Ibid.*, chap. viii.   [2] *Ibid.*   [3] *Ibid.*
[4] *Ibid.*   [5] *Ibid.*

know, know as we know hardly anything else, that our success and our triumph were due to superiority in strength by just a grain, no more, of our better self over the raging rebellion beneath it? It was just a tremble of the tongue of the balance: it might have gone this way, or it might have gone the other, but by God's grace it was this way settled—God's grace, as surely, in some form of words, every-body must acknowledge it to have been.[1]

And back in her bedroom she cursed herself, 'prayed for strength to resist temptation, and longed for one more chance of yielding to it.'[2]

It is at this most appropriate moment in the novel, a moment when the struggle of higher and lower, flesh and spirit, has thus nakedly disclosed itself, that we read, along with Catherine, a story the minister has written on what turns out to be the same theme. He had mentioned it to her in the garden and has offered it to her as to the one person worthy of the trust. Its title is 'Did he Believe?' and it tells of the conversion to Christianity of Charmides, a Grecian sculptor, living in Rome about A.D. 300.

Charmides is described as one whose own nature, whose delight in art and philosophy, and whose reading of Plato, have taught him that man has a self higher and better than his sensual self. He feels that art embodies Divine ideas and even that beauty is a form of virtue, and this feeling is confirmed by the way every descent into debauchery seems to cut him off from his work. Roman culture of that day did not share such views. It opposed them not only by its licentiousness but by that deadly question of the Sophists: 'What is there in it?' a question which paralysed the struggle against self-indulgence and set man's noblest faculty, his reason, to making him worse than a beast. As for the religion of the Hebrews, of which he had heard, it all sounded repulsively barbaric and retrograde to such a lover of Greek philosophy, though there was a new sect which seemed a trifle more congenial.

One day, out of curiosity, he attends an illicit Christian meeting. The letters of a certain Paul, which he hears read, are 'Hebrew' to him, but a Greek slave-girl he meets there helps him to understand a little better. Having fallen among Christians, she has 'by God's

[1] *Catherine Furze*, chap. viii.   [2] *Ibid.*

grace' become convinced of sin and of the necessity of establishing God's kingdom within her. This she has done through faith in Christ. And she gives Charmides the story of Christ's life to read. This, too, seems 'rude' compared to the writings on which he has been nurtured. 'The girl's face, however, recurred to him: he could not get rid of it and he opened the biography again.'[1] Thus led by the physical, he finds what is 'higher.' This time he stumbles on the 23rd and 24th chapters of Matthew, and suddenly he realizes that in cursing the Pharisees for lack of mercy, etc., that is, for moral evil, the author has given a new centre, a new pivot, to society. From that moment the Christian philosophy grows more and more attractive to him. Its intellectual charm, however, would not alone have been enough to make him a Christian, for he can never quite accept what seems its complete break with his own culture. What enables him to take the leap is his love for the girl. This love is as different from any he has known, as she, enraptured with her faith, is different from other women. 'It was the new love with which men were henceforth to love women—the love of Dante for Beatrice.'[2] When a meeting they attend is betrayed, the two of them are martyred together, she gazing toward heaven, he only at her. And it is on a kiss that he expends his last strength. At the end we read that 'Charmides was never considered a martyr by the Church. The circumstances were doubtful, and it was not altogether clear that he deserved the celestial crown.'[3]

The irony implied by such a close is the same as that of the story's title. How sincere is a religion in which so much human love and need are mixed? But of course the meaning is double. If the religious ideal has been adulterated by the human, the human has been ennobled by that ideal: his love for her is so different from the relations he has had with other women that it has led him to embrace a religion of self-sacrifice and even enabled him to die beside her without regret. This inevitable element of the human in the spiritual, an element which may be considered an impurity (and can even lead to crime), is exactly, as I have said, the central insight of the whole novel.

There is nothing like self-denial to sharpen desire. When Catherine

[1] *Ibid.* [2] *Ibid.* [3] *Ibid.*

and the minister meet again their danger has terribly increased. Catherine has gone home for the summer holidays to find her mother successful in dropping her old friends but still unable to attract those of the class above. She now attempts to use Catherine to draw the brewer's family through their silly son. The attempt is a failure, for the girl detests him. With such rivals, moreover, the image of Mr. Cardew glows brighter than ever in her mind. And then she meets the minister while walking in the country outside Eastthorpe. Cardew has become literally a man possessed: he has thought only of her since their last encounter. Their talk is of nothing, but as they talk, they are trembling. He gazes at her while she tears a lily to pieces. And we read next:

She loved this man; it was a perilous moment; one touch, a hair's breadth of oscillation, and the two would have been one. At such a crisis the least external disturbance is often decisive. The first note of the thunder was heard, and suddenly the image of Mrs. Cardew presented itself before Catherine's eyes, appealing to her piteously, tragically.[1]

Thus awakened by—heaven, Catherine bursts into passionate praise of Mrs. Cardew ('How I envy her! how I wish I had her brains for scientific subjects!')[2] and flees. Flees to pure suffering, to rage against her own folly, by which she had lost him: we are forbidden to suppose she has even the 'poor reward of conscience or duty,' for 'left to herself, she would have kept him.'[3] What does this mean? It means that conscience or duty as they ordinarily operate bring some satisfaction to the self, the pride of choosing the right, but what did she care for the pleasures of pride—her self was all in her love. The moral principle that forbade that love seemed the self's mere enemy, a source only of pain. If she was 'saved,' in short, it was indeed at the cost of that 'absolute surrender' of the self which Mr. Cardew had taught her was Christ's demand. Nor is the surrender complete even yet.

Much of the underlying theme, so far given only in hints, grows more explicit in the chapter of analysis that follows, though the

---

[1] *Catherine Furze*, chap. ix.   [2] *Ibid.*   [3] *Ibid.*

chapter can also be read as simple character study. Cardew, we learn, had married early and by one means or another been shielded from healthy intercourse with the outside world, living, with his religion and his books, an 'entirely interior life.'[1]

His self-communion produced one strange and perilous result, a habit of prolonged evolution from particular ideas uncorrected by reference to what was around him. If anything struck him, it remained with him, deduction followed deduction in practice unfortunately as well as in thought, and he was ultimately landed in absurdity or something worse. The wholesome influence of ordinary men and women never permits us to link conclusion to conclusion from a single premise, or at any rate to act upon our conclusions, but Mr. Cardew had no world at Abchurch save himself.[2]

Is this not a way of accounting for the dangerous heretical emphases into which an Irving, or, as we shall soon find, a Cardew, could fall, the result of following out one *self-gratifying* element in Christianity without the corrective of others which life's variety would have forced them to recognize? It is his inexperience, too, that has permitted Mr. Cardew's behaviour to Catherine. Intellectual sympathy between man and woman, we are told, necessarily contains something other than intellect, something sweeter. But the trouble with Mr. Cardew is that he does not distinguish, he literally does not know what is happening or when to stop.

As for Catherine, we are at last told plainly that she was not one of those whose lives are a 'simple progressive accumulation of experience,' but one who at the proper stimulus had suddenly opened, 'seen the world differently,' and begun to ask 'strange questions.' It was a kind of 'new birth' that is common during times of religious excitement, and two hundred years earlier 'all that was in her would have found expression in the faith of her ancestors, large enough for any intellect or any heart at that time.'[3] And

[1] *Ibid.*, chap. x.
[2] *Ibid.*
[3] *Ibid.* On this page, in this connection, Hale White makes a comment which may be worth quoting as a sample of his 'digressions'—or rather, of one kind, for

because it was through Mr. Cardew that 'the word was spoken to her, and he was the interpreter of the new world to her,' she loved him.

But what is love? There is no such thing: there are loves, and they are all different. Catherine's was the very life of all that was Catherine, senses, heart, and intellect, a summing-up and projection of her whole self-hood.[1]

And it is thus made explicit what the sacrifice of her love must mean.
     Mr. Cardew has spoken 'the word' to her which taught her the moral law, but now, in his drunkenness, he is to speak a word of another kind—a word impelled (though unconsciously) by dangerous desire and leading, as its first and immediate result, to

his digressions strike more than one note. He has told us of Catherine's impatience with the bars which prevent people from coming close to one another. 'Often she knew what it was to thirst like one in a desert for human intercourse, and she marvelled how those who pretended to care for her could stay away so long: she could have humiliated herself if only they would have permitted her to love them and be near them. Poor Catherine! the world as it is is no place for people so framed! When life runs high and takes a common form, men can walk together as the disciples walked on the road to Emmaus. Christian and Hopeful can pour out their hearts to one another as they travel towards the Celestial City and are knit together in everlasting bonds by the same Christ and the same salvation. But when each man is left to shift for himself, to work out the answers to his own problems, the result is isolation. People who, if they were believers, would find the richest gift of life in utter confidence and mutual help, are now necessarily strangers. One turns to metaphysics; another to science; one takes up with Rousseau's theory of existence, and another with Kant's; they meet; they have nothing to say; they are of no use to one another in trouble; one hears that the other is sick; what can be done? There is a nurse; he does not go; his old friend dies, and as to the funeral— well, we are liable to catch cold. Not so, Christian and Hopeful! for when Christian was troubled "with apparitions of hobgoblins and evil spirits, even on the border- land of Heaven—oh, Bunyan! Hopeful kept his brother's head above water, and called upon him to turn his eyes to the Gate and the men standing by it to receive him." My poor reader-friend, how many times have you in this nineteenth century, when the billows have gone over you—how many times have you felt the arm of man or woman under you, raising you to see the shining ones and the glory that is inexpressible?' (Note that Hale White's reader is 'my poor reader- friend.')

[1] *Catherine Furze*, chap. x.

crime. He preaches a sermon in Eastthorpe, which Catherine attends, and this time he speaks on the Prodigal Son. The parable is intended, he says, to show 'not the magnificence of the Divine nature, but of human nature—of that nature which God assumed.'[1] And this is shown not only in the son's beautiful decision to go back to his father and simply ask for forgiveness. 'The splendour of human nature—do not suppose any heresy here; it is Bible truth, the very gospel—is shown in the father as well as the son.'[2] That is, in that love which welcomed the longed-for sinner without a word of rebuke, but with kisses—'no matter what the wrong may have been. If you say this is dangerous doctrine, I say it is *here*. . . . Is it not moving—nay, awful—to think of all the good it has done, of the sweet stream of tenderness, broad and deep, which has flowed down from it through all history.'[3]

This is certainly true—so complex is life—but there follows at this moment a brief exchange between him and Catherine when they are alone after the sermon, an exchange we are significantly kept from overhearing. What was said, we are told, 'God and they only knew,'[4] but this we know: it sends Mr. Cardew to a certain deserted place near the river to wait for her to come to him. And since she *does* try to come, must we not suppose that she would now have been 'lost'— but for the 'accident' that prevented their meeting alone? For we have seen by how tiny a grain of her better self she had conquered once before the raging rebellion beneath. And now in place of that restraining lesson to 'sell all' for Christ, to seek deliverance from 'the body of this death,' she had in her mind that 'sweet stream of tenderness,' that promise of forgiveness, which worked on the side of desire. Mr. Cardew was unconscious of what he did—and yet he knew. Why else such vehement denial of heresy and danger? The suggestion contained in his resemblance to Irving has at last reached its dramatic fulfilment, for this is exactly the heresy of that other passionate minister. It is also exactly that of Gide's minister in *Symphonie Pastorale*, with his persistent dangerous glorification of love and joy—also with scriptural authority to support it.

The meeting—the assignation—does not take place. Catherine has

---

[1] *Ibid.*, chap. xii.   [2] *Ibid.*
[3] *Ibid.*   [4] *Ibid.*

hesitated for some reason, and when at last she approaches, she has been forestalled by Tom, the blinded workman's son. He too has fallen in love with her, and feeling the intellectual gulf between them, has followed Mr. Cardew to ask his advice. He does not leave the minister until the private meeting has grown impossible. 'Accident,' Hale White remarks. 'My friend Reuben told me the other day his marriage was an accident. The more I think about accidents the less I believe in them.'[1] And it is suggested that Catherine's hesitation, Tom's presence through his love for her, all such things compose a 'web' for which she *was* in fact responsible, a web that links her fate to her nature—makes it meaningful—in a way suspiciously like that which religion would maintain. We are thus given an acceptable modern form for what might once have been described as the rescue, long since earned from a just Providence, of one of God's chosen, who after due struggle has been carried beyond her strength.

Tom, intelligent and efficient, has come to be Mr. Furze's right hand at the shop, though the simple-minded boss hates to admit it. But having seen Tom escort Catherine home from that sermon, Mrs. Furze leaps to the conclusion that there is something between them, that Tom is responsible for Catherine's treatment of the brewer's son, and therefore for their social failure, and that they must get rid of him. Without ever admitting to herself what she is doing, she bribes a disreputable fellow-workman of Tom's named 'Orkid' (awkward) Jim to collect—or manufacture—evidence of Tom's dishonesty. This he does, and Tom leaves town in disgrace.

There are four people who believe in his honesty, in spite of the 'evidence': his father, Catherine, Mr. Cardew and Mrs. Furze's little maid Phoebe, who now quits her job in indignation. Catherine, however, does nothing. Perhaps there is nothing she can do, but she does not even try, and this is because of a strange 'collapse' that has taken place within her. All cheerfulness and energy have gone, she dreams on death, and 'terrors vague and misty possessed her.'[2] Before leaving, Tom made her an offer, which she refused, and this has 'brought it vividly before her that her life would be spent without love, or at least a love which could be acknowledged.'[3] It is this,

---

[1] *Catherine Furze*, chap. xii.   [2] *Ibid.*, chap. xvii.   [3] *Ibid.*

the thought that her life must lose what is sweetest, and worse still, her lack of any definite object for all her inner force, that is at the root of the general decline in her health which now shows itself. It becomes necessary at last to call a doctor.

Dr. Turnbull is one of the novel's finest portraits. He is a doctor of the kind Hale White had often longed for in vain, for though he is a materialist by philosophic conviction, denying the existence of that separate 'soap-bubble' called the soul, he is nevertheless 'the most spiritual man in the whole district.'[1] He is spiritual, the reader may conclude, as Spinoza was spiritual, in seeing spirit and matter as aspects of the same thing. He is therefore 'spiritual in his treatment of disease,'[2] his ideas foreshadowing those of modern psychosomatic medicine. Moreover, his general ideas have the strangest resemblance to the stern principles of Calvinism—to that content in them of reality, of which Hale White was so aware. In resentment at this sternness, when it is directed later at Mr. Cardew, Catherine once reflects that he simply does not understand passion, does not know what it is to have his pulse stirred. 'Pulse stirred!' Hale White remarks. 'The young are often unjust to the old in the matter of pulsation, and the world in general is unjust to those who prefer to be silent, or to whom silence is a duty.'[3] And we are told of a passionate episode in the doctor's life in which he took a course exactly opposite to the self-deceiving self-indulgent course of Mr. Cardew, sentencing himself to eternal separation from his beloved to save her from harm that would have come to her through him. His sternness, like that of Calvinism, is thus shown to be only the hard-won knowledge that self-conquest is necessary if the passions are not to become sources of anarchy and evil.

When Dr. Turnbull finds a weakness in Catherine's chest, 'her face lighted up.'[4] What this tells him, of course, is that here is a girl who does not want to live. He reminds her that when life has grown tasteless, one can at least be of use to others, and he mentions Phoebe, who, in the windswept shack of her poverty-stricken parents, is now dying of consumption. She goes to Phoebe and is with her when she dies. The picture of this girl, of her secret love and her pathetic death

---

[1] *Ibid.*   [2] *Ibid.*
[3] *Ibid.*, chap. xix.   [4] *Ibid.*, chap. xviii.

is one of the most beautiful threads in the fabric of the novel. In her last hours the girl reveals that she loves Tom, but that she always knew where his heart lay and wishes only that he and Catherine should be happy.

The lesson of Phoebe's selflessness does not help. It reminds Catherine indeed of St. Paul's formulation of it which has so affected her life, but this in turn reminds her of Mr. Cardew—and her love flames up more intensely than ever. Going home from the house of death, she deliberately takes a path frequented by the minister, and once more they meet. It is now that they come closest to an open declaration. For when he wonders about the man a girl like her could love, she confesses that the man exists, but is unattainable. The touch of his sleeve shakes her like electricity, but once again, for the last time, she is drawn away from the very brink of her happiness by something within her stronger than herself. And continuing home in anguish, she meets Dr. Turnbull, whose conversation about Cardew, about marriage, about the Law, in short, is really a Calvinist sermon—the last sermon she is ever to hear.

To his disapproval of Mr. Cardew's self-indulgence, she replies that such men should perhaps not be judged by ordinary standards. This he instantly opposes—and as a doctor as well as a man. Nothing is more dangerous, even to sanity, than to indulge a sense of one's 'difference.' In at least the great majority of cases, originality should appear only as a better performance of what is common to all. He condemns Mr. Cardew's treatment of his wife. The woman is a saint, he says, whom the man *ought* to love. Oh, certainly, a married man will sometimes meet women he thinks will make him happier than his wife can, but indulgence of each passing temptation is the way to anarchy, and on the whole a man will go to ruin unless he learns to make the best of what is allotted him. Mrs. Cardew 'is a bit of excellence stuck down before him for *him* to value. It is not intended for others, but for *him*, and he deserts the place appointed him by Nature if he neglects it.'[1]

As it happens, Mr. Cardew has, during this conversation, found his way back to his proper 'place.' Going home after this final rejection, he is at last struck by something, 'that same Something

[1] *Catherine Furze*, chap. xix.

which had so often restrained Catherine. It smote him as the light from heaven smote Saul of Tarsus journeying to Damascus. His eyes were opened; he crept into an outhouse in the fields, and there alone in an agony he prayed.' [1] He has, in short, suddenly realized the true nature of his behaviour to Catherine and to his wife. And when he reaches home, where his wife lies ill, he looks at the flowers near her and says, 'I am really so ignorant of flowers, Doss [the name he called her before they were married]; you really *must* teach me.' [2] And with tears the husband and wife come together.

It is at this point that the old-fashioned 'conversion' takes place which underscores the meaning of the novel's main development. Tom, returning on a visit, saves the life of 'Orkid' Jim during a flood. Jim goes off without a word, but looking queer, like one struck by an overwhelming revelation, and a little later he seeks Tom out and commands him to follow him to the Furze home. There, in the presence of all, Jim confesses his part in Tom's disgrace, and on his knees begs Tom's forgiveness. We are told that he then went off to America, whence stories returned that he had become a preacher of God's word, and that 'by God's grace he had brought hundreds to a knowledge of their Saviour.' [3] This event might be accused, by the scrupulous 'realist,' of bringing Tom back to Mr. Furze's employ in time to save the older man from ruin. But there is no reason to suppose the author of such a novel could not have avoided the appearance of melodrama if he had wished. He did *not* wish, for the reason given, and because he preferred to challenge with such an episode the modern kind of simple-mindedness which recoils with a sneer from every reference to religion. 'I can also assure my in-credulous literary friends,' he remarks, after reminding us of an actual case of the same sort reported by Bunyan, 'that years ago it was not uncommon for men and women suddenly to awake to the fact that they had been sinners, and to determine that henceforth they would keep God's commandments by the help of Jesus Christ and the Holy Spirit.' [4] This describes in symbolic terms, as I have said, exactly the novel whose end is now approaching.

Catherine too has been 'saved.' But we have seen that her whole

[1] *Ibid.*   [2] *Ibid.*
[3] *Ibid.*, chap. xx.   [4] *Ibid.*

'self-hood,' including even that in her which Mr. Cardew had awakened to the moral law, was inseparably intermixed with the love which the law forbade. This is the perfectly sound thematic reason for her death, which is not, as some have thought, another device for closing up the plot. Moreover, that truth provides a reason for her death which is equally sound from the point of view of realistic fiction. The weakness in her chest grows fatal because she wants it to and will not exert herself in any way to preserve her life. This, of course, is the same connection between disease and the love of death which Thomas Mann has since dramatized with such richness and power. And there comes a bright warm summer day when the very beauty of the fields increases her contentment with death, so completely has she given up her private self, so united does she feel with all continuing creation.

Puzzling as it has been to many, the last scene between the dying Catherine and the minister, who has just returned from abroad and whom she has called to her bedside, should no longer present any difficulties. They are left alone, and after some trifling remarks, he falls on his knees beside her bed. His whole creed—'forgiveness, the atonement, heaven—it had all vanished.'

'Mr. Cardew, I want to say something.'
'Wait a moment, let me tell you—*you have saved me.*'
She smiled, her lips moved, and she whispered—
'*You* have saved *me.*'
By their love for each other they were both saved. The disguises are manifold which the Immortal Son assumes in the work of our redemption.[1]

It is after writing like this that some of Hale White's readers look up from his page and ask themselves in wonder how he came to be forgotten.

The novel ends with a brief description of the new kind of minister Mr. Cardew has become. His sermons henceforth are of 'the simplest kind—exhortations to pity, consideration, gentleness and counsels as to the common duties of life.' [2] He has been changed

---

[1] *Catherine Furze,* chap. xxi.   [2] *Ibid.*

by 'something deeper' than a theory—by love, in short, that very love which had once trembled on the edge of crime.

Some men are determined by principles, and others are drawn by a vision or a face. Before Mr. Cardew was set for evermore the face which he saw white and saintly at Chapel Farm that May Sunday morning when death had entered, and it controlled and moulded him with an all-pervading power more subtle and penetrating than that which could have been exercised by theology or ethics.[1]

[1] *Ibid.*

o

CHAPTER X

Clara Hopgood

HERE are two comments on Hale White's last novel by two warm admirers of his work. The first is by W. R. Nicoll, writing as Claudius Clear in the *British Weekly* of July 9, 1896. '*Clara Hopgood* appears to be utterly unworthy of him from every point of view. There are sentences in it which none but he could have written, but on the whole it is unsatisfactory, even in style, while the moral teaching is in sad contrast with that of his early books.'[1] The second is by Arnold Bennett, who would not of course be disturbed by the immorality of a work of art, but who did demand meaningful construction. '*Clara Hopgood* is not about Clara Hopgood, but about her sister Madge Hopgood, and Clara is only dragged in at the end.'[2] I quote these remarks because they tell us something useful about the novel. They tell us how it will look, even to admirers, when its chief meanings are missed. They express, therefore, the kind of mistakes which are most likely to recur and which it must be the business of a proper reading to correct.

Of course, it is hardly necessary to say that Hale White's moral attitudes have not changed. But he had always judged actions by their meaning to those involved rather than by their appearance to the conventional eye (for 'the symbolism of an act varies much'), and the time was bound to come when he would shock the moral reader who takes appearances at face value. Sure enough, it is the difference between appearance and reality of which he reminds Claudius Clear in his brief answer, printed in the *British Weekly* on

---

[1] Claudius Clear (W. R. Nicoll), 'Mark Rutherford,' *British Weekly*, XX (July 9, 1896), p. 185.

[2] Arnold Bennett, *The Journal of Arnold Bennett*, New York, The Viking Press, 1933, III, p. 28.

July 30, three weeks later. The note, signed Reuben Shapcott, was written mainly to deny that the novels are based on actual people, but it ends: 'I cannot help a protest against the charge of immorality brought against *Clara Hopgood*. The accusation is another proof that even in a country which calls the New Testament a sacred book and professes to read it, the distinction between real and sham morality is almost unknown.' The novel seems, indeed, deliberately fashioned to challenge sham morality, for it contains not only much irony directed against merely formal or conventional religion but also, at times, a surprising saltiness, amounting, some might say, to downright coarseness.

Nicoll's reaction must have been common, for *Clara Hopgood*, published in March 1896, is not only the least popular of Hale White's novels but it even tends to go unmentioned when they are named. Yet it represents in many ways the highest development of his genius. It has a character often associated with a master's late works, the character of an ultimate distillation. It is more packed with meaning, yields more wisdom per square inch, so to speak, than any other of his books. This, of course, is its first barrier to popularity. For though it has a story and one whose end completes its beginning through a chain of passionate action and reaction, it is so ruthlessly concentrated on essential meanings that many readers will be apt to find it a work of mere intellect, cold and difficult. It is undoubtedly more easy to follow the earlier novels, in which the strong feelings within the events and around them were, however controlled, fully expressed; here we get instead the briefest notation of what happens and the fewest possible remarks about it. Things happen so fast, indeed, that if our attention has wandered a moment we are likely to feel unprepared, and at least one development may be a little too quick for plausibility.

The impression that the novel is too intellectual could be reinforced, moreover, by the fact that its chief characters are all highly developed intelligences, capable of expressing brilliantly the hidden implications of their lives. The book is full of discussion, discussion which leaps forever away from the human particulars to what they mean. But there are three reasons why this talk does not make a 'talky,' that is a dull, idea-ridden novel, why it is, indeed, as fascinating as any action. First, in this work, as in the others, feeling and experience precede ideas, give birth to them and keep them relative. The talk is not merely right or wrong, it reveals character. Second, what the persons of the drama, like the author himself, seek to understand is the moral life, whose problems they are themselves facing in their uttermost difficulty: it is this their ideas are about. Now the moral life is precisely the life of conflicting emotions, and the most abstract utterance of character—or author—takes continual warmth from the material with which it deals. Finally, the novel's discussions are exciting because the fact that one speaker is right, rarely, if ever, means that his opponent is wrong. We are introduced by their talk, not to a systematic theory but to the complexity, the contradictions, of reality.

As for the novel's style, it is not hard to see why this too disappointed Nicoll, for it has developed in the same way as all the rest. That impatience to leap to essential facts and meanings has meant also an impatience with every word that is not absolutely necessary for their communication. This, of course, was always part of the distinction of Hale White's style. But in *Clara Hopgood* it is more strikingly obvious than ever before that he has turned away from—beauty, Nicoll would undoubtedly say, but it would be more accurate to say the beauty that carries a sign, the beauty of ornament. What we get instead, more purely than ever before, is the beauty of grace, which is the perfect performance of what is difficult in movements that are few and easy. For some readers this is the highest beauty prose has to offer, there being for them no thrill greater than that of finding, as we do here again and again, the almost too complex thought, the almost unformulable feeling, expressed in language that is concrete, clear and brief.

That the subject of the novel has so often been missed can only be because we find it hard to accept the inconclusive as an intentional meaning. For it is made perfectly plain in a short chapter of discussion between the two sisters by whom that subject is to be represented, Clara, twenty-five, and Madge, four years younger. The talk, which is also introductory characterization, starts with a game of chess. Madge, who has just received the warning of 'check!' complains that the game is not for her. Clara replies:

'The reason is that you do not look two moves ahead. You never say to yourself, "Suppose I move there, what is she likely to do, and what can I do afterwards?"'

'That is just what is impossible to me. I cannot hold myself down; the moment I go beyond the next move, my thoughts fly away, and I am in a muddle, and my head turns round. I was not born for it. I can do what is under my nose well enough, but nothing more.'

'The planning and the forecasting are the soul of the game. I should like to be a general, and play against armies and calculate the consequences of maneuvers.'

'It would kill me. I should prefer the fighting. Besides, calculation is useless, for when I think that you will be sure to move such and such a piece, you generally do not.'

'Then what makes the difference between the good and the bad players?'

'It is a gift, an instinct, I suppose.'

'Which is as much as to say that you give it up. You are fond of that word instinct; I wish you would not use it.'

'I have heard you use it, and say you instinctively like this person or that.'

'Certainly; I do not deny that sometimes I am drawn to a person or repelled from him before I can say why; but I always force myself to discover afterwards the cause of my attraction or repulsion, and I believe it is a duty to do so. If we neglect it we are little better than the brutes, and may grossly deceive ourselves.'[1]

Now if the usefulness of reason to foresee consequences and to prevent self-deception is Clara's justification, there is justification for Madge, too. It lies in the fact that life is sometimes so complex that calculation is indeed useless, and 'instinct' or accident will solve a problem reason might have given up—or handled wrong. Sure enough, Madge suddenly makes a 'lucky' move—never asking herself what will follow—and wins. This does not, however, cause Clara to yield. For to her sister's triumphant 'Have you not lost your faith in schemes?' she gives the answer that we have already met as Hale White's definition of faith: 'You are very much mistaken if you

[1] *Clara Hopgood*, chap. iii.

suppose that because of one failure, or of twenty failures, I would give up a principle.' [1]

The 'game' they have been talking about, of course, is also the game of life. When the subject shifts to love, as more interesting than 'chess,' it has shifted precisely to what, as the novel will show, is life's most revealing test of their two modes of decision. For it is the test in which emotion is most persuasive and consequences are most grave, permanent and far-reaching. As might be expected, Madge believes in love at first sight, like that of Romeo and Juliet, while Clara insists that in so vital a matter the 'whole strength of the soul' should be directed to making sure that an attractive man really suits her. 'I do not believe,' she declares, 'in oracles which are supposed to prove their divinity by giving no reasons for their commands.' [2] The risk of acting on impulse is tremendous. But Madge replies that there is just as much risk the other way, and the 'balancing see-saw method . . . would disclose a host of reasons against any conclusion, and I should never come to any.' [3] The important question to decide was whether one loved a man, and 'your reason was not meant for that kind of work.' [4] Clara is not won over, but she has smiled. 'Although this impetuosity was foreign to her, she loved it for the good that accompanied it.' [5]

As the reader may have recognized, it is Hale White's own divided nature which fills these opponents with equal conviction and sharpens their arguments. He has found, in fact, for his last novel, a subject so deeply inclusive that, without departing from the story's necessary development, he is able to make it a kind of summation of his richest, most 'contradictory,' thought. The subject of *Clara Hopgood* is the two ways of life, at last brought out into the open, which have always opposed themselves in his mind: the spontaneous life of feeling and intuition, and the deliberate life of reflection and rule. I have spoken of this opposition before. It is the opposition between the varying 'inner voice' and established principle, which their Protestantism developed in both Gide and Hale White, which so often forms the hidden conflict of their tales, and which, as each allegiance pulls against the other, creates the richness and variety of

[1] *Clara Hopgood*, chap. iii.   [2] *Ibid.*   [3] *Ibid.*
[4] *Ibid.*   [5] *Ibid.*

their thought. Now Hale White himself chiefly honoured and tried to live the reflective life; for him, as for Clara, faith in well-grounded principles (*self*-chosen, it is true, but thereafter disciplining the self) was of the first importance. And in his earlier novels it is this life that gets the best of it, the spontaneous life being shown as too often the life of selfish passion. His novels have been novels of self-conquest.

At the same time, however, that which opposed this tendency in him was *almost* of equal strength, and even in those novels there have always been hints that the way of life which is most right can sometimes be wrong. In *Clara Hopgood* this insight is for the first time put in the centre: he now faces squarely the difficult truth that for life as a whole the way of foresight and rule no more constitutes a royal road to righteousness—or to evil—than that of unexamined impulse. Instead of showing them in such a manner that one must yield to the other, he has dared to give the best possible cards to each, to represent them by two protagonists equally desirous of righteousness, equally hard to condemn, equally 'sympathetic.' And instead of asking which is right, he now asks something deeper: he asks what are the advantages and the disadvantages of each, what each can win from life and what each must lose. His tolerance goes so far, indeed, that he even insists—the point occurs twice—that it is wrong to impose one way on a nature to which the other is appropriate, that only our own way can provide the true morality for each of us.

This having been established, however, his meaning goes a little further. When the chain of actions which flows from the two ways of life and their delicate necessary interrelationship has been completed, though neither can be called wrong, one has risen above the other. I have already suggested that, in spite of Arnold Bennett, the novel's true subject involves both sisters, not one. The reading which follows may explain why it is in fact Clara who deserves the final accolade given her by the title.

As the significant opening pages show, it is not only by temperament but by background that the sisters have been shaped to play their parts in the story. They have grown up during the first half of the nineteenth century in a town near Eastthorpe (or Bedford), but the late Mr. Hopgood, their father, was a cultured man without religion who believed that girls needed exact knowledge and disci-

pline even more than boys, and he sent his daughters to finish their
education in Germany. In his house, moreover, 'thought was vocal'[1]
and everything was discussed. This did not mean that they learned
from him, or from Germany, any disrespect for religion. On the
contrary, their mother, who was deeply religious but not dogmatic,
felt that her husband's beliefs were 'in substance' the same as hers, and
of course in Germany iconoclasm joined hands with an idealism
which revered religion as a language for truths if not as literally true.
Certainly no Puritans could have exceeded the girls in their preoccupation with moral questions.

The education of Madge, however, contained an episode which
intensified her natural bent for 'insurgency' and which prepares us
for her great act of freedom to come. She spent a year of her girlhood in a Brighton boarding-school run by two ladies who were
'low Church and aggressive'—so much so, indeed, that she was
finally expelled for the crime of not having been baptized. The
account of what she learned there reads strangely like a parody of
Catherine Furze. For like Catherine, Madge was introduced by her
religious instruction into a 'new world.'

She was just beginning to ask herself *why* certain things were right
and other things were wrong, and the Brighton answer was that the
former were directed by revelation and the latter forbidden, and that
the 'body' was an affliction to the soul, a means of 'probation,' our
principal duty being to 'war' against it.[2]

Is this not exactly the lesson that 'saved' Catherine, and that her book
was designed to show as profoundly true? Yet here the tone is
significantly different, and what its irony tells us is that the lesson can
also be nonsense, when, as mere 'revelation,' it is imposed mechanically from without. Madge learns only how such formulae can be
irrelevant to life, and this means too that she has been deprived of the
guidance amid the passions which they might have given her as
taught by a Mr. Cardew. 'She had learned a good deal . . . not
precisely what it was intended she should learn, and she came back

[1] *Clara Hopgood*, chap. i.
[2] *Ibid.*, chap. ii.

with a strong insurgent tendency, which was even more noticeable when she returned from Germany.' [1]

It is she, of course, who precipitates—and naturally, by falling in love—the crisis that is to test their two ways of living. The man in the case is Frank Palmer, a travelling salesman from London. Frank is 'generous and courageous, perfectly straightforward,' [2] but he is handicapped in his relations with people like the Hopgoods by his mediocrity of mind and heart. He chats pleasantly, but he does not think, and his only strong feeling (a feeling which does, for that matter, obscure many deficiencies) is his love for Madge. There are two episodes that win him her love in return. They are episodes, it will be noted, of a kind which does indeed make the see-saw of reason appear an impertinence—and nothing more proper than the simple response of feeling. The first comes as the completion of another significant discussion.

Clara has received a letter telling her the story of a man whose daughter was periodically attacked by the mania of stealing, and who himself took the blame one day when she was caught. He was sent to prison, his daughter got well and married, and he left a letter justifying himself, but only to be opened if she died childless. She did die childless and the truth came out, though she never knew it. Now Clara has earlier expressed her views on the matter of sacrifice, saying that the world's opinion was as nothing to her beside the human affections, and that she would sacrifice the greatest fame for the love of a brother or sister 'who perhaps had never heard what it was which had made me renowned.' [3] This time, however, she declares it is useless to ask beforehand if one would be capable of that father's heroic unselfishness. What interests her is whether his lie was a 'sin.' Madge's answer is vehement. It is ridiculous to measure an act of love by such a 'contemptible two-foot measuring tape.' In such a case, 'do what you feel to be right and let the rule go hang.' [4] Some clever logician will no doubt be able to find 'a higher rule' by which you have acted. But Madge has judged her sister too hastily. What Clara

[1] *Ibid.*
[2] *Ibid.*, chap. iv.
[3] *Ibid.*
[4] *Ibid.*, chap. v.

has really asked is whether love—or any passion—justifies the betrayal of a principle. And her answer is no.

'As for my poor self,' said Clara, 'I do not profess to know, without the rule, what is right and what is not. We are always trying to transcend the rule by some special pleading, and often in virtue of some fancied superiority. Generally speaking the attempt is fatal.' [1]

As usual in the company of the Hopgoods, poor Frank is beyond his depth. He would turn Catholic, he says, rather than decide such matters for himself, and he would choose Mrs. Hopgood as his priest. But though that lady had agreed with Clara that it set a dangerous precedent to dispense with a fixed standard, she now rebukes Frank. 'The worth of the right to you is that it is your right,' she says, 'and that you arrive at it in your own way.' [2] And she asks him if he has never had to decide promptly for himself what was the right thing to do.

He remembers a case, but a more exciting answer is what happens on the walk he takes with the girls after their discussion—the first of the two episodes mentioned above. While crossing a field, they are attacked by an ox. There is not quite time for them all to run to safety, and, pointing the way to the girls, he waits, stuns the ox with his cane, and then follows them. There was only one thing to be done, he later explains, while Clara says she would have seen half a dozen—'that is to say, nothing'—and Madge that she would have acted promptly, but wrongly, for she would have run away.

The effect of his swift simple male rightness is strengthened when he and Madge play a love scene from *The Tempest* at a charity entertainment in the town—and this is the second of the episodes which win her to him. The morning after their shared triumph, just before leaving, he takes her in his arms for the first time. And though he has frequently failed to rise to his occasions verbally, so important with a cultivated, literate girl like Madge, he now has the help of Shakespeare. He murmurs a loving line of Ferdinand's and she falls on his neck.

Shakespeare, however, is not always at hand to help. During the

---

[1] *Clara Hopgood*, chap. v.   [2] *Ibid.*

period that follows, his constant little failures to meet her whole mind, to share her feeling for poetry, for instance, cause Madge some disturbing doubts. In her effort to crush them, she turns against the culture—the literature—which has meant so much to her.

What a miserable counterfeit of love, she argued, is mere intellectual sympathy, a sympathy based on books! . . . Love . . . is an attraction which has always been held to be inexplicable, but whatever it may be it is not 'views.' She was becoming a little weary, she thought, of what was called 'culture.' [1]

Thus her philosophy of the rightness of impulse discloses in her own experience its first difficulty. The impulse—and now even the undoubted passion—which drew her to him are not her whole self; fidelity to one part of her could apparently mean betrayal of another. It could mean, too, betrayal of those she loves. Sensing that her doubt was shared by Clara, she defends Frank too vehemently from anticipated criticism, and for the first time fails in honesty and closeness to her sister, wounding Clara deeply.

The climactic self-betrayal comes during a day's outing with her lover in the country. It appears that Frank, to please her, has memorized Wordsworth's Ode on *Intimations of Immortality*. Her first response is to express her view of the poem's inferiority to the best of Wordsworth. But suddenly she realizes how much his learning it reveals. Her heart overflows, she calls the poem 'lovely' and she is more attracted to him than ever before. A storm rises and they take refuge in a barn. Here, less restrained than Catherine Furze by temperament, by education and by principles, she yields where Catherine resisted; her faith in the rightness of the moment's feeling has carried her to 'dishonour.'

It is surely not this event alone, however, that contains the moral teaching in such 'sad contrast' for readers like Nicoll to that of his earlier novels. It is what follows. Immediately afterward, with the same impulsiveness that led her to yield, she comes to another decision. When they reach home, she sends him tenderly, but firmly, away. And to the letter that soon comes from him asking forgive-

---

[1] *Ibid.*, chap. viii.

ness and pleading for marriage, she answers that the wrong has been hers, for she now knows she does not love him, and that they must part forever.

> Whatever wrong may have been done, marriage to avoid disgrace would be a wrong to both of us infinitely greater. I owe you an expiation; your release is all I can offer, and it is insufficient. I can only plead that I was deaf and blind. By some miracle, I cannot tell how, my ears and eyes are opened, and I hear and see. It is not the first time in my life that the truth has been revealed to me suddenly, supernaturally, I may say, as if in a vision, and I know the revelation to be authentic. There must be no wavering, no half-measures, and I absolutely forbid another letter from you.[1]

That 'the revelation is authentic,' that this has indeed been, to use a phrase we will later be invited to apply to it, Madge's 'vision of God,' her continuing story will make unmistakable. Now, after such a 'fall,' that epoch's conventional morality would naturally have expected the author to plunge so decent a girl into shame, with marriage as the only possible mitigation. Instead, he has suddenly turned her into a moral heroine, whose *refusal* of marriage is her greatest act. He has shown us, in short, that conventional (or 'sham') morality can stand opposed to the true: Madge has dared to accept worldly dishonour—and the world's possible vengeance—precisely on behalf of a deeper honour, which constitutes her nobility.

He has shown us, too, something even more subtle: that if her reliance on impulse led Madge to self-deception, and the crime of self-betrayal, we are not therefore free to condemn it—life is not so simple—for it has also led her to the deepest truth. From now on, in fact, her story is to be precisely a drama of heroic faith in a true personal intuition of right against enemies of such faith both gross and subtle, both without her and within. And this grasp of the changing moral value of things which is so large a part of Hale White's genius will go further still. For we shall see that the sister one might have expected him to favour, the reflective high-principled Clara, so often in the right, will herself, in all innocence,

---

[1] *Clara Hopgood*, chap. x.

turn into the Tempter; and that if the spontaneous life can err, so can the other.

That self-betrayal, however, must be paid for. For Madge the payment is double. As we are told when the Hopgoods are suffering from the gloom of London, to which Madge's situation has forced them to move, 'Madge was naturally more oppressed than the others, not only by reason of her temperament, but because she was the author of the trouble which had befallen them.'[1] The latter sorrow she feels at its most intense on the day she confesses to her mother that, as far as appearances are concerned, she 'has gone the way of the common wenches whose affiliation cases figured in the county newspapers.'[2] There is a short period of agonizing struggle while Mrs. Hopgood tries to retain her faith in her daughter—in the value of the nurture she has given her: the passage is another example of the power and beauty of Hale White's simple statements. At last, without a word, Mrs. Hopgood embraces her daughter. 'So was she judged.'[3]

One day, a day of exceptional depression, Madge goes out alone into the country for relief. It is beautiful autumn weather, and when she sits down to rest on the porch of a little church, beauty lies all about her.

Sick at heart and despairing, she could not help being touched and she thought to herself how strange the world is—so transcendent both in glory and horror; a world capable of such scenes as those before her, and a world in which such suffering as hers could be; a world infinite both ways. The porch gate was open because the organist was about to practise, and in another instant she was listening to the *Kyrie* from Beethoven's Mass in C. . . . She broke down and wept, but there was something new in her sorrow, and it seemed as if a certain Pity overshadowed her.[4]

The secular reader must not too hastily reject that significant capital letter. For does it not refer to the infinite whole (the same glimpsed by Miriam) of which she has now seen herself to be a part, and the

[1] *Ibid.*, chap. xi.
[2] *Ibid.*, chap. x.
[3] *Ibid.*
[4] *Ibid.*, chap. xi.

thought of which reduces—as it can for all of us—the self-absorption which intensifies pain? And as if sent by that very Pity, who should come trudging toward her at this moment, a wicker basket on her arm, but the wonderful Mrs. Caffyn.

Mrs. Caffyn, a simple country woman of fifty, proprietor of the only shop in her parish, is to utter some of Hale White's sharpest challenges to 'sham morality,' and must have poured much salt on Mr. Nicoll's wounded sensibilities. Madge faints before her on the porch, and though she guesses her trouble, the girl's lack of a wedding-ring does not prevent the purest ,most unjudging sympathy and the readiest help. And this is not all. For we are told that when the town rector condemned a certain drunkard and his fallen daughter, she pointed to the extenuating circumstances of their poverty and their temptations, and dared to add 'I don't believe the Lord A'mighty would be marciful to neither of *us* if we was tried like that.' She does him the courtesy of going on, 'Leastways, speaking for myself, sir,' [1] but he is hardly conciliated.

When Mrs. Cork, the Hopgood's landlady, finds out the 'kind of woman' Madge is, and virtually drives them from their lodgings, it is Mrs. Caffyn who helps them to a refuge. They move into the home of her London daughter, Mrs. Marshall. But the brutality of that landlady has forced them to move on a day when Mrs. Hopgood, who has caught a bad cold, should have been in bed. 'On the morrow she was seriously ill, inflammation of the lungs appeared and in a week she was dead.' [2] Another of those deaths in Hale White which imitate the brutal suddenness of many actual deaths, and again he turns instantly from the painful fact to a kind of precise reflection upon it more powerfully effective than most bursts of feeling. And though one significance of Mrs. Hopgood's death is nowhere stated, it is surely the most important. It is the fact that Madge is partly responsible, that it belongs on the chain of consequences which her mistaken passion had begun.

But the censure of a world of Mrs. Corks is not the worst thing Madge has to face in her struggle to be faithful to her 'revelation.' Far more terrible is the temptation to doubt it. The first temptation comes from Frank. Madge is being replaced in his heart by a rich

[1] *Clara Hopgood*, chap. xii.   [2] *Ibid.*, chap. xiv.

pretty musical cousin, but he cannot forget that he owes Madge something, or that the world would think so, and that if the truth were known he would be ruined. He seeks her out for a last appeal that they marry, and his mere presence, because of what had passed between them, because of his coming child, profoundly shakes her. But then he begins to speak, and his lack of conviction instantly reveals his true feelings. She remembers what he is and her strength is restored. Their marriage would be a crime, she says, and when he hints at the conventional view that it is rather the rectification of a crime, she stops him. 'I know what is the crime to the world; but it would have been a crime, perhaps a worse crime, if a ceremony had been performed beforehand by a priest, and the worst of crimes would be that ceremony now.'[1]

The most powerful temptation, however, comes from Clara, and the scene in which it occurs is one of the novel's greatest discussions. Clara is, of course, deeply troubled by her sister's situation, and when Madge tells her of Frank's visit, she suggests, speaking 'slowly,' that it does at least show his continued love. Now we have just seen how Madge, in her instinctive—that is, swift and not easily formulable—judgment of Frank, had been right. In Clara's hint we are shown how reason, working as so often from insufficient evidence, can be wrong. 'You doubt?' Madge asks, and the word 'doubt' must surely be heard in all its connotations: this is the doubt with which reason forever tries man's faith—no matter in what. 'You hesitate; you reflect?' Madge continues, underscoring this meaning. 'Speak out.'

Characteristically, Clara begins by stating a principle which admits Madge's right to her own view, eager to defend her sister thus even from her own criticism.

'God forbid I should utter a word which would induce you to disbelieve what you know to be right. It is much more important to believe earnestly that something is morally right than that it should be really right, and he who attempts to displace a belief runs a certain risk, because he is not sure that what he substitutes can be held with equal force. Besides, each person's belief, or proposed

---

[1] *Ibid.*, chap. xvii.

course of action, is a part of himself, and if he be diverted from it and takes up with that which is not himself, the unity of his nature is impaired, and he loses himself.'[1]

This—to many of us—is deeply true, but it *can* be a defence of wrong, and for this reason Madge, so sure of her right, rejects it. 'Which is as much as to say that the prophet is to break no idols,' she replies—that is, some beliefs are *not* beliefs in the real thing, and the prophet does well to attack them. She insists again that Clara speak out, and again Clara's statement is worth quoting, both because of its wisdom and because its occurrence here shows Hale White's to be deeper still, for he knows that even such wisdom can be wrong.

'I have sometimes wondered whether you have not demanded a little too much of yourself and Frank. It is always a question of how much. There is no human truth which is altogether true, no love which is altogether perfect. You may possibly have neglected virtue or devotion such as you could not find elsewhere, overlooking it because some failing, or the lack of sympathy on some unimportant point, may at the moment have been prominent. Frank loved you, Madge.'[2]

Clara's point here is not only true, it is one of Hale White's favourite truths, and one which Mark Rutherford, it will be remembered, wishes he had learned earlier. But it is just as true that such a 'reasonable' argument can work against *any* faith—not only those which are quixotic but equally those which, adhered to, will gloriously justify themselves. Madge silences her sister with a terrifying cry of agony, but there can be no doubt that to Hale White it is now Madge and not Clara, who is most to be honoured. It is hinted in this scene and the point is made even more explicit later on when Madge is 'tempted' in the same way by Mrs. Caffyn.

Her foes again ranged themselves over against her. There was nothing to support her but something veiled, which would not altogether disclose or explain itself. Nevertheless, in a few minutes,

---

[1] *Clara Hopgood*, chap. xviii.   [2] *Ibid.*

her enemies had vanished, like a mist before a sudden wind, and she
was once more victorious. Precious and rare are those divine souls,
to whom that which is aerial is substantial, the only true substance;
those for whom a pale vision possesses an authority they are forced
unconditionally to obey.[1]

Madge's struggle to retain her faith is at last rewarded by the peace
of certainty. She gets a final letter from Frank in which his coldness
and shallowness are fully revealed. It changes Mrs. Caffyn's mind,
and when Mrs. Marshall reads it, her warning to Madge against the
marriage is even violent. For Mrs. Marshall is already suffering from
a marriage without love, and she knows, like Zachariah Coleman,
that there is nothing worse. By then, however, she no longer has any
reason to fear for her friend. The tone of Madge's assurance is final.

With the baby coming, it has been necessary for Clara to go to
work, and a job in a bookshop was found for her by Mr. Marshall's
brother-in-law. It is about this man that the rest of the story will
revolve. He is Baruch Cohen, a man of Jewish ancestry, whose
Jewishness is most apparent, we are told, in his thinking.

He believed after a fashion in the Jewish sacred books, or, at any
rate, read them continuously, although he had added to his armoury
defensive weapons of another type. In nothing was he more Jewish
than in a tendency to dwell upon the One, or what he called God,
clinging still to the expression of his forefathers although departing
so widely from them. In his ethics and system of life, as well as in his
religion, there was the same intolerance of a multiplicity which was
not reducible to unity. He seldom explained his theory, but everybody who knew him recognized the difference which it wrought
between him and other men. There was a certain concord in everything he said and did, as if it were directed by some enthroned but
secret principle.[2]

Such a 'Jew,' of course, was Hale White himself—and the other
'weapons' in Baruch's 'armoury' certainly came, like those of his
author, from his namesake Spinoza, as well as from Stoics like

[1] Ibid., chap. xx.   [2] Ibid., chap. xix.

P

Epictetus, whose *Manual* seems sometimes almost to describe him. Baruch is, in fact, one of the best of Hale White's self-portraits: he shares with his author not only his mind, and a tendency to reflection in the midst of feeling, but a capacity for feeling of the most intense sort. Though 'repulsed into reserve' by life, like Mark Rutherford, he too is devoured by a longing for love, and it is Baruch who is described in the sentence already quoted: 'It is not those who have the least but those who have the most to give who most want sympathy.' [1] This makes him, like his author, specially vulnerable to the pain which parents feel when their children turn away from them. He has a grown son, and one day when he, his son and the son's sweetheart are overturned in a row boat, the boy sees first to her safety, though his father cannot swim. This marks an epoch in Baruch's life, and it is as one thus freshly reminded of his loneliness that he pays his second visit to Clara in her shop.

On his first visit he had asked for a little book of moralizing essays and maxims called *After Office Hours*, which he had left to be repaired. Clara has read some of it and it is her talk of the book's author with Baruch which establishes their relationship. Now in the page of quotations Hale White sees fit to give from that book we have again the kind of thing some might call a 'rambling' on the part of an author who likes to scatter his ideas but is impatient with the disciplines of fiction. This would be wrong. In fact, 'although these passages were disconnected, each of them seemed to Clara to be written in a measure for herself,' [2] and no wonder, for they express precisely the underlying ideas of the novel. This means, too, ideas which belong among the most important in her creator's life. It is no accident, therefore, that the author of *After Office Hours*—a late friend of Baruch's called Morris—should be described in such a way as to hint at his identity with Hale White. The work is published under a pseudonym. Hale White's books, too, were written 'after office hours.' And though, in a stroke of slyness, we are told that Morris was not a clerk as the title suggests but an usher in a private school, Hale White also held that job—if only for two days. Moreover,

[1] *Clara Hopgood*, chap. xix.
[2] *Ibid.*

. . . although he was original and reflective, he had no particular talent. His excellence lay in criticism and observation, often profound, on what came to him every day, and he was valueless in the literary market. A talent of some kind is necessary to genius if it is to be heard. So he died utterly unrecognized, save by one or two personal friends who loved him dearly. He was peculiar in the depth and intimacy of his friendships.[1]

That kind of genius and that capacity for friendship belong, of course, to Hale White, and though his 'talent' was greater than this says, it is true that it was not the kind to win him a large public. As final proof of their identity, the first three of the five maxims quoted are to be found among the 'notes' in *More Pages from a Journal*, having been taken from our author's own private journal.

Here they are:

A mere dream, a vague hope, ought in some cases to be more potent than a certainty in regulating our actions. The faintest vision of God should be more determinative than the grossest earthly assurance.

I knew a case in which a man had to encounter three successive trials of all the courage and inventive faculty in him. Failure in one would have been ruin. The odds against him in each trial were desperate, and against ultimate victory were overwhelming. Nevertheless, he made the attempt and was triumphant, by the narrowest margin, in every struggle. That which is of most value to us is often obtained in defiance of the laws of probability.

What is precious in Quakerism is not so much the doctrine of the Divine voice as that of the preliminary stillness, the closure against other voices and the reduction of the mind to a condition in which it can *listen*, in which it can discern the merest whisper, inaudible when the world, or interest, or passion, are permitted to speak.

The acutest syllogizer can never develop the actual consequences of any system of policy, or, indeed, of any change in human relation-

[1] *Ibid.*,

ship, man being so infinitely complex, and the interaction of human
forces so incalculable.

Many of our speculative difficulties arise from the unauthorized
conception of an *omnipotent* God, a conception entirely of our own
creation, and one which, if we look at it closely, has no meaning. It
is because God *could* have done otherwise, and did not, that we are
confounded. It may be distressing to think that God cannot do any
better, but it is not so distressing as to believe that He might have
done better had He so willed.[1]

Our reading of the novel so far has made detailed comment on the
first three maxims unnecessary: though they are of wide general import, they also clearly formulate the ideas of Madge's story. The first
identifies her great revelation, the second describes the unreasoning
faith which sustains her until her improbable happiness, and the third
distinguishes, like her story, between the Divine voice which the
individual can hear, if he listens, and those, much louder, of the
'world or interest or passion.' The next two, however, carry us
deeper. The fourth tells us why it is impossible to prove that one
sister's 'system of policy' must lead to success (of any kind) and the
other's to failure. The reason is that future ends are unknowable and
present means can therefore be justified only by each individual's
sense of their present rightness. As Mrs. Hopgood and Clara have
pointed out, this can only be a private matter. The fifth maxim
explains that choice in such affairs is impossible anyway. The two
sisters' differing 'systems of policy,' with all their consequences,
belong to a chain of necessities which could not conceivably have
been otherwise. It is absurd—the idea is also Spinoza's—to think that
God's omnipotence means the power to break His own laws; it is
rather His nature to do what *must* be done. And so with those por-
tions of His will which are manifested in the character and fate of
His people—of Madge and Clara. We have no right, in short, to
expect that either girl *could* have chosen the character and fate of her
sister.

It is necessary to add at once that Hale White knows as well as the

[1] *Clara Hopgood*, chap. xix.

cleverest of his readers the difference between acceptance of the inevitable order of nature and that mechanical and premature fatalism which is the alibi of the weak. When Frank, after a last attempt to win Madge, which fails because he does not want it to succeed, yields to the current and marries his cousin, he is much consoled by the sentence: 'To what is inevitable we must submit.'

It did not strike him [Hale White remarks] that it was generally either a platitude or an excuse for weakness, and that a nobler duty is to find out what is inevitable and what is not, to declare boldly that what the world oftentimes affirms to be inevitable is really evitable, and heroically to set about making it so. Even if revolt be perfectly useless, we are not particularly drawn to a man who prostrates himself too soon and is incapable of a little cursing.[1]

This first conversation between Baruch and Clara, full of a concentrated profundity which is to mark all the others, surprises them both. Both are usually reserved with strangers, yet they have suddenly shared most intimate thoughts and feelings, and been promptly understood. For Baruch it takes only one more meeting to convince him of the unique value of what he has found. This occurs at the Marshalls, and though Clara says little and the talk is on politics, cool and impersonal, the next chapter wonderfully begins, 'Baruch was now in love.'[2] This does not make him happy,

[1] *Ibid.*, chap. xxv.

[2] *Ibid.*, chap. xxiv. The paragraph is worth quoting in full, as an example of Hale White's late style, and of his characteristic interweaving of 'passion' and 'reflection,' as well as for its meaning. 'Baruch was now in love. He had fallen in love with Clara suddenly and totally. His tendency to reflectiveness did not diminish his passion: it rather augmented it. The men and women whose thoughts are here and there continually are not the people to feel the full force of love. Those who do feel it are those who are accustomed to think of one thing at a time, and to think upon it for a long time. "No man," said Baruch once, "can love a woman unless he loves God." "I should say," smilingly replied the Gentile, "that no man can love God unless he loves a woman." "I am right," said Baruch, "and so are you." '

What we have been told, with such intense concentration, is that without being informed by some view of life which subordinates the purely physical, the coming together of men and women is not love but an animal coupling, while unless one

for, as we have been told, 'he was now . . . at a time of life when a man has to make the unpleasant discovery that he is beginning to lose the right to expect what he still eagerly desires, and that he must beware of being ridiculous.'[1] The thought of a young man, a friend of Marshall's, whom he once found talking to Clara, torments him. As it happens, however, he has nothing to fear. Clara 'had never received any such recognition as that which had now been offered her [by Baruch]: her own self had never been returned to her with such honour.'[2] And she begins to love him in return.

Accident has so far prevented his meeting Madge, though he has heard her story. It is at this point in his developing relationship with Clara that he meets Madge for the first time. He finds her in Clara's bookshop, reading a volume of Shelley, and he is struck with her beauty, which suffering has matured not dimmed. While waiting together, they have a significant conversation, ostensibly about the poet. Madge, it appears, no longer likes Shelley's poetry, and as a man she dislikes him altogether. His treatment of Harriet she considers unforgivable. Perhaps, Baruch suggests, he felt justified in leaving her because he had ceased to love her. Madge looks at him—this comes uncomfortably close to her own case. It is, in fact, a possible view of it, and one which does it least honour. Madge's answer, however, and the whole conversation, is designed to establish the difference.

'I should put it this way,' she said, 'that he thought he was justified in sacrificing a woman for the sake of an *impulse*. Call this a defect or a crime—whichever you like—it is repellent to me. It makes no difference to me to know that he believed the impulse to be divine.'[3]

Not every impulse is equally to be honoured. Hers had led her not to sacrifice another for the luxury of freedom but rather, at the price of

is capable of human love (in which the physical is a source of heat and spontaneity), his love of God is mere cold philosophic assent. Note, by the way, that it is the Jew who emphasizes God, the abstract principle, and the Gentile the human intermediary, a touch which could make the passage an apt epigraph for *Catherine Furze*.

[1] *Clara Hopgood*, chap. xix.
[2] *Ibid.*, chap. xxiv.   [3] *Ibid.*, chap. xxvii.

her own suffering, to save him, as well as herself, from the infinite wrongs of a loveless marriage. (If this sounds like sophistry or mere ingeniousness, is it not true that the moral life leads inevitably to borderline cases where only the finest reason, logic-chopping, if you like, can make the necessary distinctions between act and act?)

Clara is delayed in her work, and since Madge has an errand, Baruch offers to accompany her and then return for her sister. It is at this moment that the seed of what Clara is to do drops into her mind. It is announced in a sentence very easy to pass by on a first reading. 'Clara looked up from her desk, watched them as they went out the door, and for a moment, seemed lost.' [1] Baruch returns, and when he walks Clara home, he is drawn closer than ever before to an open declaration. 'Do you know, Miss Hopgood,' he says at last, 'I can never talk to anybody as I can to you.' What follows is for the present writer the greatest single moment in all of Hale White's work.

Clara made no reply. A husband was to be had for a look, for a touch, a husband whom she could love, a husband who could give her all her intellect demanded. A little house rose before her eyes as if by Arabian enchantment; there was a bright fire on the hearth, and there were children round it; without the look, the touch, there would be solitude, silence and a childless old age, so much more to be feared by a woman than by a man. Baruch paused, waiting for her answer, and her tongue actually began to move with a reply, which would have sent his arm around her, and made them one for ever, but it did not come. Something fell and flashed before her like lightning from a cloud overhead, divinely beautiful, but divinely terrible.

'I remember,' she said, 'that I have to call in Lamb's Conduit Street to buy something for my sister. I shall be just in time.' [2]

At the shop she leaves him, and he goes home to face a future in which there seemed 'nothing to be done but to pace the straight road in front of him, which led nowhere so far as he could see.'

[1] *Ibid.*
[2] *Ibid.*

What came to Clara in that flash of awful light was a call to self-sacrifice, a self-sacrifice inhumanly terrible—and inhumanly beautiful. She has seen the possibility of giving Baruch up to her sister. For only an exceptional man could ever love a woman 'dishonoured' like Madge, and it is only an exceptional man that a woman like Madge could love. Baruch is that man, and Clara's insight in the shop was that these two, given the time and the circumstances, could discover each other's quality. I have said that love is to be the great test of each sister's way of life. The behaviour of each in her love is a kind of dramatic self-expression, and what follows from that behaviour the fate appropriate to each nature. Now, in spite of the novel's care to show that Madge's way is for her inevitable and that it can lead to God like any other, the fact remains that in her love she had deceived herself and that her characteristically impulsive response to it was an act which brought misfortune to herself and her family. The time has come for the elder sister to receive her test, and her nature its appropriate expression and fulfilment. And Clara, feeling, as we have seen, the claims of her own desires as strongly as any Madge, can yet see beyond them the claims of others. To see these is for her to place them first. For her *this* is characteristic. *Her* ultimate self-expression is self-sacrifice.

But there is one thing more to be said: there is meaning also in the way these two characteristic acts are related. That of Madge brings misfortune while that of Clara repairs the damage. There must be payment for what Madge has done—the payment here is a loving husband and a home—but Madge will get both, because it is Clara who will pay. Hale White omitted, perhaps intentionally, to formulate among those maxims from *After Office Hours* this deepest meaning of the novel. But he had formulated it in another place. It is a passage already quoted from *The Autobiography* and it foreshadows exactly the theme of his last novel.

Virtue [is] martyred every day, unknown and unconsoled in order that the wicked might somehow be saved. . . . The consequences of my sin, moreover, are rendered less terrible by virtues not my own. I am literally saved from penalties because another pays the penalty for me. The Atonement, and what it accomplished for man, is therefore a sublime summing up, as it were, of what sublime men have to do for their race.[1]

The rest of the novel is devoted chiefly to Clara's delicate maneuvering to bring Baruch and Madge together, her ultimate purpose—their falling in love—being accomplished during a long week-end with Mrs. Caffyn and the Marshalls in the country. This is the development whose speed is perhaps a little excessive. It seems to leave Baruch open to the same charge of shallow fickleness which the novel has earlier brought against Frank. The flaw, however, is not really fatal. If any second love is possible for Baruch, it is this one. To say it happens too quickly is not as serious as to say it could not have happened at all.

The day after their return from the country, Clara completes her sacrifice by arranging to leave them forever. Marshall had once taken them all to visit the saintly Italian exile Mazzini, then conducting his operations from London, and Clara had asked him if volunteers were ever needed for dangerous assignments. (That she should choose this form for her sacrifice is not arbitrary, by the way, for it has always belonged to her seriousness to be interested in politics, and she has uttered some of Hale White's final political conclusions.[2]) Now she returns to Mazzini and offers her services as a spy. And though he guesses that her motives are more personal than political, he accepts her, for, as he remarks, 'The devotion of many of the martyrs of the Catholic church was repulsion from the world as much as attraction to heaven.'[3] She is sent to Italy, and about eighteen months later Mazzini tells Baruch that his sister-in-law is dead. The novel ends:

All efforts to obtain more information from Mazzini were in vain, but one day when her name was mentioned, he said to Madge—

'The theologians represent the Crucifixion as the most sublime

[1] *The Autobiography*, chap. ii.
[2] Talking to Marshall, a 'radical' who is violently Chartist and anti-clerical, she suggests that the superstition of a modern newspaper reader can be as dark as that of the most benighted Spanish peasant, and that a tyranny of the majority is not only possible but is coming, which will be worse than that of the Inquisition.
[3] *Clara Hopgood*, chap. xxix.

fact in the world's history. It was sublime, but let us reverence also the Eternal Christ who is for ever being crucified for our salvation.'

'Father,' said a younger Clara to Baruch some ten years later as she sat on his knee, 'I had an Aunt Clara once, hadn't I?'

'Yes, my child.'

'Didn't she go to Italy and die there?'

'Yes.'

'Why did she go?'

'Because she wanted to free the poor people of Italy who were slaves.' [1]

Many have found the last page of the novel either pointless or a mere 'realistic' trailing off. In fact, it is a final necessary step in the development of the central theme. It is also the saddest of Hale White's endings. That story Clara had told of the father who goes to his grave misunderstood by the beloved daughter for whom he has sacrificed himself has now become her own. For she lies in the earth, and Baruch, whom she loved, calmly repeats that error behind which her love and her sacrifice will now be concealed forever. The obliteration of the act which most completely expressed her nature, and might well have crowned her life with glory, is a second death, and it is a kind of death which, for Hale White, has always added a special horror to the first. To be forgotten or misjudged after death— a despairing fear of this recurs often in his work. That he visits it upon Clara, however, is a sort of final honour. It is as though only the most terrible, the most total, of earthly martyrdoms would be commensurate with the spiritual majesty to which she has been lifted by her sacrifice.

It should now be clear why the book has Clara's name, rather than her sister's. Madge's 'way' has brought her the happiness of earthly fulfilment. Clara's has brought her nothing but death. But though we might not choose the latter for ourselves, we cannot fail to see which is the nobler. The triumph of Madge is human; that of Clara is divine.

[1] *Clara Hopgood*, chap. xxix.

CHAPTER XI

Last Writings

I

IT has been said that Hale White's creative life—he lived to the age of eighty-two—came to an end with *Clara Hopgood* in his sixty-fifth year. It would be more accurate to say only that his writings decreased in size. The development which was already evident in that last novel—his growing concentration on essentials—turned him more and more to direct exposition or to shorter fiction in which he could move straight to some vital point. This fiction, and this expository writing, however, are rarely inferior in quality to the novels that came before. On the contrary, in wisdom, force and beauty the three volumes of *Pages from a Journal* (the chief work of his later years) are among his best writings, and because he goes in them to the heart of so many matters, they are the works which bring us closest to him and which make available most quickly and easily the best he has to offer. One reads his novels and puts them aside for a time, but the *Pages from a Journal* belong on one's desk or near one's bed.

That concentration on essentials, in style and meaning, is only a part of the reason for his late excellence. Far more striking in a man of his age was his capacity for fresh response. A note in *More Pages* tells us: 'The long apprenticeship has ended in little or nothing. What I was fifty years ago I am now; certainly no better, with no greater self-control, with no greater magnanimity.'[1] This admission of defeat is also the statement of a triumph. What kept his talent alive is the fact, already conveyed in our account of his life, that his old age was as beset by longings, exaltations and agonies as his greenest youth had been; that his writing was as much as ever a conquest over warring emotions and the complexity of life they create. The power

---

[1] *More Pages*, p. 258.

to feel such love as we find in *The Groombridge Diary* is exactly the power behind his last writings.

The chief works that followed *Clara Hopgood* were *An Examination of the Charge of Apostasy against Wordsworth* (1898); *John Bunyan* (1904); two prefaces (in 1907), one to his selections from Johnson's *Rambler*, and the other to the World Classics edition of Carlyle's *Life of Sterling*; and the *Pages, More Pages* and *Last Pages from a Journal* (1900, 1905 and 1915). These last three volumes contain essays on literature, philosophy, religion, morality and nature—as well as on people like Galileo; Bradley, the eighteenth-century astronomer; and Captain James, the seventeenth-century explorer—aphoristic notes on similar themes, but mostly on conduct, and short stories. What is most remarkable about the variety of this production is its uniformity of tone. 'In our determination of our own actions, and our criticism of other people,' he said in the *Pages*, 'we should use the whole of ourselves, and not mere fragments.'[1] He was speaking of the conduct of life, but he might equally have been speaking of his writing. This is the point, in fact, with which we began: we get in every essay the thought not of a specialist pursuing merely his subject or his theory but of a whole man interested above all in life, the response to the subject of his undivided humanity. In his case, as I say, this generally means a response of unusual intensity. It is precisely because his experience is so vivid to him, and hits him so hard, that the conduct of life preoccupies him and he always asks of the works of the mind the question already mentioned: Do they help us to live? And whether we share his need, or his sense of what is helpful, it is impossible to miss that wholeness of response, that note of experience, which characterizes every page of these last works as much as of the earlier. We find it not merely in the fiction, still so passionate in subject and attitude. It is almost always an intense feeling which he expresses in his literary criticism. And it is constant loyalty to the emotional life that determines the nature of his general ideas. Not only does it drive them deep, since the emotional life is complex: it often gives them the appearance of self-contradiction. For, 'Truth is not one,' as Hazlitt said, 'but many; and an observation may be true in itself that contradicts another equally true, according

[1] *Pages*, p. 77.

to the point of view from which we contemplate the subject.'[1] And Hale White's loyalty to felt experience, which is precisely his 'sincerity' and which is the same 'sincerity' as Gide's, results, like that of Gide, in a continual recognition of the claims of different points of view, in the willingness to admit into the life of mind the un-systematic variety of that of feeling. The reader who considers some statement of either writer one-sided can therefore be pretty sure that the writer knows it too and that he is asking him to recognize another possible truth, not deny his own.[2]

It might be said that writing and thinking necessarily originate in experience. But most often in the intellectual life it becomes a point of pride that they do not stay there, that our own feelings and needs should be sacrificed to consistency, to fashion, to the goals and standards peculiar to our specialty. 'How seldom,' Hale White re-marks—it is an almost obsessive complaint—'is that which is spoken the result of experience!'[3] This attitude accounts for a certain im-patience with culture which recurs throughout his work (in spite of his own helpless addiction to it), a sense that 'if we fly to books as an opiate our brains will become atrophied and we neglect the more wholesome and infinitely more amusing entertainment to be obtained from objects and people near us.'[4] And because of it his essays on Spinoza, on 'Talking about our Troubles,' on astronomy, on 'The Faerie Queene,' are likely to be interesting in much the same way as his fiction, even to those whom such subjects generally bore.

II

His short stories may be divided into three kinds, and two of them will perhaps disappoint readers who like stories to be dramas fully

---

[1] Quoted by Catherine M. Maclean, Born Under Saturn: A Biography of William Hazlitt, London, Collins Clear-type Press, 1934, p. 96.

[2] Writing to his son Ernest on February 21, 1889, of a work of Carlyle's, Hale White says: 'It is a strong, somewhat one-sided statement of a great truth; one-sided because all statements are one-sided and cannot be otherwise.' (Unpublished letter in the possession of Mrs. Irene White.)

[3] Last Pages, p. 278.

[4] Ibid., p. 1.

worked out. The first provides situations which, almost fable-like in
their simplicity, are frankly designed to convey a moral or to raise a
moral question. An example is 'Conscience.' In this the narrator,
having affirmed in conversation Hale White's own notion of the
power for right decision of the uncoerced 'inner voice,' hears a tale
which ironically questions it. Phyllis, a governess treated by her kind
employers as one of the family, encourages the shy daughter of the
house to love a young man whom all regard as the girl's suitor. A
moment comes when she finds to her dismay that she loves the man
herself. She spends a night in vain 'sophistry,' wondering if the Devil
or Providence is responsible for this glimpse of a possible happiness.
But the next morning, when the man actually proposes to her, she
instantly refuses him. Two years later he marries her friend, and the
marriage, though not tragic, is not happy, while she herself remains
a spinster. We are left with the question, did her 'conscience' lead
her right? It will be seen that if the method is simple, the conception
of life's possibilities which is dramatized is not. Such morality is not
narrowness but depth. And the story has the added charm of perfection in the telling; there is not a stroke too much or too little or
imprecise.

The second kind dispenses with narrative development altogether
and records instead a state of mind or feeling. Appropriate situations
are provided, but these are merely basic life-situations, not stories,
and what matters is the qualities of the experience and the reflections
to which it gives rise. An example of this is 'Letters from Aunt
Eleanor' (in *Pages*), in which a woman who has luxuriated in that
completeness of shared love which is Hale White's ideal, loses first
her husband and soon afterward her daughter. Her letters to the
daughter, and then her diary after the daughter's death, give us not
'happenings' but a picture of her almost wild passion for both, and
then of the struggle of her mind with the supreme agony of their
deaths. 'How trouble tries words!' [1] the woman exclaims. The story
is like a white-hot crucible in which human relationships and the
common consolations for suffering are tested and everything burned
to ashes but what is real. Composed as it largely is of reflections, it
could perhaps have been done as an essay like his 'Time Settles

[1] *Pages*, p. 185.

Controversies' or his 'Patience.' What justifies the resort to fiction is
that fiction is the best device available for catching thoughts and
feelings in their living state, preserving their particular illuminating
history and all their force. Here too the late style is at its best, and
this story, for all its lack of drama, is as moving and beautiful as any
of his writings.

Hale White does, however, provide 'real' stories too, though they
will satisfy admirers of Chekhov sooner than those of Maugham. The
best of these are 'Mrs. Fairfax' and 'The Governess's Story' in *Pages*;
'A Bad Dream,' 'Mr. Whittaker's Retirement' and 'Kate Radcliffe'
in *More Pages*; and in *Last Pages* 'The Sweetness of a Man's Friend,'
'The Love of Woman' and 'A Dream of Two Dimensions' (this an
early story, rewritten in his age). Some are in the vein of his first
books, 'Mrs. Fairfax,' for example, a vivid ironic re-creation of a
provincial society within which a drama of love takes place. It is the
love of an elderly minister for a widow—lost in an intellectual desert,
he is excited by her intelligent literacy—and a chief note is the
delightful, confusing admixture of the physical in the love of this
elderly man of mind. Other stories concentrate wholly on one or
two individuals and the passion or injustice in their relations. A
typical example of the latter—the last story he wrote, as far as is
known—is 'The Love of Woman,' a treatment of the subject
peculiarly intense for a man in his eighties. A Mark Rutherford type,
through his paralysing irresoluteness, has let slip out of his life a
woman he loved, and afterwards, through what is really the same
flabbiness of character, 'plunged blindfold' into a loveless marriage.
Now a widower, and dying, he calls the first woman to his bedside
to utter at last the feeling that had never faded, and he discovers it is
still returned. They marry, though it be for hours, and he lives on
for many happy years. This might seem unpromising, and yet the
story is most powerful. It is not a psychological drama full of
interesting turns of development; it is a poem of celebration. Its
quality comes from the absoluteness of its commitment to the idea
of the supreme value of love and the restrained *violence* with which
it is told; the fact that it stays always on the level of passion, omitting
life's prose, its transitions not 'realistically' gradual but leaping.
This passion breaks through at the end in strange parenthetical

exclamations which interrupt the reflections of the narrator, the man's friend.

I, Philip Dixon, conclude with a word:
All these years Margaret's love had lain unseen, unexpressed, unsubdued, alive, although encompassed with mortality. It was not killed by violence offered to it, nor did it decay through rot and damp.
[I bend my knees and worship.] I have heard of seeds which will remain in a storehouse in darkness and cold for years, and when placed in the earth will bloom in gorgeous colour. [God is great.] [1]

(The reader will remember Mark Rutherford for whom the love of woman also spoke of God.)

III

Hale White's literary criticism, too, as I have said, had its origin in strong feeling. This made it very different from the kind to which we have lately grown accustomed. It is not a criticism concerned with passing judgment from above. The same readers who call his novels 'artless' will therefore be likely to find his criticism 'unsophisticated,' and it may be well to begin by assuring them that they would, once again, be too hasty. There is plenty of evidence that he could have brought to the game of discriminating between good and bad writing, or of formulating the rules for such discrimination, a sufficiently developed literary intelligence. He knew, as we have already seen, that 'what is said' cannot be distinguished from 'the way it is said,' which is to say he was aware of the most unlikely places where a writer's meaning might lie concealed. And he knew that from the meaning comes the form. 'Whether this judgment is just,' he tells us of Johnson's complaint that Samson Agonistes had a beginning and end but no middle, 'depends upon the discovery of the true theme of the poem.' [2] This understanding of the meaning of form involves a certain view of the significance, as well as the beauty,

---

[1] Last Pages, p. 242.
[2] Ibid., p. 183.

of economy. Of a poem of Wordsworth's he remarks in his Black Notebook, 'The last two lines contribute nothing, and contributing nothing, they subtract.' He knew, in spite of Mr. Baker, how his own kind of fiction attained to organic unity.

In a play or story not only should there be progress to an inevitable conclusion, but progress in the development of character. The personality, closed at the beginning, should gradually expand and attain full expression in the crisis.[1]

He knew above all that art must be at once particular and general.

In all works of art the finite should represent the infinite, but to attempt to represent the infinite without a most concrete finite is absurd.[2]

It should be added that his reliance upon experience rather than upon *a priori* ideas would naturally increase his skill as a judge of literary excellence, for it would enable him to contradict himself, to see success where the rules have been broken and it comes in a new form. Thus he can criticise a novel of Sterling's for lack of 'construction' and praise another (*Martha Vine*, by Viola Meynell) that does without it.[3]

But he was not interested, as I say, in the usual kind of criticism. There is a note in *More Pages* which tells us what his critical emphasis was.

There is much which is called criticism that is poisonous, not because it is mistaken but because it invites people to assert beyond their knowledge or capacity. . . . If we will be content with admiring, we are on much surer ground. It is by admiration and not by criticism that we live, and the main purpose of criticism should be to point out something to admire which we should not have noticed.[4]

[1] *Ibid.*, p. 295.
[2] *Ibid.*, p. 256.
[3] He does the first in his preface to Carlyle's *Life of Sterling*, and the second in an unpublished review of *Martha Vine* in the possession of Mrs. D. V. White.
[4] *More Pages*, p. 257.

Q

To this can be added a remark from the essay on George Eliot in *Last Pages*: 'We need to be taught to admire, to surrender ourselves to admiration. "If you call a bad thing bad," says Goethe, "you do little; if you call a good thing good, you do much." '[1] It is, of course, easy to argue with this, to show how important to the health of literature is the capacity to discriminate bad from good, and the rejection of the bad. But we are perhaps more fruitfully occupied in grasping the truth such an emphasis contains. To find something to admire is to enlarge the mind, to enlarge the possibilities of life. (Indeed, it is our admiration, in the sense of our belief in them, of certain ideas and certain forms of being, that enables us to act at all: we will see below that this attitude to criticism is in fact the same as his attitude to life.) Admiration, as it functions in Hale White's literary essays at any rate, involves exactly such a relation with great works and such a profit gained from them. And this is the reason, though his letters show a literary culture of wide scope, that his published criticism is limited to the few writers who have most deeply affected him. Marked often by the added warmth which comes from defending them from fashionable attack, it is devoted to showing with visible gratitude the wisdom, or simply the life-enhancing beauty, by which they have helped him to live.

Two apparently contradictory results flow from this. The first is that his writings on literature are peculiarly modest and self-effacing. It belongs almost to morality for him to refrain from using his beloved subject as an occasion for personal display: for instance, for showing off some private 'theory in order to attract attention and prove originality.' The words 'striking' and 'brilliant' are, in his vocabulary, terms of abuse. Of his *John Bunyan*, he wrote to a friend:

Complaint has been made that I have given too much of Bunyan and too little of myself, but this is no reproach. If a biographer really is in earnest about his subject his object will be to present him and not to use him as a peg on which to hang matters of no consequence whatever.[2]

[1] *Last Pages*, pp. 134-5.
[2] *Letters*, p. 127.

And so he is fond of the quotation by which the actual literary facts are presented to the reader, or of the detailed synopsis. This means that that same hasty reader, deprived of so many of the obvious signs of the active intelligence, will often be unaware of its presence. But in fact it is there, and in a higher degree than self-glorifying 'brilliance' generally requires. The quotations are chosen and the work gone over in a way that lays bare with unusual intimacy what is important. To do such criticism justice we must restrain our eagerness for large portable generalizations, we must share his own 'love of fact.' We must be willing, in short, to attend his careful presentation of that 'most concrete finite' without which any aspiration toward the 'infinite' is absurd. If we are, however, we will find that the 'infinite' never fails to make its appearance.

But the second result of his dealing mainly with what he has intensely admired appears, as I have said, a contradiction of the first. It is that, for all their modesty, his literary essays are the purest *self*-expression. He loves what answers his personal need, and revealing its nature, reveals his own. His essays on Bunyan, Carlyle, Johnson and George Eliot, and equally those on Spenser, Wordsworth and Byron, are full of passages that can be applied to him and to his writings. And this is so, even though they sometimes emphasize contradictory ideas and qualities: it is then to different aspects of himself that they must be applied. This means that his literary essays are full of human rather than purely literary wisdom. And it means that his style, in spite of the restraint and impersonality enjoined by his respect for the 'facts,' is, paradoxically, full of feeling. It is moved, and it is moving.

Not want of 'sophistication,' then, but its affirmative import, its emotion and its general wisdom, are what distinguish his criticism from the kind that nowadays fills many of us with respect—and impatience. In examining some of the literary criticism of his last years we will therefore be killing two birds with one stone. We will not only be discovering what he was as a critic; we will also be completing our portrait of him as a thinker and as a man.

'A Visit to Carlyle in 1868' in *Pages* begins as the report of a visit he paid with his father, a report full of telling detail and actual conversation which sets the great man before us alive. He then turns to 'a reflection or two' still strikingly at variance with the common view of Carlyle, who has come to be judged by the worst construction that can be put upon his utterances rather than the profound best.

Carlyle is the champion of morals, ethics, law—call it what you like—of that which says we must not always do a thing because it is pleasant. There are two great ethical parties in the world, and, in the main, but two. One of them asserts the claims of the senses. Its doctrine is seductive because it is so right. It is necessary that we should in a measure believe it, in order that life may be sweet. But nature has heavily weighted the scale in its favour; its acceptance requires no effort. It is easily perverted and becomes a snare. In our day nearly all genius has gone over to it, and preaching it is rather superfluous. The other party affirms what has been the soul of all religions worth having, that it is by repression and self-negation that men and States live.[1]

The reader will notice that for Hale White *both* parties are right. What he opposes is the fragmentary, the lopsided, and when he bears down on one side, it is only to counterbalance an excess on the other. For most of us in ordinary life, as he says, the tendency is always against self-negation, and this accounts for the frequency of his moral emphasis. It accounts, too, for his reverence for the quality of courage, which, for him, is always closely allied to faith. Courage is Carlyle's chief lesson: it is the theme of what Hale White calls his greatest work, the *Frederick*.

The *Frederick* [is] the biography of a hero reduced more than once to such extremities that apparently nothing but some miraculous intervention could save him, and who did not yield, but struggled on, and finally emerged victorious. . . . [It describes] the struggle of the will with the encompassing world. . . . It is interesting to note how attractive this primary virtue of which Frederick is such a remarkable representative is to Carlyle, how *moral* it is to him; and, indeed, is it not the sum and substance of all morality?[2]

[1] *Pages*, pp. 8–9.   [2] *Ibid.*, p. 11.

But we need more than will and courage, we need delight. In 'September, 1798'—also in *Pages*—we are told that the great worth of *The Lyrical Ballads*, what unites the homely poems of Wordsworth with the exotic *Ancient Mariner*, is that they restore our interest in life, they show us again the world's beauty and mystery which tend to disappear beneath a film of custom. And this too helps us to live.

The help to live, however, that is most wanted is not remedies against great sorrows. The chief obstacle to the enjoyment of life is its dullness and the weariness which invades us because there is nothing to be seen or done of any particular value. If the supernatural becomes natural, and the natural becomes supernatural, the world regains its splendour and charm. Lines may be drawn from their predecessors to Coleridge and Wordsworth, but the work they did was distinctly original, and renewed proof was given of the folly of despair even when fertility seems to be exhausted. There is always a hidden conduit open into an unknown region whence at any moment streams may rush and renew the desert with foliage and flowers.[1]

Note here how the lesson of literature's unforeseeable renewal is extended to become a source of encouragement in the struggle of life.

It is not odd that Hale White should be drawn to the Puritan Spenser, even apart from the music. (This he found can be 'as sweet as Mozart' at the same time that it conveys meaning more completely than 'the most expressive penetrating prose.') Yet the degree of their closeness is greater than, in our first thought, we might have imagined. It is this that accounts for the essay 'Spenser and Kilcolman,' in *Last Pages*, written near the end of his life. The title, it turns out, suggests the theme, and it is the theme of the story of Mark Rutherford. For Kilcolman was Spenser's Irish home, and Ireland was for the poet what Victorian England was for Rutherford, a place of brutal ugliness from which he was impelled inwardly to fly. The *Faerie Queene* was Spenser's mode of *escape*—Hale White quotes and

---

[1] *Pages*, p. 108.

italicizes the line 'My tedious travell [I] doe forget thereby'—it was
for Spenser, as it is for us, 'pure romance.' But we must not, in the
pride of our knowledge of all the poem contains, too hastily reject
the word 'romance,' for its meaning deepens as the essay goes on.

> [What] attracted and pacified Spenser in his tower . . . was
> *romance*, the contrast between [his poem's] world of noble miracle,
> of faith, and the world of Desmonds, Tyrones and English incapacity
> in which his outer life was passed. The Red Cross Knight, who over-
> comes a dragon after a three days' fight, may be totally impossible
> fiction, but he is more profitable company than the politician whose
> achievements fill the newspapers of today. The knight is real and the
> politician is not.[1]

He is real in that he is true to the reality of our deepest feelings and
ideals, he embodies and helps us realize them, whereas the politician
negates them. Romance, in short, 'is really his "religion." It is in
romance that the strength of a religion lies. Britomart may be a
saving creed: a mere code or collection of propositions cannot.'[2]
And though such romance, like religion, embodies what is best in
the inner life in images of appropriate and magnetic beauty, it does
not, any more than religion, mean a denial of reality. 'Most attractive' to Hale White is Spenser's picture of the 'constant desperateness
of the struggle. Paynim, giant and dragon are not overcome till the
knight has made his last effort, and defeat, if it be not ultimate, is
acknowledged.' Not ultimate because—

> Victory, even in the *Faerie Queene*, is not everywhere complete.
> Archimago, the great Adversary, Satanas, true to fact, is not only
> ubiquitous, but can assume countless disguises and, at any rate in that
> half of the *Faerie Queene* which we possess, always eludes us. Each of
> his machinations for the time is foiled and this is all we can expect.[3]

Even more self-revealing, however, is Hale White's preface to his
selection from Johnson's *Rambler*. What lay behind that preface was

---

[1] *Last Pages*, pp. 12-13.   [3] *Ibid.*, p. 14.
[2] *Last Pages*, p. 17.

not only that, with Walter Raleigh, he considered Johnson 'England's greatest *man* since Bacon.' It is that, more directly than any other writer, Johnson had uttered his own thoughts and experiences, had expressed his own sense of life's terror, his own need for relief and support, his own concern with the problem of right conduct. This is why he could remark to a friend as he worked on the selections:

Some of the things he says are so terribly close to fact that I can hardly get through them. Sometimes he is so pathetic, all the more so for his stateliness and restraint, that 'the mother swells up towards my heart.' I feel, and have for years felt, a burning desire to express *my* truth about Johnson, that is to say, his truth for me.[1]

His view of Johnson was not the common one of his day (and still, to a large extent, of ours) due to Macaulay and Boswell. He tells us that Macaulay's Johnson, a grotesque combination of powers and fatuities, was 'a false and ridiculous phantasm' and 'the affirmation of impossible existence.'[2] It is not enough to point in amusement to apparent contradictions: one must grasp what the warring ideas and attitudes meant to the man himself and how they were related in his character. Macaulay 'does not discern that, although a belief in the intercession of the dead may be folly, it may also be an indication of greatness.'[3] He is equally wrong in regarding Johnson's style as pointlessly artificial, as 'systematically vicious.' 'Each member of Johnson's balanced sentences conveys a new idea or is a double stroke on the head of the nail.'[4] And Boswell's *Life* is also misleading, in spite of its greatness, because it was not in conversation that the best and deepest of Johnson was to be found. He often talked for effect or for polemical triumph, but his writing came from his heart. For the rest, let Hale White speak for himself. I quote at some length because he is describing almost exactly the kind of man I have attempted to describe in this study, and what he says, in language, moreover, which is itself a revelation of what he was, will etch in more deeply the lines of his own portrait.

[1] *Letters*, p. 247.
[3] *Ibid.*, p. ix n.
[2] *Rambler*, p. x.
[4] *Ibid.*, p. xi.

Johnson was a moralist, not in the narrow sense in which we now use the word, but signifying the student and critic of all that is good and evil, pleasant and unpleasant in human nature. . . . This is a study which is now out of fashion. The preacher who should preach (like Socrates) upon the various modes of virtue and relations of life would have but a small following, and the author who discussed them would not find it easy to obtain a publisher. Undoubtedly Johnson presents us only with a half-truth when he teaches self-knowledge and condemns curious physical and metaphysical research. . . . Man is born to know everything which can be known, to love all that is lovely, and science or art may have a very practical effect on his character and his happiness. Nevertheless, Johnson's doctrine is a half-truth as sufficient as it is possible for any doctrine taught by a finite creature to be. It is wholesome to turn, at least occasionally, from the speculation of the twentieth century to the *Rambler* and *Idler*. There we are on mother earth and learn how to do what must be done today. It does harm to busy ourselves with that which is beyond our strength, we become giddy and may fall. . .

Johnson does not examine the foundations of morals, nor has he any consistent method of dealing with human affairs. The *Rambler* is none the worse because it is a series of miscellaneous tracts. It is worthy of notice that men who have had no distinct errand or purpose, no new philosophy or religion to propose, should have left such deeply scored marks. The universe is so complex that nothing is true save a word fitted to a particular occasion. The systems decay; the cause for which the reformer preached is discovered to have for the most part no relationship with fact, and becomes a dead cause, but some casual speech in a field of lillies, a parable, essay, or fable survives and will survive as long as the race lasts. . . .

Although Johnson is a moralist he is not censorious. He is human; his experience of life is wide and deep; he is an apologist for natural propensity. . . . Johnson's morality is also hatred of the oppressor, and pity for the unfortunate. . . . Johnson is not a priest but a man, a man like his Master, a man to whom mercy as well as judgment are 'the weightier matters of the Law.' There is an infinite depth of tenderness in him. . . .

[His orthodoxy] is amazing to us, for everybody now, unlearned as well as learned, is supposed to be entitled to the doubts and denials of all the sceptics, German, French, and English. The superstition of credulity has given place to a superstition of incredulity, or rather of credulity in a different form. It is by no means asserted that the scholars are wrong, but the acceptance of their conclusions, so far as most of us are concerned, is essentially in no way more respectable than the faith of a cowherd in 1750. The fashion for poems, essays and stories which exult in the Contradiction or Antinomy of the Universe is now more than ever prevalent, and we are all of us heaven-storming blaspheming Titans. We have forgotten that there is no gospel but that of the Reconciliation and that the man who brings us into agreement with the smallest fact which was hostile does greater service than a sublime genius depicting through volumes rebellion or despair. Every brave man strives in some fashion or other to come to terms with himself and the world. . . .[1]

The *Rambler* is neglected because its philosophy is nothing more than everybody knows . . . but is there any consolation in sickness which is not a platitude? When we endure pain and depression week after week, doubting the issue of each weary day, has any support been revealed to us unknown to all the sons of men? Johnson has found nothing better, but what he has found he feels. He is wise enough not to discard that which is common because it is common: he has discovered that it is our duty to put life and meaning into the common; that the only salvation attainable lies therein.[2]

There is also a brief essay on Johnson in *Last Pages*. In this Hale White admits certain limitations and defects in his author, among

---

[1] 'To reconcile man as he is to the world as it is, to preserve and improve all that is good, and destroy or alleviate all that is evil, in physical and moral nature— have been the hope and aim of the greatest teachers and ornaments of our species. I will say, too, that the highest wisdom and the highest genius have been invariably accompanied with cheerfulness. . . . But now the little wisdom and genius we have seem to be entering into a conspiracy against cheerfulness.' (Thomas Love Peacock, *Headlong Hall and Nightmare Abbey*, London, Everyman's Library, J. M. Dent and Company, 1908, p. 269.)

[2] *Rambler*, pp. xvi-xxx.

which the 'gravest defect perhaps of all' is that 'he seems to have cared nothing for music and painting, nor indeed for beauty in any shape as beauty.' But he goes on:

And yet it is to him I pay especial homage, such as I do not pay to poet, philosopher, saint or artist. He was not a this or a that; he belonged to the small class who live for the sake of living, and whose object is to cultivate the art of living wisely. He walked through the world observing men and their ways, and caring for nothing else.[1]

IV

I have left Hale White's two longest critical essays for last because together they represent the most complete and most explicit statement of his ideas. They serve, therefore, as a useful point of departure for a final summary of his 'message.'

The Examination of the Charge of Apostasy against Wordsworth attempts to prove that when the poet turned from the French Revolution and the Whigs to a position resembling that of the Tories, and from Godwinian rationalism to religion and the Church, he was not really betraying his own deepest beliefs, though cultivated people were finding it modish to say so.

Cultivated men and women feel that they must have something to say about [Wordsworth], and so they take up 'Lucy Gray' and '1815,' and pass on, summing him up in a phrase, 'inspired poet, dullest of renegades.' The antithesis does not exist and could not have existed, but it saves them much trouble, not only in criticism and conversation, but in their own thinking. It is also seductive, because it is so much more brilliant to shut up a man like Wordsworth in a formula than to confess we can but put down a point here and there which cannot be connected by any circumscribing outline.[2]

Now it is to be remembered that Hale White, too, began with a rebellion against religious orthodoxy and political conservatism, and

---

[1] Last Pages, p. 79.

[2] W. H. White, An Examination of the Charge of Apostasy against Wordsworth, London, Longmans, Green and Company, 1898, p. 62.

that in his maturity he too saw fit to emphasize what was alive in religion and what was mistaken in liberal politics. There remain differences, but the principles of the defence are clearly applicable to himself.

We are told that the poet's radical theories had always been those of the 'thinker,' and accompanied by 'the doubt which infects all abstractions, the suspicion that there are limitations and equally valid counter-abstractions.'[1] Even in his radical youth he had written to the Bishop of Lincoln: 'In my ardour to attain the goal I do not forget the nature of the ground where the race is to be run.'[2] More important than theories, or than 'the persons or places' which seem from time to time to be the champions of the right, is what lies beneath both, what must be the measure by which they are judged. Thus, in a letter of 1821 to Loch, Wordsworth wrote:

If I were addressing those who have dealt so liberally with the words renegade, apostate, etc., I should retort the charge upon them, and say, *you* have been deluded by places and persons, while *I* have stuck to *principles*. I abandoned France and her rulers, when *they* abandoned the struggle for liberty, gave themselves up to tyranny and endeavoured to enslave the world.[3]

This view had placed Wordsworth beside the Tories in opposition to Napoleon. And his alliance with them seemed strengthened by his loss of faith in what seemed to many the magical virtues of universal suffrage. He began to feel that, if this were granted, power would be wielded by unreflecting masses rather than by thinking individuals; the House of Commons would not be a deliberative assembly but 'mere slavish delegates, as they now are in America, under the dictation of ignorant and selfish numbers, misled by unprincipled journalists.'[4] It is clear, however, that he had not lost interest in political liberty but had only begun to foresee new forms of tyranny which universal suffrage would indeed make possible. His Toryism, in fact, would not have pleased the Tory party. Speaking of the New Poor Law Act in 1834 in an 1835 appendix to

[1] *Ibid.*, p. 4.   [2] *Ibid.*, p. 5.
[3] *Ibid.*, p. 10.   [4] *Ibid.*, pp. 13-14.

his poems, he says that the poor, if they are to be asked to fight for their country, have a *right* to its support when they can't work. 'If Wordsworth had been in the House of Commons,' Hale White remarks, 'he would have been considered dangerous, for it is a recurrence to first principles which has produced every great revolution, whether in religion, morals, politics or art. They may be ridiculed, but they are always feared as the most insurrectionary of realities.'[1]

As for Wordsworth's religion, we are told that he never attempted to 'prove' it, like Coleridge; what he emphasized in his writing was always what the heart could feel and the imagination perceive, that in religion which spoke to him of realities and helped him to express them. 'Wordsworth's religion was not a thing *constructed* by a professional theologian or metaphysician, but was rather a group of convictions and hopes incapable of reduction to a coherent system.'[2] In turning to this he has left behind nothing essential, but only certain forms of thought which limited his power to see and express what meant most to him. 'Happy for us,' the poet wrote in the argument to the 4th Book of *The Excursion* (1814 edition), 'that the imagination and affections in our own despite mitigate the evils of that state of intellectual slavery, which the calculating understanding is so apt to produce.' And here is Hale White's comment:

To understand the importance which Wordsworth assigns to the Imagination, we must remember what he had suffered from destructive analysis. It was the root of all evil to him, and he insists, therefore, on the authority of the Imagination, which is nearly, if not quite, the same as faith. He believes that there are presentations, perceptions, which, if we like we can reduce to nothings, but which are nevertheless realities—in fact the essential realities of life. He goes very little further than this: for him it is enough, and he leaves to each man to obtain for himself what increase of definiteness he needs. He thought that superstition was nearer the truth than 'the formal inference where feeling hath no place'; that any religion was better than the mere 'repetition wearisome of sense,' and that when the

---

[1] *An Examination of the Charge of Apostasy against Wordsworth*, p. 19.
[2] *Ibid.*, p. 44.

Greek mother offered up her hair to the river Cephisus in thankful-
ness for her child's return, a message was delivered to her through
the rite more precious to her than any which 'uninspired research'
could bring and of greater validity.[1]

Thus, the religion that might very possibly mean intellectual bond-
age for some, for Wordsworth meant emancipation. It was precisely
to leave his mind *free* to hear and deliver such messages, such
'presentations, perceptions,' that he needed to rest it, as it were, upon
Anglican orthodoxy. For Hale White, it is true, no orthodoxy could
ever have been endurable. And yet, as will grow clearer below, the
difference between their final positions is not so great as those who
make much of religious orthodoxy would suppose. What Hale
White wrote of Caleb Morris, the great Calvinist minister who
influenced him so deeply, is here pertinent:

He believed undoubtedly in the chief doctrines of Christianity, but
he was one of the freest of men, if freedom is the largeness of the
space in which we move and live. We may deny that Leviticus was
written before the Captivity, or dispute the authenticity of the
Gospel of Saint John, and be narrower than a rigid Calvinist.
Thomas à Kempis and Bunyan were infinitely free.[2]

Religion, that is, can leave some people free—indeed it can help them
—to see and describe certain profound realities of the human spirit,
a kind of freedom that does not automatically accompany religious
emancipation. This, in fact, is the theme of *John Bunyan*.

John Bunyan, in spite of the amazing perfection of its style, is
perhaps the easiest of Hale White's books to underrate, and the
reason is given in that letter of his already quoted: it seems to contain
so little of the author, and so much mere synopsis of works we could
read for ourselves. As I have suggested, however, his kind of reading
we do not always do for ourselves. The synopses of Bunyan's four
principal works are in fact masterly, not merely because of the large
amount in them which had been opaque—mere theology—and which
grows transparent under his hands, but because of the beautiful

---

[1] *Ibid.*, p. 33.   [2] *Last Pages*, pp. 247-8.

delicacy and precision of his touch. This work requires, indeed,
the same ability to take a hint as does his fiction. For though he
chooses what he will retell with care, he tends to let Bunyan's
symbols speak for themselves. And though the single sentence in
which he often comments on a bit of narrative may be full of
emotion and may require, for paraphrase, many more sentences than
one, it may also be so brief it will seem to the hasty cold and insignificant. As for the book's lack of the personal, it is interesting
that it was an early gift to the woman who was to become his second
wife. And she tells us: 'He said I should see in it some sort of explanation of our strange affinity.'[1] What he surely expected it to show
the young woman, who, as we know, united devotion to her religion
with a most mature, a most subtle human wisdom, was the amount
of reality he could still see in that religion, though he could accept
none of its institutions. For, as he says in his opening paragraph,
while Bunyan has great value as an 'expositor and preacher' of
Puritanism

we are now, however, beginning to see that he is not altogether the
representative of Puritanism, but the historian of Mansoul, and that
the qualification necessary in order to understand and properly value
him is not theological learning, nor in fact any kind of learning or
literary skill, but the experience of life, with its hopes and fears,
bright day and black night.[2]

And since for Hale White it is Puritanism itself which is concerned
with Mansoul, what his study of Bunyan reveals is the permanent
human truths out of which its dogmas were evolved. These rise
continually from the synopses of the works. And they are summed
up in the last chapter, a wonderful essay which might alone ensure
the book's survival, called 'Some Reflections on Bunyan and
Puritanism.'

In his 'reflections' on the first, Hale White denies the view of
Froude that Bunyan could allegorize as he did because his religion
was no longer real to him, and he therefore felt free to add new
stories to the old.

[1] *The Groombridge Diary*, p. 2.   [2] *John Bunyan*, p. 2.

It does not disprove the reality of Bunyan's temptation that he represented it as a struggle with a fish-scaled monster. The articles of his creed required a concrete expression. Religion is dead when the imagination deserts it. When it is alive abstractions become visible and walk about on the roads.[1]

And further:

It is a test of a religion that genius is not only able to live with it but is necessarily transformed by it.[2]

Hale White himself has taught us how to understand this. He means it is a test of the depth and scope of reality the religion takes in, and of its consequent power to direct and keep busy a great mind. This is why he can go on to say:

So profound . . . was the influence of Christianity on Bunyan that without it he is not conceivable. The effect of religion on those for whom it is alive is the same as it was for him. It increases the value of the whole man; it deepens love, it exalts the stature, and adds force to every faculty. When it ceases to make us wiser and more passionate, when it does not confer greatness, it is a mere accretion.[3]

The genius of Bunyan is held to be 'tainted with vulgarity,' we are told, for a very simple reason: 'the inseparable association of non-conformity with vulgarity, and of gentility with the church, [which] is a curious characteristic of the English "imperfectly educated."'[4] Nevertheless, he was in his own way well educated, and he was the reverse of a 'Dissenter' in the sense of one who cares much about dissent. Though his chief school, for literature and for life, was the Bible, he made better use of it than most of us do of a university education.

He knew how to write his mother tongue with purity and force. . . . Properly speaking he has no style, that is to say nothing comes

[1] Ibid., p. 231.
[2] Ibid., p. 282.
[3] Ibid., pp. 233-4.
[4] Ibid., p. 235.

between us and the thing which is in his mind; the glass is not coloured. Although he was not technically a poet, his prose is distinguished by a quality of the best poetry. The word which goes straight to the mark is used, evidently without any search for it. We never find in him any of those dead phrases which the best authors nowadays cannot avoid, so tyrannical is the power of cheap and easy literature. To attempt to imitate Bunyan would be foolish, but we may learn from him to speak simply and not mechanically.[1]

The Bible also concentrated his powers, 'gave him character, and armed him at every point in every encounter,' supplying him 'with those sure maxims, *certa vitae dogmata*, which Spinoza advises us to commit to memory and "constantly to apply to the particular cases which frequently meet us in life." '

This is the art of living, the only education of much account. Saint Francis of Assisi directs his disciples that their aim in their studies is to be not that they may know what to say, but that they may act. . . . We read, even the best of us nowadays, in order that we may gain ideas, that we may 'cultivate the mind.' We do not read that we may strengthen the will or become more temperate, courageous or generous. The intellect undoubtedly has its claims, but notions have become idols. It is easier to get notions than to practise self-denial.[2]

As for his 'dissent':

Bunyan . . . is not a Dissenter in the sense that he is much taken up with dissenting. He is an Assenter, or Assertor. Religion is the vital air he breathes, and religion is affirmative. He is the poet of Puritanism, but also of something greater, that is to say of a certain class of experiences incident not especially to the theologian, artist or philosopher, but to our common nature. He was enabled to become their poet because, although he was shaken to the centre by them, he could by Grace abounding detach himself from them and survey them. This is his greatest service to us. He takes us by the hand and

---

[1] *John Bunyan*, pp. 235-6.
[2] *Ibid.*, pp. 236-7.

whispers to us, *Is it thus and thus with thee?* and then he tells us he has gone through it all and by God's mercy has survived.[1]

Again it will be noted that he has described exactly the kind of writer I have been trying to show him to be himself, though in this case, unlike that of Johnson, the similarity reaches also to the style.

The 'reflections' on Puritanism are a reply to the three common charges against it: that its doctrines are inhumanly harsh and cold, like the ethics of that capitalist business which it is supposed particularly to glorify; that these doctrines are contradictory; and that Puritans are peculiarly given over to 'cant.' The book's chief disproof of the first charge is of course to be found in the preceding analysis of Bunyan's works, where we are shown again and again the human truths embodied in the theological symbols, truths which apply not only to 'Economic Man' but to man. But here Hale White's views are summed up, and their final statement is directed chiefly against Matthew Arnold, whose *St. Paul and Protestantism* elicits a rare note of anger. This work affirmed that

our Puritan churches came into existence for the very sake of predestinarian and solifidian dogmas [the latter maintain that we are justified, not by works, but by faith alone] and that 'the Puritans are, and always have been, deficient in the specially Christian sort of righteousness.' More amazing still, Paul's righteousness before his conversion 'was, after all, in its main features, Puritan,' and Puritan theology 'could have proceeded from no one but the born Anglo-Saxon man of business, British or American.' It is needless to dwell on the folly of this wild talk. We have seen what was the theological form of Puritanism, and that it was not due, as Mr. Arnold supposes, to mere speculation. Heaven, hell, and the Atonement were the results of the conception that there is a generic, eternal and profoundly important distinction between right and wrong.[2]

It is true that the insistence on the difference between right and wrong, and the accompanying idea of our responsibility to God—which for Hale White is a form of the insight that moral laws have

[1] *Ibid.*, pp. 237-8.   [2] *Ibid.*, pp. 238-9.

R

a more than conventional or temporary authority—belong to all of Christianity. (They belong equally, it can of course be added, to Judaism.) But Puritanism dwelt on them. 'Reformations do not create; they do but re-establish that which is nearly effaced.'[1]

Here is how Hale White deals with the famous contradiction:

> Puritanism strove more earnestly than any other religion to reform men and to save them from sin. This is remarkable, seeing that pre-destination was so firmly held. Why should we bestir ourselves if it be true that we cannot alter what is ordained? And yet Bunyan was never for a moment held back in his efforts to turn the wicked from their evil ways by his theory that God had judged them from eternity. He knew, although not explicitly, that we must accept both the reasoning and the impulse to interfere and must not trouble our-selves with their apparent contradiction.[2]

To this point has Hale White been brought by his preference for the testimony, however various, of felt experience over the conclusions of systematic reasoning. He *accepts* the contradiction. And in doing so he hints that it need not matter, that it is not intellectual consis-tency that is required of a faith by which men can live but rather that its opposing elements have each their share of validity, their support from the facts of experience. This particular contradiction ought really to have been spared our modern scorn, for it is surely one by which we all live. Expressing it differently, we too affirm, on appropriate occasions, each of its opposing ideas. It is the opposition between the necessity life teaches to accept one's own limits and those of life, and the frequent advisability, which it also teaches, of struggling on for what is desirable in spite of them; or, in the form in which it runs through all Hale White's work, between the idea that wisdom lies in reconciliation with the inevitable, and the idea that the inevitable (or the apparently so) can be reversed and 'miracles' be performed by a faith which maintains one's own vision against the 'evidence.'

As for the Puritan's 'cant':

---

[1] *John Bunyan*, p. 245.
[2] *Ibid.*, p. 240.

Cant differs in degree. The question is, not whether we cant, but how much. There may be a soul of honesty in our belief although a thick husk of cant envelop it. If the blood did not reach to the extremity of the Puritan's creed, it went a long way. He, no doubt, was guilty of cant. It follows all great movements, religious or secular, and their apostles become tainted with it. They are obliged to go on, to define and organize: they unfurl a flag, enlist disciples, phrases are caught up, and cant begins. Cant! The charge is not one which the twentieth century should prefer. . . . Is not society a mass of cant? Do not the people cant who 'entertain' and are 'entertained' and repeat as their own thought the leading article of a newspaper? Strange that we should be sunk in cant, and that nevertheless we should profess such repulsion from it in Puritanism.[1]

This is another of those insights of his wonderfully calculated to check the complacency of modernity, one to place beside Clara Hopgood's that we are not to congratulate ourselves on our freedom from superstition because we do not share that of a Spanish peasant. We too pretend to beliefs we don't feel or live by, and, on the other hand, the Puritan, or any believer, may often feel deeply the content of reality in his religion, in spite of the mechanical piety into which the conditions of life may cause him to sink.

Finally, 'although the Puritan's religion was a religion of right doing and not an idle intellectual exercise, he thought it was of the greatest importance that we should have true notions about the being of God.' And again Hale White instantly translates this religious idea into language that shows its general meaning. It means that the Puritan thought we should seek reliable general ideas about the nature of life—of reality—as a whole. 'The Puritan thought that life is controlled by our relationship to that which is beyond this lower world and though he may have been wrong in details he was right in principle. Society is at this moment kept together by habits which were formed by ideas.'[2]

We have already seen, however, that the intellectual allegiances of Hale White, like those of Gide, are never absolute or permanent. Loyal to experience, he could never forget the incompleteness of

[1] *Ibid.*, pp. 246-7.   [2] *Ibid.*, p. 249.

every idea and every system. If he emphasized most what seemed most to require his emphasis, he was always aware of that other side which might, in its turn, call for his defence. And this is the point with which he beautifully ends his book.

One last word. Puritanism has done noble service, but we have seen enough of it even in Bunyan to show that it is not an entirely accurate version of God's message to man. It is the most distinct, energetic and salutary movement in our history, and no other religion has surpassed it in preaching the truths by which men and nations must exist. Nevertheless we need Shakespeare as well as Bunyan, and oscillate between the *Pilgrim's Progress* and *As You Like It*. We cannot bring ourselves into a unity. The time is yet to come when we shall live by a faith which is a harmony of all our faculties. A glimpse was caught of such a gospel nineteen centuries ago in Galilee, but it has vanished.[1]

[1] *John Bunyan*, pp. 49-50.

CHAPTER XII

Conclusion

THE ideas in Hale White's last books we have, of course, met in his work before. We have now seen how they persist and come together in spite of occasional contradiction, into a more or less unified attitude to life. We have seen, too, what is surely the most important cause of his failure to win a large public. For this attitude went directly against one which has characterized English and American culture since he began to write: our faith in the power of reason to lead us, in every sphere, to all we need to know. This faith is perhaps the defining element in that tradition of liberalism to which it has seemed a matter of pride, as well as of good sense, for large numbers of our educated classes to belong. As always, however, times are changing, and this tradition is now being challenged not only by unthinking reaction but by intelligent liberals themselves. Witness the following statement from a recent work devoted to just such criticism from within, a statement most pertinent to our study of Hale White:

As it [liberalism] carries out its active and positive ends it unconsciously limits its view of the world to what it can deal with, and it unconsciously tends to develop theories and principles, particularly in relation to the nature of the human mind, that justify its limitation. Its characteristic paradox appears again, and in another form, for in the interests of its great primal act of imagination by which it establishes its essence and existence—in the interests, that is, of its vision of a general enlargement and freedom and rational direction of human life—it drifts toward a denial of the emotions and the imagination. And in the very interest of affirming its confidence

247

in the power of the mind, it inclines to constrict and make mechanical its conception of the nature of mind.[1]

The extension of modern awareness represented and assisted by such a perception may mean that we have arrived at last at the moment for which Hale White's work has, as it were, been waiting.

As I have suggested, it was our author's desire to remain true to felt experience in all its complexity that determined the nature of his ideas. Now a first result of such an awareness of complexity is that it leads to scepticism, to doubt of established formulae. Here, of course, we have the most important aspect of his similarity to Gide. I have written elsewhere: To 'the peculiarly Protestant sincerity with which [Gide] examined a self too wide and too much in motion for any formula that stood still . . . has been due a mistrust of formulae equal to his interest in them.' [2] But if this sense of 'the doubt which infects all abstractions, the suspicion that there are limitations and equally valid counter-abstractions,' led Hale White first to play Gide's role of critic of culture—as such he tended to rebel in his youth against the pressure toward religious and political conformity —he did not, like Gide, stop in that role. 'It is not by criticism, but by admiration that we live,' he said, and this means, as his work for-ever shows us, not by scepticism, but by faith. For Hale White, how-ever necessary 'destructive analysis' might often be, the chief business of the human mind was to *add* to what we can believe, what we can affirm, what gives us courage and confidence and hope. 'We ought to struggle earnestly to increase our beliefs,' he wrote in *Last Pages*. 'Every addition to them is an extension of life, both in breadth and depth.' [3]

He had, as we have seen, good reason for this emphasis. Was not that 'hypochondria' which overshadowed his life precisely scepticism in its extreme form? It simply extended the agile ('Protestant') mind's perception of the incompleteness of formulae into a sense

[1] Lionel Trilling, *The Liberal Imagination*, New York, Viking Press, 1950, pp. xiii-xiv.

[2] Irvin Stock, 'A View of Les Faux-Monnayeurs,' *Yale French Studies*, Number 7, 1951, p. 72.

[3] *Last Pages*, p. 318.

that *all* the beliefs which make life tolerable were delusions, a 'painted veil,' hiding a reality opposed to every human purpose, hiding especially that final mockery of all: the fact that man is flesh heading rapidly for putrefaction in the grave. Hale White could not, on the whole, deny that this insight of his hypochondria was true, a revelation of the 'dread abyss' which does indeed 'underlie the life of man.' But what was most significant to him was that it was the truth of illness, of insomnia at three o'clock in the morning, and that it crippled and worked against life. It was an array of reason and evidence that was generally vanquished, he had learned not by argument but by sunlight and health, the health which automatically brings courage. And it was his search for help which the stronger Gide did not require that turned him away from 'criticism'; it was because he *needed* to, that he sought to find what would oppose the truth of scepticism, what would weaken its authority. He found this answer to scepticism in that very complexity of life which had begun by leading him to it. He found that experience teaches us to doubt even the conclusions of sceptical reasoning itself, and that it thereby sets us free to maintain our faith in those 'presentations, perceptions,' often apparently unreasonable, which answer our needs and help us to live.

It teaches us first of all how reality stretches always further than we can reach; there is always more in every direction, a more that pours forth endlessly the unforeseen to mock our pretensions to complete and final truth. It is to be remembered that Hale White's concern is with wisdom applicable to the basic eternal problems of daily living. He, too, would be aware that generalizations like this one cannot be transferred mechanically to more limited fields, like gardening, for example, or the question of whether a particular union should go on strike. In such fields we must take the short view; it is the business of wisdom to take the long. In the matter of our judgments of ourselves, of our friends, of the possibilities of life, our successive rational hypotheses, each masquerading as the voice of changeless reason itself, are usually too narrow, leave out too much. Limiting our views, they can inhibit energies which untroubled faith in a mere 'dream' might release to work 'miracles.' In the second place, that same complexity makes for another difficulty. A gift for reasoning will often disclose reasons equally valid on many of the sides of every issue, and thus lead to constant vacillation. For:

> There are always a multitude of reasons both in favour of doing a thing and against doing it. The art of debate lies in presenting them; the art of life in neglecting ninety-nine hundredths of them.[1]

And another note tells us: 'Under every reconciliation opens presently an unfathomable chasm. We shall never reach immovable peace by thinking.'[2] Finally, subtle psychologist that he was, Hale White knew that, for all its pretensions to autonomy, reason was only a tool, the tool of moods or motives often unconfessed even to oneself. This insight, which so enriched his characterization, is part of the great nineteenth-century exploration of the role of the unconscious mind; it is the insight that our reasons may, far more often than we know, be merely 'rationalizations.'

We see, of course, that his scepticism of 'reason' is not an affirmation of unreason. It is, on the contrary, reason itself which leads him to it. It is precisely the superior intelligence which remains forever aware of that 'variousness, possibility, complexity and difficulty'[3]— Lionel Trilling's significant phrase—which a too simple-minded faith in 'reason' has tended to miss. For this faith is actually a faith, not in reason but in those particular current theories that are offered, one after another, as speaking in its name. It is not their wisest adherents who make such a pretension, and not, often enough, their inventors. Marx, we know, was provoked by certain of *his* followers into denying that he was a Marxist. It is always those who seek to escape the endless necessity to *go on* reasoning who delight to proclaim that at last some theory permits them to know, to define—and therefore to limit and reduce—once and for all. Moreover, to think that by virtue of current theories we know all we need to know, or that we could know it with the proper reading, is not merely to be *un*reasonable, to fall short, intellectually, before life's complexity. There are two disadvantages even worse. It is to lose that awareness of mystery, of the wonderful, which keeps life interesting. And it is

[1] *More Pages*, p. 247.   [2] *Last Pages*, p. 315.
[3] Trilling, *op. cit.*, p. xv.

to relax one's guard before life's waiting terrors. 'Reason' can be the opium of the people.

A note in *More Pages* formulates the next step in his argument. 'If you are very short-sighted or half blind, it is safer in the twilight to shut the eyes and depend entirely on the touch in moving about.' [1] Reason—or rather the successive particular theories by which alone we know it—being so often 'short-sighted or half blind' in this 'twilight' of life in which we move, feeling may sometimes be more dependable. It follows that the assertions of faith do not differ from those of reason only and always as the pleasantly false from the necessarily true; they can differ also as those validated by feeling from those which pretend—and not every time, as we have seen with justice—to be logically deducible from all the relevant evidence. And the faith which adheres to the former is not only and always the credulous acceptance of old wives' tales; it can also be strength of character. It can be the strength to hold on to what we have felt to be true in our healthiest moments, in spite of the alleged evidence which life's variety must inevitably throw up against it. Life sooner or later throws up everything: the question is, upon what will we choose to come to rest? And this is determined by what is other than reason, by what we love and need, by our values, ideals and aspirations. Faith can be the strength to keep *these*, rather than our doubts and fears, the masters and the users of our powers of reason. Without such faith, which must often, as I say, seem unreasonable, nothing of any worth can ever be accomplished. But more important than that, we can never without it attain even to simple peace.

This is why Hale White's writing leads us persistently back to religion. For, as he shows us, religion is not the mere history or promise of supernatural doings which it appears to those who take it literally—whether devotees or scorners. It is rather a great accumulation and organization, expressed in symbolic language, of those affirmations about the universe and man and the relations between them which we must all come to in some form in order to live. As one of those who rise periodically to enlighten the provincialism of modernity, Hale White reminds us that in the past, too, men learned, as we learn, what life is like; that though their epochs provided them

[1] *More Pages*, p. 239.

with a religious language in which to utter what they learned, this does not mean it differs essentially from what life teaches us today. It follows, of course, that, like any language which time or distance has rendered foreign, the language of religion must for most of us be translated. Now there is a tendency to bridle at the thought of translation: perhaps we resent the insinuation that truth can be uttered in other forms as well as our own; and—its corollary—that our own, too, are historically conditioned and will some day need to be interpreted. But translation is in fact essential to all communication, not only between separate cultures, epochs and countries but also between friends. Words are private as well as public things, and we must first grasp what realities they correspond to for him who utters them, rather than for ourselves, before we can judge them rightly. If the translator is a traitor, as the Italian proverb has it, he surely does not, except in poetry, betray what is most important. It would be more just, if less clever, to call him a preserver; it is to him we owe the continuity of civilization. Hale White, seeking like certain others of his time to make religion 'intelligible,' has in fact taken rank with the preservers of civilization. He has made available to us a treasure of our heritage from which many of us, especially nowadays, have been cut off.

It is not, however, only the difficulties of translation which have cut us off from that treasure. Even translated, it is a kind of thing not easy to take up. What prevents us—great numbers of us at least—is simplemindedness; or it is pride; or it is weakness. For, as Hale White shows, there are two great lessons which religion chiefly teaches. The first is that God is greater than we, that though man proposes, God disposes, and this, being translated, means that reality contains so much more than we can know that we must be humble and tentative in all our judgments. 'Charity, charity!' exclaims Melville's Confidence Man. (And if his motives for saying it are impure, this does not mean his statement is any the less true.) 'Never a sound judgment without charity. When man judges man, charity is less a bounty from our mercy than just allowance for the insensible leeway of human fallibility.' [1] And religion's second lesson is that, appearances to the contrary notwithstanding, all will be well. Such a statement

---

[1] Herman Melville, *The Confidence Man*, New York, Grove Press, 1949, p. 186.

can come from Pangloss and be easily contradicted, as Candide, to our amusement, keeps on learning. But in the perspective of a whole life we generally find that it is timidity or childish rebelliousness which leaps to contradict it, and that the strong always take it, in some form, for granted. It is thus that strength of character might be translated into words.

The wisdom of religion, the wisdom of Hale White, is not the only kind of truth it is possible to draw out of life's infinite variety. But as it rises from the struggle for support against life's common hurts and terrors, it has a special value for those who suffer from them. At one time or another this means all of us.

BIBLIOGRAPHY

I. WORKS BY W. HALE WHITE[1]

An Argument for an Extension of the Franchise. London, F. Farrah, 1866.

A Letter Written on the Death of Mrs. Elizabeth Street. London, W. P. Griffith and Son, 1877, privately printed and circulated.

The Autobiography of Mark Rutherford, Dissenting Minister, edited by his friend, Reuben Shapcott. London, Trübner and Co., 1881.

Mark Rutherford's Deliverance, Being the Second Part of his Autobiography, edited by his friend, Reuben Shapcott. London, Trübner and Co., 1885.

The Revolution in Tanner's Lane, by Mark Rutherford, edited by his friend, Reuben Shapcott. London, Trübner and Co., 1887.

Miriam's Schooling and Other Papers, by Mark Rutherford, edited by his friend, Reuben Shapcott. London, Kegan Paul, Trench, Trübner and Co. Ltd., 1890.

Catherine Furze, by Mark Rutherford, edited by his friend, Reuben Shapcott. London, T. Fisher Unwin, 1893.

Clara Hopgood, by Mark Rutherford, edited by his friend, Reuben Shapcott. London, T. Fisher Unwin, 1896.

An Examination of the Charge of Apostasy against Wordsworth. London, Longmans, Green and Co., 1898.

Pages from a Journal with Other Papers. London, T. Fisher Unwin, 1900.

John Bunyan. London, Hodder and Stoughton, 1904.

More Pages from a Journal with Other Papers. London, Oxford University Press, 1910.

The Early Life of Mark Rutherford by Himself. London, Oxford University Press, 1913.

Last Pages from a Journal with Other Papers, edited by his wife. London, Oxford University Press, 1915.

Letters to Three Friends, edited by his wife. London, Oxford University Press, 1924.

II. WORKS TRANSLATED, EDITED AND PREFACED BY W. HALE WHITE

Ethic, by Benedict Spinoza, translated from the Latin by William Hale White. London, Trübner and Co., 1883.

Tractatus de Intellectus Emendatione et de Via, Qua Optime in Veram Rerum Cognitionem Dirigitur, by Benedict Spinoza, translated by William Hale White. London, T. Fisher Unwin, 1895.

---

[1] See Simon Nowell-Smith, *Mark Rutherford: a Short Bibliography of the First Editions*, Supplement to *The Bookman's Journal*, 1930.

The Inner Life of the House of Commons, by William White, edited with a Preface by Justin McCarthy, M.P., and with an Introduction by the author's son, two vols. London, T. Fisher Unwin, 1897.

A Description of the Wordsworth and Coleridge MSS. in the Possession of Mr. T. Norton Longman, edited with Notes by W. Hale White. London, Longmans, Green and Co., 1897.

Coleridge's Poems, A Facsimile Reproduction of the Proofs and MSS. of Some of the Poems, edited by the late James Dykes Campbell, with Preface and Notes by W. Hale White. Westminster, Archibald Constable and Co., 1899.

Selections from Dr. Johnson's 'Rambler,' edited with Preface and Notes by W. Hale White. Oxford, The Clarendon Press, 1907.

The Life of John Sterling, by Thomas Carlyle, with an Introduction by W. Hale White. London, Henry Froude, Oxford University Press, 1907.

III. THE MORE IMPORTANT UNREPRINTED CONTRIBUTIONS BY W. HALE WHITE
TO NEWSPAPERS AND MAGAZINES

'Births, Deaths and Marriages,' *Chambers's Journal*, IX (March 6, 1858), pp. 155-7.

'The Priesthood *vs.* the Human Mind and Science' (letter), *Exeter and Plymouth Gazette*, January 6, 1864.

'Metropolitan Notes' (weekly column), the *Aberdeen Herald*, from May 11, 1861, to January 27, 1872.

'Below the Gangway' (weekly column), the *Morning Star* (London), from February 12, 1865, to July 10, 1866.

'Sketches in Parliament' (weekly column), the *Birmingham Journal*, the *Birmingham Daily Post and Journal* and the *Birmingham Daily Post* (these three changes in name occurred while Hale White wrote for this newspaper), from February 3, 1866, to January 31, 1880.

'Letters by a Radical' (weekly column), the *Rochdale Observer*, from January 19, 1867, to March 30, 1872.

'Sketches in Parliament' and 'How it Strikes a Stranger' (weekly column), the *Nonconformist*, from February 14, 1872, to August 6, 1873.

'Our London Letter' (weekly column), the *Norfolk News*, from March 2, 1872, to March 17, 1883.

'Genius of Walt Whitman,' the *Secular Review*, March 20, 1880.[1]

'Marcus Antoninus,' the *Secular Review*, July 3, 1880.

'Ixion,' the *Secular Review*, September 11, 1880.

'Heathen Ethics,' the *Secular Review:* November 21, 1880.

---

[1] This and the three items which follow from the *Secular Review*, were found in Hale White's Scrapbooks. Since no issues of this magazine dated earlier than 1885 are available in New York, I have been unable to add the volume and page number.

'Two Martyrs,' *Bookman*, III (February, 1893), pp. 153-4.
'Mr. W. S. Lilly and *The Times*' (letter), the *Speaker*, XIII (February 10, 1906), pp. 457-8.
'The Golden Nail,' the *Rochdale Observer*, February 17, 1906.

IV. CHIEF UNPUBLISHED WRITINGS BY W. HALE WHITE

'The Black Notebook.' A private journal of literary, moral and philosophic reflections and of quotations from his reading, kept by Hale White between 1894 and 1904; in the possession of Mrs. D. V. White, Sherborne, Dorset, England.

'The White Notebook.' The same journal continued until his death; in the possession of Mrs. D. V. White.

'The 1910 MS.' An account by Hale White, written in 1910, of his relationship with his second wife; in the possession of Mrs. D. V. White.

Two Scrapbooks. Large books in which Hale White kept clippings of his own early periodical writings and of articles of others which interested him; in the possession of Dr. R. Hale-White, London.

Three letters to his father, dated March 6, 1852, May 3, 1853, and September 20, 1880; in the possession of Dr. R. Hale-White.

Letters to his eldest son (Sir William) and his eldest son's wife, written between 1874 and 1911; copies in the possession of Dr. R. Hale-White.

Letters to his second son (Jack) and his second son's wife, written between 1882 and 1912; copies in the possession of Dr. R. Hale-White.

Letters to his third son (Ernest), written between 1886 and 1911; in the possession of Mrs. Irene White, St. Albans, Hertfordshire, England.

Letters to Viscountess Robert Cecil, written between 1909 and 1913; in the possession of Viscountess Robert Cecil, Chelwood Gate, Uckfield, Sussex, England.

Letters to Mabel Marsh, written between 1897 and 1910; copies in the possession of Mrs. D. V. White.

Letters to Mrs. Gladys E. Easdale, written between 1906 and 1910; in the possession of Mrs. Easdale, London.

Letters to George Jacob Holyoake, written between 1865 and 1882; copies in the possession of Dr. R. Hale-White.

V. CRITICAL AND BIOGRAPHICAL WORKS ON W. HALE WHITE

Buchman, Ursula Clare, *William Hale White* (Mark Rutherford). *The Problem of Self-Adjustment in a World of Changing Values*, University of Zürich dissertation. Zürich, Juris-Verlag, 1950.

Hale-White, John, 'William Hale White, "Mark Rutherford," 1831-1913. Notes by his Second Son, Geneva, February 1931.' Unpublished MS. in the possession of Dr. R. Hale-White.

Hale-White, Sir William, 'Notes about William Hale White (Mark Rutherford), Personal Reminiscences by his Eldest Son W. Hale White. Made May 1932.' Unpublished MS. in possession of Dr. R. Hale-White.

Klinke, Hans, *William Hale White, Versuch einer Biographie*, Griefswald dissertation. Frankfort, Buchdrukerei Wilhelm Bohn, 1930.

Maclean, C. M., *Mark Rutherford: A Biography of William Hale White*. London, MacDonald & Co., 1955.

Nicoll, William Robertson, *Introduction to the Novels of Mark Rutherford*. London, T. Fisher Unwin, 1924.

Nicoll, William Robertson, *Memories of Mark Rutherford*. London, T. Fisher Unwin, 1924.

Smith, Henry Arthur, *The Life and Thought of William Hale White*, Ph.D. dissertation, University of Birmingham, England, 1938.

Stone, Wilfred H., *Religion and Art of William Hale White* ('Mark Rutherford'), Ph.D. dissertation, Harvard University, 1950. Revised and published in Stanford, California. Stanford University Press, 1954.

Warner, Alan John, *Mark Rutherford, A Victorian Pilgrim. A Study of the Mind and Writings of William Hale White* (1831-1913), Ph.D. dissertation, University of the Witwaterstrand, Johannesburg, South Africa, 1949.

Wright, J. Ernest T., *W. Hale White (Mark Rutherford)*, Ph.D. dissertation, University of Pittsburgh, 1932.

VI. THE MORE VALUABLE SHORTER ESSAYS ON W. HALE WHITE IN BOOKS AND MAGAZINES

Baker, Ernest A., 'Mark Rutherford and Others,' in his *History of the English Novel*, Vol. IX (London, H. F. and G. Witherby, Ltd., 1938), pp. 97-121.

'C,' 'The Art of Mark Rutherford,' *The Academy*, LVI (February 4, 1899), pp. 161-3.

Chevrillon, André, 'Ruskin et la Vie,' *Revue des Deux Mondes*, XLVI (August 1, 1908), pp. 564-90.

Howells, W. D., 'The Editor's Study,' *Harper's New Monthly Magazine*, LXXII (December, 1885, to May, 1886), pp. 485-7.

Low, F. H., 'Mark Rutherford: An Appreciation,' *Fortnightly Review*, XC, Old Series, or LXXXIV, New Series (September 1, 1908), pp. 458-73.

Massingham, H. W., 'Memorial Introduction' to *The Autobiography of Mark Rutherford*. London, T. Fisher Unwin, 1923.

Murry, J. M., 'The Religion of Mark Rutherford,' in his *To the Unknown God* (London, Jonathan Cape, Ltd., 1924), pp. 260-75.

Sperry, W. L., 'Mark Rutherford,' *Harvard Theological Review*, VII (April 1914), pp. 166-73.

Taylor, A. E., 'The Novels of Mark Rutherford,' *Essays and Studies by Members of the English Association*, Vol. V. (Oxford, The Clarendon Press, 1914), pp. 51-60.

Taylor, W. D., 'Mark Rutherford,' the *Queen's Quarterly*, XXV (October 1917), pp. 153-71.

VII. WORKS BY W. HALE WHITE'S SECOND WIFE, DOROTHY V. WHITE AND BY HIS FATHER, WILLIAM WHITE

Smith, Dorothy V. Horace (Mrs. White's maiden name), *Discourses on Character, Completeness, The Fatherhood of God, Life Everlasting* (pamphlet). Beckenham, Kent, T. W. Thornton, Printer and Publisher, 1902.

Smith, Dorothy V. Horace, *Miss Mona*. London, Methuen and Co., Ltd., 1907.

Frank Burnet. London, John Murray, 1909.

White, Dorothy V., *Twelve Years with my Boys* (published anonymously). London, Methuen and Co., Ltd., 1912.

Isabel. London, Mills and Boon, Ltd., 1910.

'Occasional Notebooks' (Mrs. White's unpublished diary).

'The Dorothy Book.' Unpublished collection of Mrs. White's letters and sayings made by W. Hale White between 1907 and 1913 and now in the possession of Mrs. White.

The Groombridge Diary. London, Oxford University Press, 1924.

White, William, *To Think or Not to Think* (pamphlet). Bedford, John G. Nall, 1852.

INDEX

81, 83-9, see also White, Mrs. D. V.;
and the ministry, 35, 38, 42, 54-5,
96-7, 98-9; his love of music, 66;
his name, 28; his love of nature;
67; and New College, Calvinist
seminary, 1, 9, 34, 38-9, 40, 42,
in his novels, 162, 211-12; his old
age, 80-1, 221-2, 225; his politics,
56-60; and religion, 8-9, 27-32,
33-4, 38-40, 43-7, 55, 63, 84, 85, 127,
251-3, see also Religion; his scholarship, 69-70; as schoolmaster, 40-1,
107; and science, 67-9; his self-
effacement, 169, 228-9; his temperament, 62-3, 64, 65, 81, 87-8, 94;
his thought, 19-27, see also under
subject, e.g. Faith; wholeness of, 14-
15, 222

As a writer:
his anonymity, 2, 79, 80, 91; his art
and skill, 13-16, 142; his creative
life, 221; criticism of, 131-3, 196-
198; his 'digressions,' 131-2, 187 n.,
212; some distinguished opinions on,
3-5; his irony, 45, 116, 151-2, 182,
185, 202; as literary critic, 222, 226-
236; his motives for writing, 12,
14-15; his narrative skill, 126-7, 131,
146, 175, 197, 219; his short stories,
223-6; his sincerity, 6, 12, 223; as
social historian, vi, 16-19, 92, 110-11,
133, 134, 148; starts writing, 6, 55-
56, 75; his style, 4, 5, 11, 12-13,
33, 84, 115, 198, 215 n., 221, 229,
239; his writings listed, 2

White, see also Hale-White
Whitman, Walt, 75, 76
Wilhamstead, 28
Wordsworth, influence of, on White
39-40, 95; mentioned, 112, 128 n.,
205; White on, 2, 69-70, 227, 229,
231, 236-9
Wordsworth, Dorothy, 70

Yale French Studies, 248 n.
Yeats, 81